Service-Oriented Architecture

for Enterprise and Cloud Applications

Service-Oriented Architecture
for Enterprise and Cloud Applications

Shankar Kambhampaty
Chief Technology Officer — Investment Banking Services
Polaris Software Lab

Wiley India

Service-Oriented Architecture
for Enterprise and Cloud Applications
Second Edition

Other Wiley Editorial Offices:

John Wiley & Sons, Inc. 111 River Street, Hoboken, NJ 07030, USA

Wiley-VCH Verlag GmbH, Pappellaee 3, D-69469 Weinheim, Germany

John Wiley & Sons Australia Ltd, 42 McDougall Street, Milton, Queensland 4064, Australia

John Wiley & Sons (Asia) Pte Ltd, 2 Clementi Loop #02-01, Jin Xing Distripark, Singapore 129809

John Wiley & Sons Canada Ltd, 22 Worcester Road, Etobicoke, Ontario, Canada, M9W 1L1

Reprint: 2013

Second Edition: 2010
ISBN: 978-81-265-1989-7
www.wileyindia.com
Blog for the book at: http://soa4entandcloud.blogspot.com/

Printed at: *Radha Offset, Delhi*

To my Mother

Foreword

Service Oriented Architecture (SOA) offers powerful environment to deliver technology solutions. I picked up the power of SOA and its application in renovating business legacy applications – step by step over the last 8 years. Our team of SOA architects at Polaris learnt the smart way of leveraging SOA in building appropriate solutions for our global customers. SOA ensures the metamorphosis of technology becoming the value creator for business. More importantly this is being delivered at a cost that impresses and invites business leaders to adapt such technology. SOA coupled with Cloud Computing offers a brilliant mix of right technology at flexible pricing which makes "pay-as-you-go", a reality.

In the technology world a few important aspects have emerged – from the architect's perspective. Amongst such aspects "Reusability" and "Integration" have taken top priority. I am impressed the way Shankar has articulated these two important aspects in clear terms in this book. A technical architect will find significant value from this book on applying the principles of SOA and Cloud Computing. The interoperability across systems and programming languages between applications across platforms was one of the challenges the industry was facing. Shankar explains neatly how SOA and Cloud Computing help industry break this challenge with ease.

Banking, Financial Services and Insurance (BFSI) sector is largely driven around technology. BFSI entities have been pioneers in adapting technology to enhance efficiency and SOA and Cloud Computing. The emergence of Micro Finance Entities, Rural Banking – superior technology at competitive costs – will be a welcome boon for the industry.

I read Shankar's first edition with interest where he had significantly dwelled with good insights on SOA. Shankar has used his two decades plus experience in architecture and design to ably communicate the nuances of technology in simple manner. The senior architects and business leaders will find immense value from this book as to how they can build their strategies using SOA, Cloud Computing Principles. This book tries to capture few real life learnings at our customer's places.

I wish Shankar Kambhampaty the very best and congratulate him on bringing in the second edition.

Arun Jain

Chairman & Managing Director
Polaris Software Lab Ltd

Praise for the Book

As we emerge out of the severest recession of our times, technology leaders are keener than ever to squeeze the best value out of their technology spend. As they get back to investing for the future, they will, no doubt, take a very close look at two aspects; viz., robust software architecture, which has been known to secure technology investments for the long term, and newer technologies, such as cloud computing, which having moved from the research environment into mainstream industry in the past couple of years, hold out the promise of resource optimization.

In this second edition of the book "Service-Oriented Architecture for Enterprise and Cloud Applications", the author has done well to emphasize the criticality of these two aspects. He has rightly pointed out that the success of software development depends, in large measure, on the underlying software architecture. He has also explained how the synergy between software engineering and project management practices can be leveraged to ensure the success of software engineering projects.

The new chapters in this edition dwell at length on cloud computing, the tremendous opportunities that have been opened up by cloud computing and the combination of cloud and enterprise services. The author has done well to start with the basic concepts and services, cover insights into enabling technologies and platforms and move on to opportunities for platform providers, service providers, etc. It is very thoughtful on the part of the author to have included a CD with Proofs-of-Concept to help readers gain insights into application of the concepts and to have created a blog to encourage experience-sharing among the community of software architects.

I am confident that this book will serve as a useful reference for students and practitioners of software architecture alike. I hope the readers make the most of it and I wish the author the very best.

Kedarnath Udiyavar

Partner & Global Head – Investment Banking Technology Services

Polaris Software Lab Limited

Praise for the Book

Acknowledgments

This book is dedicated to my mother who encouraged me so much to share what I knew. I am indebted to my father, Shri. K. V. J. R. Krupanidhi, for all the support and encouragement to go through with this effort, especially when I had doubts on whether I would see it through. With an incredible experience of writing 50 scientific papers, he has been my "friend, philosopher and guide" throughout the exercise. I am grateful to the continuous encouragement from my sisters, Sharada and Rama, in going through with the book. I am also obliged to Govind, Prasad, Ravi and Prasanna for their support.

I would like to take this opportunity to thank Almighty and the "Line of Gurus" who have guided me right from my early schooling days. Remarkable insights have been provided to me by Dr. M. Narasimha Rao and Shri. K.M. Sastry, to whom I am very thankful.

This book would not have been possible without the unstinted support of my wife Mallika, daughter Sasirekha and son Harish Rohan. They have always been there for me inspite of the many sacrificed weekends and evenings.

I had very useful discussions on the subject of this book with the members of my team to whom I am so very thankful. My special thanks to Srinivas Konduru, Anamala Haranath who provided significant help and inputs for the book. Srinivas enthusiastically helped me in building the PoCs discussed in this book, and his review comments have ensured that the diagrams and text are consistent and correct. Haranath spent several late evening hours and weekends with me providing ideas to improve the diagrams. I am also thankful to other members of my team, Satish, Mahakash, Rajesh, Suresh, Lakshmi and Srinivas who have contributed in so many tangible and intangible ways to my understanding and thought process.

The motivation for this book has been Shri. Arun Jain, Chairman, Polaris and Shri. Kedarnath Udiyavar, Head, Investment Banking unit at Polaris. Their vision to build products and services around the principles of SOA and cloud computing with focus on BFSI sector provided me the impetus for bringing out the revised and enlarged edition on the subject. I am thankful to them in this regard.

It has been a great pleasure working with the professional team of John Wiley – Vikas Gupta, Paras Bansal and Meenakshi Bahuguna – who provided outstanding support in various stages of book writing, reviews and book production. They made it happen a second time!!

Shankar Kambhampaty

Preface

As a practicing professional, I feel that I truly learn when I write and teach. Thanks to the encouragement of my family, friends and colleagues, I began writing in small ways initially; a few white papers to start with, followed by a few papers in International conferences, a chapter in a book, the first edition of the book on SOA and now the second edition of this book on SOA for enterprise and cloud applications.

I have always been fascinated by architecting software applications. Before the term "SOA" was coined, the term "architecture" was generally used by a few specialists, mostly technical. Architecture is being increasingly seen as strategic in nature and is being discussed in direction setting initiatives. Invariably, every CIO has either already considered SOA or will do so soon, as the knowledge on this subject has substantially improved over the years.

SOA and cloud computing can be viewed and discussed from a number of dimensions and perspectives. The objective of this book is to present my perspectives drawing from numerous experiences in defining strategy, architecting service-oriented applications and recommending governance to meet customer requirements.

In the past couple of years, since the launch of the first edition of the book, I have received excellent feedback from customers, fellow professionals and students. I wish to thank one and all for the same. I have accordingly made revisions in this edition of the book.

What's New?

As Chapter 1, we now have "Software Engineering Principles" to enable beginners to get an overview of the principles of software engineering before looking at software architecture. Likewise, Chapter 3 is updated based on recent developments. With increasing adoption of SOA, organizations have taken a strategic view of SOA governance and security aspects. Also, technologies for implementing them have matured. Taking into account these developments, the Strawman architecture for enterprise-wide SOA has been enhanced in Chapter 4 and lot more content has been added to the topics of governance and security in Chapter 11.

Chapter 12 has been updated to reflect the latest trends in SOA. When the first edition of the book was launched, cloud computing was just beginning to take off. In the past year, significant progress has been made in the technologies and adoption of cloud computing. We have, therefore, included Chapter 13 that covers the concepts of cloud computing, Chapter 14 that provides an overview of key cloud computing platforms and Chapter 15 that discusses SOA with enterprise and cloud services. In this edition, one more Annexure (Annexure D) is added on EA and SOA for business-IT alignment.

Since, it is logical to include all the content related to services within an enterprise before we go beyond the enterprise, I have included all the cloud computing/services related chapters after Chapter 12 (Trends in SOA). Thus, the book is organized to provide first an understanding of services model followed by use of services within an enterprise, then about cloud and cloud services outside the enterprise and finally the combination of enterprise services and cloud services.

Who Should Read This Book

The book is meant to cater to the needs of four types of readers:

1. ***Students and Developers (Beginners)***: Chapter 1 provides the principles of software engineering, Chapter 2 an overview of software architecture, Chapter 3 gives the concepts of service-oriented architecture and Chapter 13 provides concepts of cloud computing.
2. ***Architects, Designers and Developers (Intermediate):*** Chapter 4 discusses architecture for enterprise-wide SOA, Chapter 5 introduces Enterprise applications, Chapter 6 gives details of Software Platforms for Enterprise Applications and Chapter 14 provides details of Cloud Computing Platforms.
3. ***Architects, Designers and Developers (Advanced):*** Chapter 7 provides insights into Service-Oriented Enterprise Applications, Chapter 8 explains the process of Service-Oriented Analysis and Design, Chapter 9 discusses the Technologies for SOA and Chapter 15 presents SOA with Cloud Services.
4. ***CXOs and Project Managers:*** Chapter 10 presents the approaches for computing ROI for SOA and preparation of Business Case, Chapter 11 discusses the approach for Governance, Security and SOA implementation and Chapter 12 reviews the trends in SOA.

I have structured the book keeping in mind the insights I have gathered over the past 20 years as a practicing IT professional. Although there are some textbooks available on SOA and cloud computing, it is felt that this attempt of mine provides the required conceptual clarity and knowledge of recent advances. All the chapters attempt to highlight and illustrate concepts related to various aspects of SOA and cloud computing. As a practicing engineer working in the United States and Singapore in R&D, MIS and software development organizations, I learnt the need to pay attention to detail. The code fragments in several chapters are meant to point to this aspect. In my roles as project manager, program manager and relationship manager, I have always felt that it is essential to stay aligned with customer's business. Chapters 10 and 11 have been written keeping this aspect in mind. As a practicing architect for the past 5 years and achieving the MCA certification and IBM Solution Designer certification, I stress the need for rigour in techniques and processes for architecture and design. Chapters 7, 8 and 9 focus on this aspect.

In order to get further and continued insights into SOA and Cloud Computing, a blog has been set up for the book at:

http://soa4entandcloud.blogspot.com/

This book is a humble attempt from my side to share what I know about SOA and cloud computing. I hope the readers benefit from the SOA and cloud computing concepts discussed in the book and also gain insights on the use of technologies by reviewing the PoCs on the accompanying CD-ROM. Comments or suggestions on the content or presentation of the book will be received with great interest and high appreciation.

Shankar Kambhampaty
skambhampaty@gmail.com
February 2010

List of Acronyms

ADM	Architecture Development Method
BAM	Business Activity Monitoring
BPMN	Business Process Modeling Notation
CICS	Customer Information Control System
CORBA	Common Object Broker Architecture
CRM	Customer Relationship Management
CRUD	Create, Retrieve, Update, Delete
CTQ	Cost, Time and Quality
CTS	Common Type System
CWM	Common Warehouse Metamodel
DAL	Data access layer
DCS	Development Cost Savings
EA	Enterprise architecture
EDA	Event-Driven Architecture
EIS	Enterprise Information Systems
EJB	Enterprise JavaBean
EJBs	Enterprise JavaBeans
ERP	Enterprise Resource Planning
ETL	Extract, Transform and Load
FEAF	Federal Enterprise Architecture Framework
HTTP	Hyper Text Transfer Protocol
JAF	JavaBeans Activation Framework
JAX-WS	Java API for XML Web Services
JAXB	Java API for XML binding
JCA	Java Connector Architecture
JDBC	Java Database Connectivity
JIT	Just-in-Time
JMS	Java Messaging Service
JPA	Java Persistence API
JSP	Java Server Pages
JTA	Java Transaction API
JVM	Java Virtual Machine
LMS	Loan Management System
MDA	Model-Driven Architecture

MDB	Message-Driven Bean
MTBF	Mean Time Between Failures
MTTR	Mean Time to Restore
MSIL	Microsoft Intermediate Language
MVC	Model-View-Controller
OASIS	Organization for the Advancement of Structured Information Standards
OMG	Object Management Group
OOAD	Object-Oriented Analysis and Design
PE	Portable Executable
RFP	Request for Proposal
ROI	Return on Investment
SAAS	Software as a Service
SCA	Service Component Architecture
SCM	Supply Chain Management
SDO	Service Data Object
SOA	Service-Oriented Architecture
SOAD	Service-Oriented Analysis and Design
SOAP	Simple Object Access Protocol
SSAD	Structured Systems Analysis and Design
TEAF	Treasury Enterprise Architecture Framework
UI	User interface
UML	Unified Modeling Language
URI	Uniform Resource Identifier
WCF	Windows Communication Foundation
WS-*	Web Services
WS-BPEL	Web Services Business Process Execution Language
WSDL	Web Services Definition Language
WSIT	Web Services Interoperability Technology
WF	Windows Foundation
XML	eXtensible Markup Language
XSD	XML Schema Definition

List of Figures

List of Tables

Contents

Software Engineering Principles

CHAPTER 1

CONTENTS

LEARNING OBJECTIVES

After reading this chapter, you would be able to:

- Define software engineering.
- Understand the software development lifecycle.
- Distinguish between different software engineering methodologies.
- Understand the synergy between software engineering and project management.
- Know the critical success factors for software projects.

The IEEE Computer Society defines Software Engineering as the study of approaches for the application of a systematic, disciplined, quantifiable approach to the development, operation, and maintenance of software (IEEE 1990).

Thus, software engineering involves application of engineering principles to:

1. *development* of software;
2. *operation* of the software systems;
3. *maintenance* of software to address changes required for the functionality and behavior.

1.1 SOFTWARE ENGINEERING PRACTICE

Software engineering, in many ways, is analogous to civil engineering. In order to build a house for instance, the requirements of the intended occupants of the house have to be analyzed, layout of the house has to be prepared along with design of the interiors, construction of the house has to be completed followed by testing of electrical, communication and other utility sub-systems before handing over of the house to the owner. Subsequently, the house needs to be maintained from time-to-time against defects as well as changes to the needs of the occupants. Similarly, software engineering involves gathering and analyzing of software requirements, preparation of high-level architecture and detailed design, implementation of software followed by testing to verify and validate that the requirements are met effectively. As needs of users change, the software developed to meet the needs of the users is changed accordingly while fixing any defects and limitations uncovered during the course of operation.

Over centuries, the civil engineering knowledge has increased significantly and the techniques employed have been refined resulting in a mature practice that encapsulates best practices and lessons learned from building a large number and wide variety of structures. Similarly, software engineering body of knowledge, although relatively new, has grown substantially and is continuously being enhanced through best practices observed and lessons learnt from a great number of software projects executed globally.

One of the most comprehensive efforts in structuring the Software Engineering Body of Knowledge (SWEBOK) was undertaken by IEEE. In the *Guide to the Software Engineering Body of Knowledge*, an IEEE publication that describes practices that are accepted by software professionals across the industry, the following have been defined as the key knowledge areas (SWEBOK, 2005):

1. Software requirements;
2. Software design;
3. Software construction;
4. Software testing;
5. Software maintenance;
6. Software configuration management;
7. Software engineering management;
8. Software engineering process;
9. Software engineering tools and methods;
10. Software quality.

The first five knowledge areas mentioned above, namely, definition (or finalization) of *requirements, design, construction, testing* and *maintenance* constitute body of knowledge of activities that are repetitively applied to development and enhancement of software systems and hence these represent the key disciplines (or grouping of activities) of *software development lifecycle*. The other knowledge areas support the SDLC through disciplines that provide focus to process, management and quality aspects.

The next section discusses the software development lifecycle and the related five knowledge areas.

1.2 SOFTWARE DEVELOPMENT LIFECYCLE (SDLC)

The development of software involves activities for describing the functionality to be built, designing the elements that when working together provide the functionality defined, building the elements, and validating/verifying the elements developed. Further, addressing the non-functional aspects such as scalability, availability, security and performance also comes under the scope of software development.

The activities involved in software development may be grouped based on the corresponding knowledge areas and referred to as *disciplines* or *workflows*. Accordingly, following are the key disciplines of the software development lifecycle (SDLC) as already stated:

1. requirements;
2. design;

3. construction;
4. testing;
5. maintenance.

Each of the above disciplines represents a specific area of concern in software development that can be addressed by applying a set of techniques depending on the *nature of application* (function-oriented, object-oriented, service-oriented etc.) used for implementation. Table 1-1 describes the key disciplines of SDLC and summarizes techniques employed to address the concerns of each of the disciplines (SWEBOK, 2005).

In order to benefit from consistent application of the disciplines of SDLC repeatedly to software development initiatives, it is useful to recommend a sequence of steps for each of the disciplines which represents a *process* for that discipline. In software engineering, *process* is "sequence of steps required to develop or maintain software" (Humphrey, 1995). A process model deals with the *"what"* of developing software (Visitacion, 2001).

Through processes thus defined for each of the disciplines and keeping in mind the nature of software to be developed, it is possible to come up with different types of SDLC processes. Some of the most commonly employed SDLC processes for development of software include:

1. Structure Systems Analysis and Design Process (SSAD) based on the concept of *functions* and *data stores.*
2. Object-Oriented Analysis and Design Process (OOAD) based on the notion of *objects* modeled on real world entities.
3. Service-Oriented Analysis and Design Process (SOAD), described in the later chapters of this book, based on the concept of *services*.

One of the key aspects of an engineering approach to the development of software, therefore, involves understanding the nature of application to be developed and selection of the suitable SDLC process and methodology.

1.3 SOFTWARE ENGINEERING METHODOLOGIES

Methodology is a set of principles, practices and procedures that may be repeatedly applied to develop a specific category of applications. While a software process deals with *"what"* of developing software, *methodology* deals with the *"how"* of developing software.

The disciplines of SDLC, discussed earlier, may be applied in different ways resulting in various methodologies. Table 1-2 presents the key software engineering methodologies.

The suitability of the above-mentioned methodologies for engineering a software application is determined keeping in mind the *nature of the software application* and *characteristics of disciplines* employed.

TABLE 1-1 Key disciplines and techniques of SDLC

Discipline	*Description*	*Nature of Application*	*Key Techniques*	*Responsibility*
Requirements	• Properties that a software must exhibit	Function-oriented	Requirements gathering and preparation of functional specifications	Business analyst/functional specialist
	• Maybe functional or non-functional	Object-oriented	Use-case technique	
	• Constitute the basis for establishing the scope of a software project	Service-oriented	Business process modeling, use-case technique	
Design	• Process of defining components, interfaces and relationship which when implemented will result in software that meets the functional and non-functional requirements	Function-oriented	Data flow design, structural decomposition, detailed design	Architect/ designer
	• Baseline requirements are analyzed and architecture defined	Object-oriented	Use-case realization (through identification of analysis and design classes), class diagrams, sequence diagrams, collaboration diagrams	
	• Architecture serves as a blueprint	Service-oriented	Service modeling	

(continued)

TABLE 1-1 (*Continued*)

Discipline	*Description*	*Nature of Application*	*Key Techniques*	*Responsibility*
	• Requirements elaborated and detailed design completed			
Construction	• Creation of code with reduced complexity	Function-oriented Object-oriented Service-oriented	Coding of functions Coding of classes Coding of services	Programmer
Testing	• Dynamic verification of the software on a finite set of test cases against expected behavior.	Function-oriented Object-oriented Service-oriented	Unit testing, integration testing, system testing	Tester
Maintenance	• Modification of software after delivery to correct faults, to improve performance or other attributes or to adapt software to modified environment	Function-oriented Object-oriented Service-oriented	Bug fixing Change request implementation	Programmer Business analyst/architect/designer

TABLE 1-2 Key software engineering methodologies

Methodology	*Characteristics of the Disciplines*
Waterfall	• Requirements discipline is completed fully before taking up design; construction is started only after design is complete and so on.
Incremental/iterative	• Requirements and each of the other disciplines are completed in an incremental manner with the software application being developed over several iterations.
Prototyping	• Requirements are initially detailed to the extent possible. A prototype is developed through employing the design and testing disciplines. • Prototypes are typically developed to establish the user needs and discarded in most cases.
Spiral	• Requirements are progressively elaborated along with other disciplines in an evolutionary manner. • Prototype evolves into the complete software application.
Agile	• Requirements and the application evolve through collaboration between self-organizing cross-functional teams. • Scrum, XP, Crystal, Dynamic Systems Development Method (DSDM), Feature-Driven Development (FDD) and Lean Software Development are key agile methodologies that share the same characteristics but differ from an implementation standpoint.

While software engineering is related to practices needed for software development, maintenance and operation based on the knowledge areas and disciplines discussed including techniques for effective implementation, *software project management* is related to leveraging these practices in a project context in order to meet the goals of the sponsor of the project and fulfill the needs of the stakeholders.

1.4 PROJECT MANAGEMENT PRACTICE

Project Management Institute (PMI) has structured the body of project management knowledge based on generally accepted principles and practices for effective project management. Accordingly, PMI provides guidance on project management through an offering called *"A Guide to the Project Management Body of Knowledge (PMBOK)."* These practices and principles that constitute the guidance for project management have been successfully applied to a wide variety of software projects and have become a foundation for Quality Management Systems (QMS) in a large number of organizations.

PMBOK advocates a framework with 42 processes that fall under the following knowledge areas that represent the key competencies needed for project management:

1. scope management;
2. cost management;
3. quality management;
4. integration management;
5. human resource management;
6. communications management;
7. risk management;
8. procurement management.

Each process may be described in terms of *inputs, tools and techniques* and *outputs*. A brief description of the knowledge areas is provided in Table 1-3 (PMBOK, 2008).

TABLE 1-3 Project management knowledge areas

Knowledge Area	*Description*
Project scope management	• Processes related to the scope of the project to ensure completion of all the work in the project: o features and functions in a product or service; o work done to deliver a product.
Project cost management	• Processes related to the cost of the project to ensure that project is completed within approved budget and includes: o determining resources, estimating cost and obtaining approval to arrive at a project budget; o allocating cost estimate to individual work activities and controlling changes to project budget.

(continued)

TABLE 1-3 (*Continued*)

Knowledge Area	*Description*
Project quality management	• Processes related to quality, that is, ensuring that the project needs are met. • Quality Management includes: o quality planning; o quality assurance; o quality control.
Project integration management	• Processes required to ensure proper co-ordination of activities in the project. It involves development of project plan, its execution and change control.
Project human resource management	• Processes to best leverage human resources in a project and includes: o organization planning; o recruitment; o team development.
Project communications management	• Processes to generate, collect, disseminate and disposal of project information.
Project risk management	• Processes to identify, analyze and respond to project risk.
Project procurement management	• Processes to acquire goods and services from outside the organization.

These processes may be categorized under the following five groups that represent the typical stages in a project:

1. initiating;
2. planning;
3. executing;
4. monitoring;
5. closing.

For a successful project, suitable processes from the above groups need to be chosen and applied in right manner.

1.5 SOFTWARE ENGINEERING PROJECT

In a software engineering project, usually referred to as *software project*, the practices of project management are applied to a software engineering endeavor in the context of a project in order to meet the objectives of the sponsor and the needs of the user.

TABLE 1-4 Synergy between project management and software engineering processes

Project Management	*Software Engineering*
Scope of a project has to be established as per project management practice.	Scope may be defined in terms of the *requirements* described as software engineering discipline.
Cost of a project has to be assessed and approval of the sponsor obtained.	Estimation of the effort and therefore that of the cost may be made using the software engineering techniques such as *function point estimation* method or *use case estimation* method.
Quality goals, metrics and processes for project execution have to be defined.	Software engineering processes and methodologies may be defined as the basis for defining quality goals and metrics. The processes described by *software engineering quality* discipline, namely quality assurance process, verification process, validation process, review process and audit process may be adopted for quality management.
Integration management requires various elements of project to be co-ordinated in terms of project plan development, project plan execution and change control.	The processes defined under *software engineering management* supplement the project management processes especially those related to software engineering measurement.

Software engineering and project management are two aspects of value creation of software projects. The best practices and lessons learnt from both software engineering and project management may be applied in synergistic manner for the success of software engineering projects. Table 1-4 shows some of the aspects in which software engineering and project management can be complementary and reinforcing each other.

1.6 CRITICAL SUCCESS FACTORS FOR SOFTWARE PROJECTS

While the software engineering and project management processes provide mature techniques for success of software projects, they occasionally run into major issues in organizations. There are many reasons for this; however, most often it is because the principles and techniques available are not applied the way they ought to be.

Several factors that affect the success of software projects are:

- Clarity in contract established between project sponsor and the team executing the project in terms of goals and expectations. Project team should be aware of the exact terms and conditions of the contract for timely execution of deliverables that fully satisfy the expectations of project sponsor and users.
- Focus should be more on project management practices such as scope, cost, quality and less on software engineering practices such as requirements, architecture/design and testing leading to optimal approach in application of practices of software engineering and project management.
- Mutually agreed scope of the project in terms of functional and non-functional requirements (such as performance, scalability, availability and security).
- Choice of a project execution methodology consistent with the expected deliverables and timelines. For instance, methodologies such as *waterfall*, while in existence for a long term, are less suitable for large projects on account of issues with a "big bang" release. Iterative methodology should be considered in such projects.
- Selection of technology stack for implementation that is best suited to meet the requirements.
- Adequate effort in capturing the functional and non-functional requirements and addressing them effectively in architecture and design.
- Adoption of project management processes based on generally accepted practices at industry level leveraging the best practices and lessons learnt (such as PMBOK).
- Adoption of software engineering processes based on the generally accepted practices at industry level leveraging the best practices and lessons learnt (such as SWEBOK).
- Selection of right tools for conducting techniques of project management and software engineering processes.
- Regular involvement of project sponsor and the users in reviews for validation of work products at identified milestones.

From a technology perspective, software architecture represents the foundation on which the success of software development depends.

1.7 SUMMARY

The objective of this chapter is to present the basics of software engineering. The software engineering practice is discussed with reference to IEEE's Software Engineering Body of Knowledge (SWEBOK). The Software Development Lifecycle (SDLC) and the related disciplines are described. Leveraging of the software engineering practices in a project context is next discussed with reference to PMI's Project Management Body of Knowledge (PMBOK). The synergy between the practices of software engineering and project management is brought out for software engineering projects. Factors critical to success of software engineering projects are presented. It is pointed out that the *software architecture* serves as a foundation on which the success of software development depends.

KEY TERMS

Software Engineering	IEEE Computer Society defines Software Engineering as the study of approaches for the application of a systematic, disciplined, quantifiable approach to the development, operation, and maintenance of software.
Process	Process is sequence of steps required to develop or maintain software.
Methodology	Methodology is set of principles, practices and procedures that may be repeatedly applied to develop a specific category of applications.
SDLC	The five knowledge areas, namely, requirements, design, construction, testing and maintenance that are repetitively applied to development and enhancement of software systems is referred to as software development lifecycle (SDLC).
Project management	PMBOK defines project management as the application of knowledge, skills, tools, and techniques to project activities to meet project requirements.

REFERENCES

Humphrey, W. (1995) *A Discipline for Software Engineering*, Addison-Wesley Publishing Company, Inc., Reading, MA.

IEEE (1990) *IEEE Standard Glossary of Software Engineering Terminology*, IEEE std 610.12-1990, 1990.

PMBOK (2008) *A Guide to the Project Management Body of Knowledge (PMBOK® Guide)*, 4th edn, PMI.

SWEBOK (2005) *Guide to the Software Engineering Body of Knowledge: 2004 Version* (eds P. Bourque and R. Dupuis; Chair: Leonard L. Tripp), IEEE Computer Society.

Visitacion, M. (2001) *Understanding the Difference Between Process and Methodology*, Forrester, Document ID No.: RIB-072001-00146.

Software Architecture

CHAPTER 2

CONTENTS

LEARNING OBJECTIVES

After reading this chapter, you would be able to:

- Define software architecture.
- Understand the need and objectives of software architecture.
- Distinguish between different types of IT architecture.
- Know the architecture styles and patterns.
- Recognize that Service-Oriented Architecture is an architecture style.

Software architecture is the *blueprint* for a solution that satisfies the requirements of a software application. Software applications are developed to meet the needs of the users. For example, users of airline reservation application have the need to determine the availability of seats, undertake bookings (or cancellations) and make payments. The needs of the users form the basis for arriving at the software requirements of an application.

Software requirements of an application is usually a document that clearly states the problem that is addressed by the application in terms of the specific needs and constraints expressed as a set of verifiable and measurable statements. Software requirements define the problem that the application addresses in terms of "what" the user gets from the application and not "how" the problem is solved. In the example of airline reservation, a statement that expresses the need of the user to make a booking constitutes a requirement while any description on either the user interface or the storage of booking data in a database constitutes a solution and therefore does not qualify to be a requirement.

The following two types of requirements have to be taken into account in order to completely address the needs of users of a software application:

1. ***Functional requirements:*** Functional requirements define the functionality that the application provides.
2. ***Non-functional requirements:*** Non-functional requirements define the attributes (such as performance, scalability, etc.) that are also supported in providing the functionality to the users.

A set of software requirements can be addressed in a number of ways by defining a variety of sub-systems and interfaces that leverage the underlying technology platform in different ways. Software architecture is the blueprint that defines the specific sub-systems and interfaces which when implemented fulfil the software requirements and, therefore, the needs of the users.

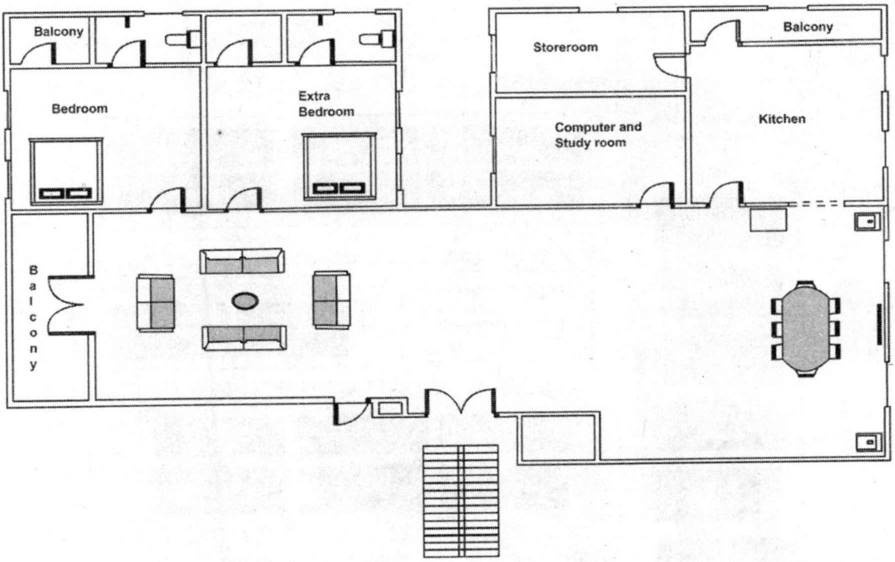

FIGURE 2-1 Layout of a house.

Illustration 1

Several analogies can be drawn from civil architecture to better understand software architecture (Alexander, 1979). Figure 2-1 shows a portion of a layout of a house.

The architecture of the house shows a living room, a kitchen, etc., the dimensions of which have been architected keeping in mind the specifications of the land and preferences and priorities of the residents. It is possible to come up with a number of solutions to address the same set of requirements.

Consider now the logical architecture of a simple Loan Management System (LMS) developed for a financial services company depicted in Figure 2-2.

The different modules – registration, loan enquiry, loan approval, etc. –address different concerns of the application. The interfaces between the layers of the application – presentation, business and data access layer – can also be clearly seen.

Going back to the analogy of the house, the rooms of the house can be seen as sub-systems of the architecture arrived at keeping in mind the preferences and priorities of residents that constitute the requirements; the doors are analogous to the interfaces, the specifications and topography of the land correspond to the characteristics of the platform on which the house is built.

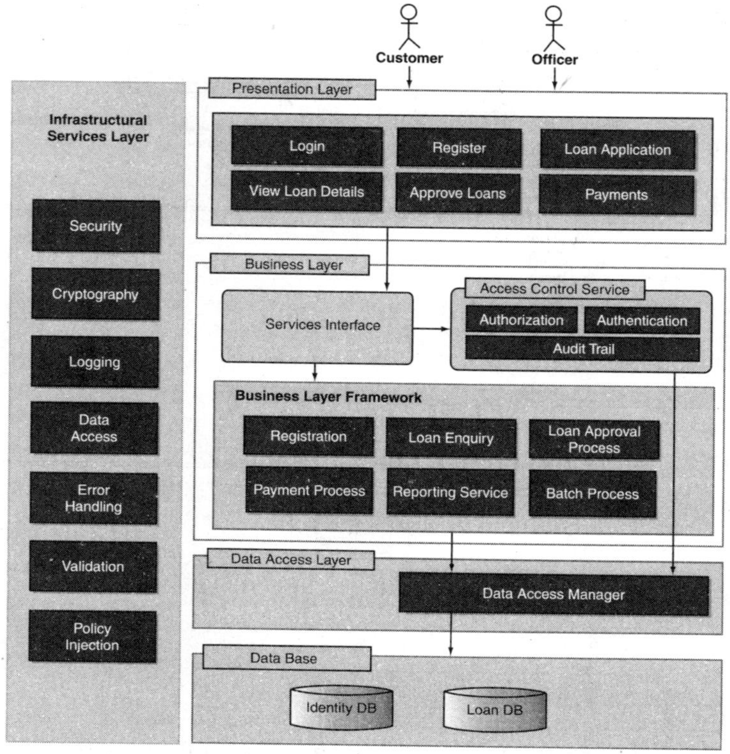

FIGURE 2-2 Logical architecture of software application.

Thus, the architecture of the application provides the blueprint that can form the basis for design and development. Just as the interior designers can develop the design of each of the room of a house on the basis of the blueprint provided by a civil architect, so can software designers develop detailed design based on the blueprint provided by the software architect. Taking the analogy further, just as interior designers take into account available constructs such as fixtures and furniture to solve the "recurring problems" of each type of the room in the house rather than develop design from scratch, so can software designers develop the designs of each layer and sub-system of an application based on established design patterns.

Formal Definition of Software Architecture

The definition of architecture as per ANSI/IEEE Std 1471-2000 is:

> *Software architecture is the fundamental organization of a system, embodied in its components, their relationships to each other and the environment, and the principles governing its design and evolution.*

On the basis of the above definition, software architecture can be specified for different types of software applications and systems. The scope of this book is limited to *Enterprise Applications* which are explained in detail in Chapter 6.

2.1 NEED FOR SOFTWARE ARCHITECTURE

Software applications vary from having a few modules with simple interfaces (similar to simple houses in civil architecture) to large enterprise applications that have large number of modules interfacing with a number of systems requiring several hundred person years of effort (akin to skyscrapers). Software applications also evolve over a period of time on the basis of changing business and user needs.

The need for a clearly defined architecture becomes apparent as the size and complexity of application increases. Every development activity involves trade-offs on *cost, time and quality* (abbreviated as CTQ); larger the application or its complexity greater the number of trade-offs and their impact on the success of the application. Architecture is key to ensuring that the trade-offs are made taking into account objectives of the stakeholders. The software architecture, thus defined, ensures that the available options are analyzed and decisions made to satisfy the goals of the stakeholders.

In order to ensure that software application is built to the required quality, established software engineering practices have to be employed for each stage of the software development lifecycle and their effectiveness measured and controlled so that goals of the application are fully met. The software engineering practices require a well-thought out foundation on which development activities can proceed in a planned manner to balance the CTQ (Jenkins, 2008). Software architecture serves to be that *foundation* on which the application can be built.

In the absence of the right architecture as a foundation, incompatibilities surface much later in the construction and testing stages of the development cycle, resulting in significant effort for correction. This effort towards rework can greatly impact the CTQs of a project and even result in failure of a project.

A well-architected solution whether in software development or civil construction

1. satisfies the functional requirements of the users;
2. meets the non-functional requirements;
3. allows for construction with available technologies and industry practices;
4. enables development to be based on established engineering principles to achieve the CTQ objectives.

2.2 OBJECTIVES OF SOFTWARE ARCHITECTURE

The functional and non-functional requirements of an application, determined by the analysis of the needs of the users, characterize the problem for which software architecture is developed. Software architecture represents the solution to the problem stated as a set of requirements.

The objectives of software architecture are to:

1. manage complexity by separation of concerns;
2. resolve concerns related to functional requirements by defining a set of layers, modules and interfaces which working together deliver the functionality required by the end-users;
3. ensure that non-functional requirements such as performance and scalability (that represent the qualities of a system) are addressed by defining necessary mechanisms (such as caching for improved performance);
4. exploit technology platform capabilities to bring down the effort required to build the application;
5. leverage reusable assets and frameworks available for the platform to reduce the cost of development;
6. lower the impact due to change of business requirements, operating constraints and technology environment;
7. apply best practices and lessons learnt in developing similar applications;
8. represent the layers, modules or sub-systems visually to make it easy for different stakeholders to validate and confirm that the architecture so defined meets the end-user's goals;
9. provide a foundation for designers to elaborate the architecture and generate design artefacts that can form the basis for development;
10. enable use of consistent terminology during software engineering lifecycle among architects, designers and developers.

Software architecture can be represented as *views*. No single view of architecture can elegantly and efficiently represent the various aspects of the architecture and meet the objectives given above. Software architecture is, therefore, represented in multiple views. The views used to represent the architecture are dependant on the type of architecture discussed in the next section.

2.3 TYPES OF IT ARCHITECTURE

In the context of an enterprise, software applications are developed, hosted, maintained and used by different stakeholders to meet the objectives discussed above. The key types of software architecture that model and address the concerns of different stakeholders in an enterprise are as follows.

Enterprise Architecture

Enterprise architecture (EA) is a collection of models that define the structure required for an organization to achieve its objectives. The scope of EA is business of the organization and the IT systems needed to support the business along with policies and principles for its governance. From an IT standpoint, one of the key aspects of EA is that its focus is on enterprise-wide concerns and on how IT systems fit into the "big picture" of the enterprise.

Enterprise Architects deal with future state business and IT vision explicitly stated and inferred from interactions with CXOs (short form for CEO, CIO, CTO, CFO) and other stakeholders in an organization. Using insights in business trends, technology trends, regulations and compliance requirements, Enterprise Architects translate business strategies to IT strategies for the enterprise. Several decisions related to rationalization, migration and retiring of applications are made by Enterprise Architects to ensure that IT applications enable and stay aligned with business processes and goals of the enterprise.

The models that represent the EA include:

1. Business model;
2. Application model;
3. Information model;
4. Infrastructure model.

There are several frameworks for defining EA of which the following are the key:

1. Zachman's Framework;
2. TOGAF's Architecture Development Method (ADM) Framework;
3. Federal Enterprise Architecture Framework (FEAF);
4. Treasury Enterprise Architecture Framework (TEAF);
5. C4ISR/DoD Framework.

Business Architecture

Business architecture is the blueprint of the business concerns of IT systems (or an enterprise). It involves developing a model based on the following:

1. business drivers;
2. business rules;
3. business processes.

Business architecture is defined by *Business Architects* (variously called *Business Analysts* or *Business Consultants* in some organizations). The business architecture so defined is mapped to technology elements for developing solution architecture of the software applications that implement the business model.

In developing the business architecture, Business Architects initially focus on the current state business strategy, business processes, rules and policies and define "AS-IS" business architecture for the IT system (or the enterprise). "TO-BE" architecture is then developed keeping in mind the business trends, competitiveness and vision for future state of the business.

The following are some of the key standards/frameworks for developing business architecture:

1. TOGAF's ADM – Phase B;
2. IBM's Business Architecture Description;
3. Microsoft Motion.

Solution Architecture

Solution Architecture represents the solution to the business problem that needs to be implemented by IT system(s) and is key to aligning business with IT. The business problem is stated as a set of business requirements and the solution architecting process involves mapping of functionality envisaged in IT system(s) to technical elements while ensuring that the non-functional attributes (such as performance, etc.) are suitably addressed.

The focus of a Solution Architect is on a specific business area from a functional perspective for which a solution needs to be developed and from a technical perspective defining those elements which when working together will deliver the required functionality with the defined quality attributes (non-functional requirements of the system). The Solution Architect ensures that the solution, which is typically one or more IT systems for a business owner, integrates into the target environment and, where EA has been defined for an organization that solution architecture aligns with it. In doing so, the Solution Architect evaluates "Build" vs "Buy" options and enables a decision to be made with buy-in from key stakeholders.

Before the advent of the component models, software applications were primarily confined to mainframe and super-mini computer environments and it was a common practice to represent software architecture of such applications in three different views: *Processing*, *Data* and *Connection* (Perry and Wolf, 1992). However, the enterprise applications developed with component models require more views to bring out additional detail. Solution architecture is, therefore, represented initially using at least the following views to describe what the solution is and how it would be implemented (Kazman, 1998):

1. conceptual view;
2. logical view;
3. physical view.

When the functional and non-functional requirements are defined clearly during the software development lifecycle, more views are needed to specify the architecture so that design activities can elaborate on the architecture to produce detailed designs.

Solution architecture is critical when developing solutions that are domain-intensive such as those developed for vertical industry segments (banking, financial services, insurance, etc.). Understanding the domain and mapping the business processes and workflows that represent the functionality of a system to technology elements and meeting integration requirements are key to getting the solution architecture right and also to the success of the IT system(s) developed.

The IEEE 1471-2000 is a standard for software architecture and can be the basis for architecture representation. More details of solution architecting process to represent architecture are provided in Chapter 5.

Technical Architecture

Technical Architecture, as the name suggests, is a blueprint of the solution described in terms of the technical elements, their structure and relationship with each other and with that of the underlying technology platform. The technical view of a solution architecture of an IT system corresponds to the technical architecture.

Technical Architects focus on specific technologies such as J2EE and .NET. Since technical architecture is based on elements that can be constructed through programming, design patterns have been used in many cases as technical elements in the architecture. A *design pattern* is a solution to a recurring problem in specific design situations (Buschmann et al., 1996).

On account of the wide range of technologies and products available in the market place, technical architecture (or technical view of solution architecture) for a given set of requirements can have a number of variants on the basis of the products chosen and reusable components or frameworks employed. Also, as technologies get outdated and the support for products withdrawn by their vendors, it becomes imperative to revisit the technical architecture for the same set of functional and non-functional requirements.

Infrastructure Architecture

Infrastructure Architecture provides the blueprint for the underlying hardware, operating systems, network, messaging and security that constitute the application of infrastructure on which solutions that meet business needs are hosted.

Infrastructure Architects review the technical architecture (or technical view of solution architecture) and focus on sizing and capacity planning of the application hosting and storage systems. Identification and implementation of systems for monitoring, provisioning and fault tolerance are activities

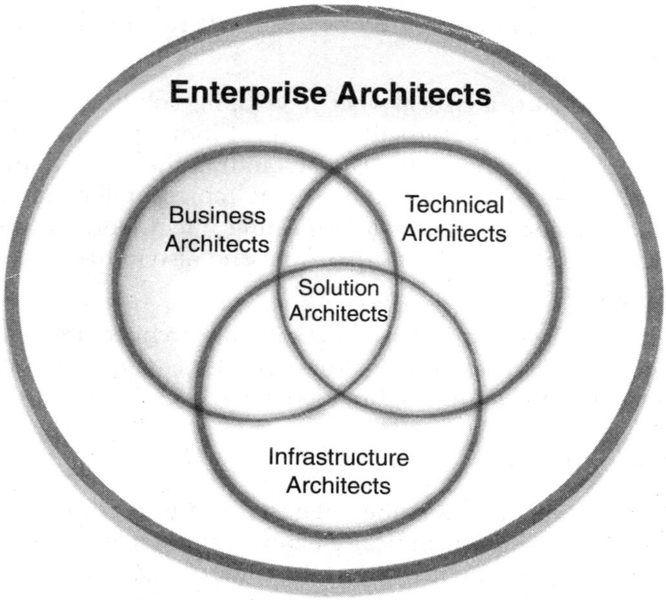

FIGURE 2-3 Types of architects.

taken up by an Infrastructure Architect. Definition of policies for application deployment and security compliance also come under their purview.

Types of Architects

While the scope of enterprise architecture, solution architecture, technical architecture and infrastructure can be clearly defined, the competencies required in different types of architects is often overlapping as shown in Figure 2-3. For instance, Technical Architects need to have an understanding of the strengths and limitations of infrastructure and should factor infrastructure dependencies appropriately into the solution. Likewise, Infrastructure Architects need to have the necessary insights into the technologies and products that would be hosted on the infrastructure.

2.4 ARCHITECTURAL PATTERNS AND STYLES

Software architecture represents functional and non-functional characteristics attributed to the requirements of the application it fulfils. Software applications with common functional and non-functional characteristics will share similar architectural properties (such as separation of concerns, encapsulation, etc.).

A notion of an *architecture style* emerged in software engineering to represent a set of architectural properties exhibited by an element or component of architecture. Architectural style provides an abstraction for an element or component of architecture with a defined set of architecture properties (Shaw, 1990). Thus, architecture for a software application comprises multiple architecture styles. This implies that architecture of a software application can be developed by identifying relevant architecture styles and applying them suitably. An architectural style is represented in terms of components, connectors and constraints related to control and data flow (Shaw and Clements, 1997).

Table 2-1 lists the seven commonly used architectural styles (Shaw and Garlan, 1996) with a brief description on what constitutes components and connectors.

A term in software architecture that is often used synonymously to architectural style is the *Architectural Pattern* which grew out of the efforts of the object-oriented programming community to describe solutions to recurring problems encountered in development.

A pattern can be defined as "an idea that has been useful in one practical context and will probably be useful in others" (Fowler, 1997). "Architectural Pattern is a description of *element* and *relation* types together with a set of constraints on how they are used" (Bass et al., 2003). An architectural pattern is described in terms of context, problem and solution with a supporting rationale. The difference between architectural pattern and design pattern is that

TABLE 2-1 Architecture style

Architecture Style	*Description*
Pipes and filters	Data flow is central to this style. Components have inputs and outputs and are called *filters*. Connectors join the components and are called *pipes*. Component (filter) reads data through its inputs, processes the data and writes the data to outputs that are transmitted as input to the next component through the connector (pipe). *Example:* Concurrent processing scenarios such as in Unix.
Objects	Data encapsulation is key aspect of this style. *Object* is an abstract data type that encapsulates data and its operations. Components are instantiations of the object data type and interact by *method* calls that serve as connectors. *Example:* Objects in OO languages.

(continued)

TABLE 2-1 (*Continued*)

Architecture Style	*Description*
Implicit invocation	Event-driven approach to invocations is a significant aspect of this style. Component invocations in this style are implicit, that is they generate signals called *events*. Connectors are *callbacks* that on receiving components bind in a static or a dynamic manner. *Example:* Event-based UI handling approach in MS Windows and Apple Macintosh systems.
Layering	Separation of concerns is fundamental to this style and this is accomplished through definition of *layers*. *Layers* are components and *protocols* are connectors that define how layers interact with one another. *Example: N*-tier web application.
Repositories	The focus in this style is on a central data structure that is widely accessed. The *central data store* and the *elements* that access it constitute the components and the mechanisms for their *interactions* form the connectors. *Example:* Database and Blackboard.
Interpreters	The concept of a virtual machine is central to this style which separates the invoking element from the execution element for portability and extensibility. *Invoking element, interpreting element* and *execution element* form the components while the *command language* of the invoking element is the connector. *Example:* Execution of scripting languages such as Perl.
Process control	Tuning of information state from the current state to a targeted future state is the focal point of this style. The elements that *process* and *control* information state are the components and the *input, output* and *feedback loop* correspond to the connectors. *Example:* Cruise Control.

the architectural pattern is course-grained and is described at the level of subsystems or modules while the design pattern is fine-grained and is described at the level of language classes (McGovern et al., 2003).

Architectural patterns, being synonymous to architecture styles, many of the architecture styles have also been identified as architectural patterns

(Shaw, 1996). Both architecture styles and architecture patterns describe abstractions of elements with specific architecture properties that can be applied in developing software architecture. However, there is one key difference in each of the perspectives. In the architecture styles perspective, focus is on components, connectors and their interactions and not on the rationale. Architectural patterns, on the other hand, not only require the rationale to be provided but also must capture common use and be aesthetic (Avgeriou and Zdun, 2005).

Table 2-2 provides architectural patterns and also a brief description in terms of context, problem and solution for each pattern (Buschmann et al., 1996). While in many cases architectural patterns are same as architectural styles, the purpose in discussing them is to present the architectural pattern perspective.

In the past few years, a new architectural style, Service-Oriented Architecture, has been added to the classical styles listed above. This book discusses various aspects of Service-Oriented Architecture with focus on Enterprise Applications.

TABLE 2-2 Architectural patterns

Architecture Patterns		*Description*
Layers	*Context:*	Decomposition of a system.
	Problem:	System to handle multiple levels of abstraction.
	Solution:	Group elements into layers with each layer interacting with the next layer.
Pipes and filters	*Context:*	Data flow with multi-step processing.
	Problem:	Sequential stages in data processing.
	Solution:	Components defined with inputs, outputs and processing such that output of one component feeds the input of the next component of the next stage.
Blackboard	*Context:*	Algorithmic problem solving not feasible.
	Problem:	Multiple problem-solving agents to cooperate.
	Solution:	Problem-solving agents interact with shared data store.
Broker	*Context:*	Distributed system with autonomous interacting components.
	Problem:	Mechanism to loosely couple interacting components.

(continued)

TABLE 2-2 (*Continued*)

Architecture Patterns		*Description*
	Solution:	Introduce mediator component that facilitates clients and servers.
Model–view–controller	*Context:*	User interfaces (UI) are prone to change and often need to be ported with different "look and feel" considerations.
	Problem:	Model to allow for changes to UI without affecting the functional part.
	Solution:	Separate application into model, view and controller.
Presentation–abstraction–control	*Context:*	Interacting components that use agents.
	Problem:	Model-interactive components as a set of cooperating agents.
	Solution:	Structure the model as a tree with presentation, abstraction and control agents.
Microkernel	*Context:*	Components with stable functional core that need to adapt over time.
	Problem:	Coping with functional and technology changes.
	Solution:	Encapsulate core services in a microkernel component.
Reflection	*Context:*	System providing modification of its own persistence.
	Problem:	Expose modifiable elements while hiding core elements.
	Solution:	Mechanism to allow change of structure and behavior dynamically.

2.5 SUMMARY

The objective of this chapter is to lay a foundation for discussion on software architecture, on service-oriented architecture and enterprise applications in subsequent chapters. The general concepts of software architecture are presented in this chapter. The need for software architecture and the possible impact on cost, time and quality aspects of a project due to lack of software architecture focus is discussed. The objectives of software and the types of software architecture, namely, enterprise architecture, business architecture, solution architecture, technical architecture and infrastructure architecture, are defined. Finally, the different architecture styles and patterns are summarized and *Service-Oriented Architecture* is described as an architecture style.

KEY TERMS

Software Architecture	IEEE Std 1471-2000 defines Software architecture as the fundamental organization of a system, embodied in its components, their relationships to each other and the environment, and the principles governing its design and evolution.
Enterprise Architecture	Enterprise architecture (EA) is a collection of models that define the structure required for an organization to achieve its objectives.
Architecture Framework	Open Group defines an architecture framework as a tool that can be used for developing a broad range of different types of architecture.
Zachman Framework	Zachman framework is an architecture framework for information systems development that can be applied to enterprise architecture. It is represented as a matrix where the rows correspond to the different perspectives (planner, owner, architect, designer and builder) and the columns correspond to the dimensions of system development effort (data, function, network, people, time, motivation).
TOGAF Framework	TOGAF is an industry standard architecture framework that includes a detailed method and a set of supporting tools for developing an enterprise architecture.
Business Architecture	Business architecture is the blueprint of the business concerns of IT systems (business drivers, rules, processes).
Solution Architecture	Solution architecture represents the solution to the business problem that needs to be implemented by IT system(s).
Technical Architecture	Technical architecture defines a solution described in terms of the technical elements, their structure and relationship with each other and with that of the underlying technology platform.
Infrastructure Architecture	Infrastructure architecture represents the solution for the underlying technology platform to include hardware, operating systems, network, messaging and security on which solutions that meet business needs are hosted.

Architectural Pattern	Architectural patterns are solutions to architectural problems in software engineering.
Architecture Style	Architectural style provides an abstraction for an element or component of architecture with a defined set of architecture properties.

REFERENCES

Alexander, C. (1979) *The Timeless Way of Building,* Oxford University Press, New York.

Avgeriou, P. and Zdun, U. (2005) *Architectural Patterns Revisited – A Pattern Language.* 10th European Conference on Pattern Languages of Programs (EuroPlop 2005), Irsee, Germany.

Bass, L., Clements, P. and Kazman, R. (2003) *Software Architecture in Practice,* 2nd edn, Addison-Wesley, Boston, MA.

Buschmann, F., Meunier, R., Rohnert, H., Sommerlad, P. and Stal, M. (1996), *Pattern-Oriented Software Architecture – A System of Patterns,* John Wiley & Sons, Ltd., Chichester.

Fowler, M. (1997) *Analysis Patterns – Reusable Object Models,* Addison-Wesley, Boston, MA.

Jenkins, N. (2008) *A Project Management Primer: Basic Principles – Scope Triangle,* Project Smart, UK.

Kazman, R. (1998) Representing software architecture, *The Architect, SEI Interactive,* **1**(3).

McGovern, J., Ambler, S.W., Stevens, M.E., Linn, J., Sharan, V., et al. (2003) *Practical Guide to Enterprise Architecture,* Prentice Hall, New Jersey.

Perry, D.E. and Wolf, A.L. (1992) Foundations for the study of software architecture, *ACM SIGSOFT Software Engineering Notes,* **17**(4), 40–52.

Shaw, M. (1990) Toward higher-level abstractions for software systems, *Data & Knowledge Engineering,* **5**, 119–28.

Shaw, M. (1996) Some patterns for software architecture, *Pattern Languages of Program Design,* Vol. 2 (eds J. Vlissides, J. Coplien and N. Kerth), Addison-Wesley, Boston, MA, pp. 255–69.

Shaw, M. and Clements, P.C. (1997) *A Field Guide to Boxology: Preliminary Classification of Architectural Styles for Software Systems.* COMPSAC '97: Proceedings of the 21st International Computer Software and Applications Conference, IEEE Computer Society, pp. 6–13.

Shaw, M. and Garlan, D. (1996) *Software Architecture: Perspectives on an Emerging Discipline,* Prentice-Hall, New Jersey.

CHAPTER 3

Service-Oriented Architecture

CONTENTS

LEARNING OBJECTIVES

After reading this chapter, you would be able to:

- Understand the concepts of SOA.
- Understand SOA using an analogy from daily life.
- Determine the drivers for SOA.
- Know the dimensions of SOA.
- Identify the key components of SOA.
- Become familiar with different perspectives of SOA.

Service-oriented architecture (SOA) is an architecture style that supports communication between services. It is based on the concept of *services*. A service is a unit of functionality that exists autonomously and whose access is through a defined interface. Services are coarse-grained elements that are stateless, loosely coupled and communicate via *messages*. In the service-oriented model, services are exposed by *service-provider* applications and invoked by *service consumers*.

Service-provider and service-consumer applications are loosely coupled by the use of *service contract* and *data contract*. A service contract is an interface that defines the message types used by service providers and service consumers to exchange messages (Skonnard, 2005). Service contracts specify one or more operations that represent individual message exchange or a request/reply message exchange. A data contract is a formal agreement between a service and a client that abstractly describes the data to be exchanged (MSDN, 2007). A service consumer invokes the operations provided by a service contract as part of the service call and exchanges data as per the data contract.

One of the key aspects of the service model is that service providers and service consumers are loosely coupled to each other. The definition of contracts enables loose coupling because service providers and service consumers can base all interactions on contract definitions than make any assumptions of each other. It also allows service providers to register their services with a *service registry* that service consumers can look-up to dynamically discover the services offered by the providers as shown in Figure 3-1.

3.1 SERVICE ORIENTATION IN DAILY LIFE

There are many examples of service orientation in everyday life. Consider the services provided by mail order companies and how the principles of service orientation apply to the business of providing goods in response to orders received by mail.

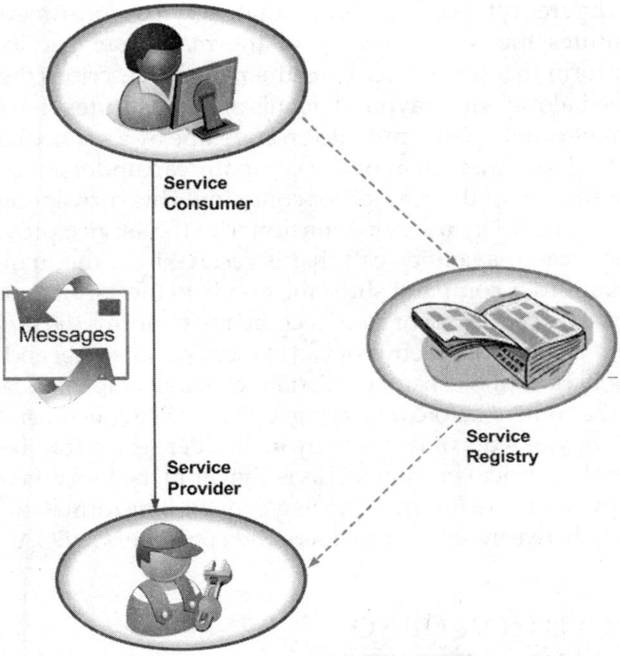

FIGURE 3-1 Service-oriented model.

Mail-Order Service

Figure 3-2 depicts pictorially a typical mail-order process.

1. Mail-order companies provide the service of ordering goods via mail. They are *service providers* of goods advertised by them.
2. Mail-order service providers publish catalog of goods in newspapers and magazines. The catalog constitutes a *service registry.*
3. People availing the mail-order service are *service consumers* who browse the mail-order catalog to determine the product of their interest.

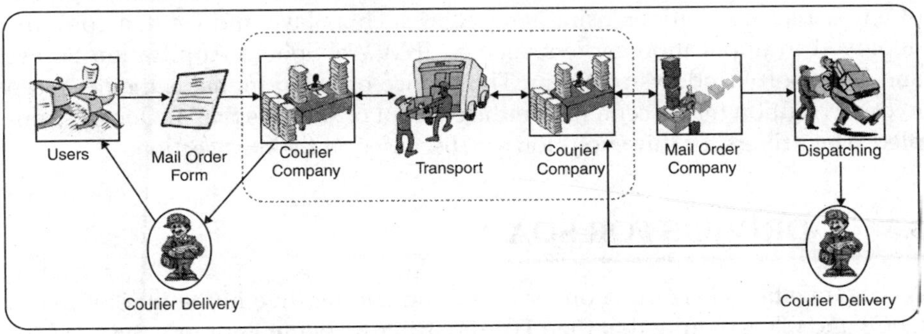

FIGURE 3-2 Mail-order business.

4. The different types of orders that service consumers can make constitutes the *service contract* of the mail-order service. The mail-order form that the service consumer fills in describes the goods to be shipped along with payment details and constitutes the data *contract*.
5. The mail-order form is put into an envelope by a service consumer that a postal department or a courier company can understand and shipped to the address of the mail-order company. This corresponds to a *service call* being made by a service consumer to the service provider.
6. In response to a service call that is received via the mail-order form, the mail-order company ships the goods to the service consumers.
7. The postal department or courier company performs the function of routing and delivery of the envelope to the service consumer and transporting goods back to the consumer. Certain courier companies can also transform the content before delivering to the service consumer. For example, a soft copy of a document sent by mail-order service can be printed and sent to the service consumer. This is similar to the function performed by Enterprise Service Bus in providing content transformation, routing and delivery between service providers and consumers in SOA.

3.2 EVOLUTION OF SOA

SOA is the next logical step in the evolution of programming paradigms (Nickull, 2005). Figure 3-3 depicts the evolution of software programming approaches. Software applications were developed on the basis of structured programming approach before the arrival of the object-oriented technologies. The object-oriented programming languages such as Smalltalk and C++ resulted in a programming paradigm that involved modeling of applications based on real-world objects. The development of languages such as Microsoft Visual Basic to support rich user interface resulted in client–server applications. The limitations of client–server solutions resulted in enhancements to languages and tools to support *N*-tier applications. The innovations in managing the life-cycle of objects resulted in development of component models for development of enterprise applications using languages such as Java and C# that could be deployed in application servers such as IBM WebSphere Application Server and Microsoft Windows platform. The service-oriented model is the next step in this evolution that is centered on the concept of services that are loosely coupled. The drivers for this evolution are discussed in the next section.

3.3 DRIVERS FOR SOA

As organizations become more efficient and competitive in the market place, CEOs and CIOs require that their IT infrastructure better supports the needs of the business better. A review of several SOA projects in different organizations

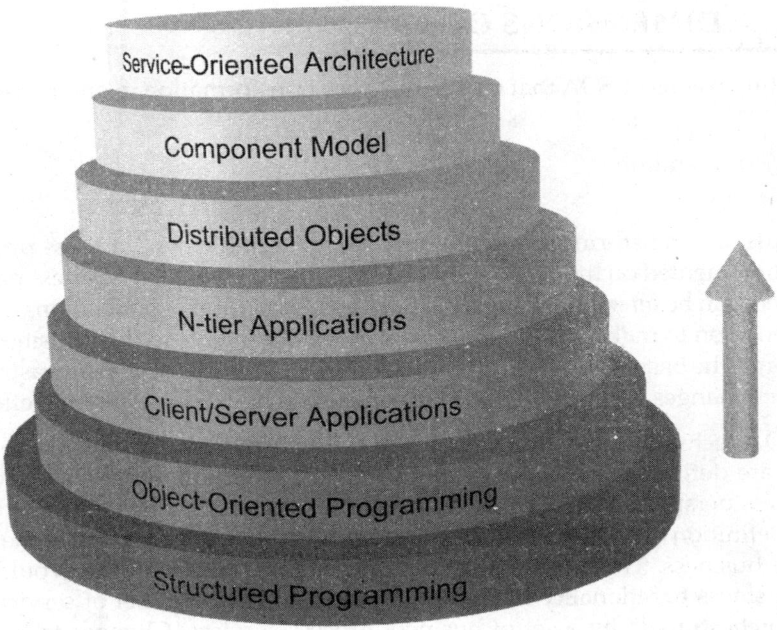

FIGURE 3-3 Evolution of SOA.

brought out the following as key drivers for SOA from business and technology perspective:

Business

1. Rapid business process changes.
2. Reduction of process cycle times.
3. Promotion of business through multiple channels.
4. Protection of investments in legacy applications.
5. Lower total cost of ownership.

Technology

1. Application modernization.
2. Technology change management.
3. Integration and interoperability for enterprise-wide heterogeneous applications.
4. Support by product vendors.

These drivers are a result of the need for an enterprise to be able to transform its business to adapt itself to changes in marketplace and can be broadly divided into three categories that represent the different dimensions of SOA.

3.4 DIMENSIONS OF SOA

The dimensions of SOA that enable business transformation in enterprises are:

1. reuse;
2. integration;
3. agility.

Business transformation in enterprises is possible when business processes are implemented on the basis of *reusable elements* defined from business perspective that can be *integrated* using an *agile* IT infrastructure. Organizations are then in a position to make strategic and tactical enhancements to their business processes on the basis of changes in the market place. The use of agile infrastructure enables changes to business processes with relative ease and minimal effort.

SOA techniques provide reusability through the concept of services. Services are defined to be *coarse-grained* to provide reusable functionality from a business perspective. The agility is brought about in SOA through an externalized definition of business processes that can be changed according to the needs of the business. The architecture of an enterprise based on SOA would have the business functionality of the applications exposed as a set of services that are "orchestrated" by a set of business process services. Changes to business functionality of any of the business applications do not impact the rest of the application infrastructure of the enterprise. Likewise, changes to the orchestration element of the business process services do not also impact the business applications in a well-architected SOA solution for an enterprise. Thus, the complexity and agility of the business processes can be more easily managed than if they had been "hard-wired" using traditional programming languages.

Integration of service providers and service consumers in SOA is addressed efficiently through the *Enterprise Service Bus* (ESB) pattern. It has several advantages over the alternative *Hub-and-Spoke* architecture used for application integration. In the *Hub-and-Spoke* architecture too, a centralized "hub" acts a message broker that accepts requests from multiple applications that are connected to it via connectors as "spokes." The hub has capabilities for message transformation, validation, routing and asynchronous message delivery. However, the hub constitutes a single point of failure. Also, most of the vendors provide hub and spoke architecture through expensive proprietary products (Bakker, 2005). Hence, the bus architecture of ESB, with distributed services of message routing, transformation and event handling, provides the capabilities needed for loose coupling and service-level integration between providers and consumers of services more efficiently.

SOA, therefore, has reusability, agility and integration as three dimensions that are critical to business transformation in organizations. The use of SOA techniques can also bring about other possibilities. As organizations go through mergers and acquisitions and also make collaborative arrangements with other enterprises for competitive edge, restructuring of the business takes place that would result in business processes supported by existing business applications to be moved to different/newer applications within the same organization or to those of the collaborating partners outside the organizational boundaries. SOA techniques allow for the degree of agility such business transformations demand by maintaining focus on the business processes and their orchestration rather than be limited by the technology used for implementing the applications.

3.5 KEY COMPONENTS OF SOA

The key components of SOA would be those that support the three dimensions discussed in the previous section: reuse, integration and agility.

Services

Service is the basic component of service orientation that provides reuse. A service exposed by a service provider is coarse-grained in the business functionality it provides and is defined by a service contract and a data contract. Service consumers invoke an operation published by a service as a part of the service contract and provide data as per the data contract. Characteristics of services include autonomy, loose coupling, statelessness, composability and discoverability. These are discussed in greater detail in Chapter 8.

Services can be implemented using a number of technologies such as *web services*. Web services are described using WSDL and are invoked using XML messages embedded in a SOAP envelope over a standard protocol such as the HTTP.

While web services (SOAP over HTTP) is the most popular technology to implement a service, it is important to note that the use of web services does not amount to SOA. The following four tenets of service orientation need to be met (Evdemon, 2005):

1. Service boundaries are explicit and services interact through explicit message-passing over well-defined boundaries.
2. Services are autonomous in terms of data isolation and loose coupling.
3. All interactions are based on service contract, data contract and associated policies.
4. Service compatibility is based on policy expressions (such as those of WS-Policy) when service contract cannot completely specify all aspects of service interaction.

Enterprise Service Bus (ESB)

An ESB is an architectural pattern that acts as the mediator/broker between the service provider and the service consumer. It forms the communication infrastructure for services to interact with one another across locations, supporting different transports, and across organizational boundaries. It provides integration capability through content routing, transformation and delivery between service providers and service consumers and has several advantages over alternative integration approaches such as *Hub and Spoke*.

ESB is an architectural pattern which by definition does not impose a specific implementation approach. The current scenario is that major vendors have tools/products that support the ESB concept and though ESBs from different vendors support the core requirements of content routing, transformation and delivery, they are significantly different from one another in the implementation aspects.

Orchestration

Business process orchestration brings agility to the enterprise. To create a business process consisting of a set of services, a workflow is defined that invokes the appropriate service at each stage in the business process. To execute a business process, the workflow defined is "orchestrated." Orchestration controls the process-level integration and automation of services.

Business Process Execution Language (BPEL) is gaining wide acceptance as the orchestration standard. BPEL is a language to specify business process as a workflow. Major vendors/open-source projects support BPEL and have orchestration engines that automate the process flow.

3.6 PERSPECTIVES OF SOA

SOA has received considerable attention from several quarters of the industry. While technology providers are defining SOA reference models and developing products to support those standards, standards bodies are keen to see increased standardization. With a significant growth expected in the adoption of SOA, analyst organizations have been conducting surveys and providing insights into trends noticed across the industry. This section discusses the perspectives of standards bodies and industry analysts.

Perspectives of Standard Bodies

The World Wide Consortium (W3C) has published a set of standards for web languages and protocols such as XML and SOAP in order to establish compatibility between fundamental web technologies and allow for any hardware and software to access the web and work together. Web services based architecture (W3C, 2004) is central to W3C's standardization and SOA is defined and applied by W3C in the context of web languages, protocols and web services architecture. W3C has also published Service Modeling Language (SML) standard for creating models of complex services and systems including their structure, constraints, policies and best practices (SML, 2009).

Organization for the Advancement of Structured Information Standards (OASIS) has developed number of web services standards such as WS-Transaction, WS-Reliability, etc. OASIS has been developing standards for SOA based on the

Service Component Architecture (SCA) and Service Data Objects (SDO) initially put forth by IBM and incubated by Open SOA Collaboration, an informal group of 18 software vendors. OASIS will be advancing SCA and SDO through the open standardization process (OASIS, 2007). SCA brings in the notion of assembling services to create a business solution thus separating the role of a programmer who develops the service from that of an architect who assembles the services. This allows for lifecycle management of services to be driven from an architecture level rather than from a UML or code level (Thompson, 2006). Further, OASIS has developed a standard reference model for SOA with the goal of coming up with a vocabulary and a common understanding of SOA. The reference model is an abstract framework that provides an understanding of the entities and their relationships for SOA (SOA-RM, 2006). Based on the concepts and relationships of the standard reference model, a reference architecture for SOA has also been developed with three main views:

1. service eco-system view related to participants of a SOA eco-system;
2. realizing services view with focus on requirements for SOA;
3. owning view related to governance and management of SOA systems (SOA-RAF, 2009).

OMG has developed or adopted several standards for modeling such as Business Process Modeling Notation (BPMN) for business processes, Unified Modeling Language (UML) for service and component modeling and Common Warehouse Metamodel (CWM) for modeling databases and business intelligence systems. It recently formed a special interest group on SOA to coordinate OMG's SOA efforts with other standards bodies. OMG has taken a platform-independent view based on its Model Driven Architecture (MDA) standards. According to OMG, "*Each of the SOA layers can be driven from models. MDA standards offer the capability to design a complete SOA solution through models, and minimize the effort invested in specific technologies or protocols*" (OMG, 2006). An UML Profile for SOA and a metamodel specification called SOAML has been developed by OMG with stereotypes such as ServicePoint, ServiceChannel, ServiceContract, ServiceInterface, etc. to model SOA solutions using extensions to UML (SOAML, 2009).

Future Trends

Adoption of SOA results can result in significant improvement to meet the specific and varied needs of an enterprise. The recent technology and business trends have opened up new vistas in the application of the principles of SOA for enterprise solutions. On size of the market for SOA, IDC projects that "by 2010 global SOA-based services spending will reach $33.8 billion" (IDC, 2006). This shows that the demand for SOA is string and growing.

According to Rosenthal, a leading SOA Consultant, "*The most important trend will probably be the emergence of SOA in the Virtual Enterprise. SOA will not be limited to an Enterprise Architecture, but will be manifested also as part of Cloud Computing and especially SaaS.*" (Rosenthal, 2009).

On the biggest trend or development for SOA, Morrison, Chief Architect of Layer 7 technologies, indicates that *"A growing recognition that the cloud *-as-a-Service (*aaS) model and SOA are not incompatible, but represent a logical progression…."* (Morrison, 2009).

On priority for enterprises, Forrester indicates that *"One top priority for enterprises is improving business processes, either by directly automating steps in a business process (such as order management) or by providing the right information at the right time to people who participate in the business processes."* (Bartels and Rymer, 2006).

Gartner states that *"Use SOA when designing most large, new business applications and processes, or when integrating some combination of purchased packages, legacy applications and services from other business units"* (Shulte, 2006).

Further, Gartner defines a more mature version of SOA called *Advanced SOA* that involves the addition of *"business event and event-driven architecture (EDA) model to its original request/reply interactive business service model"* (Natis and Schulte, 2006).

The next chapter discusses SOA at enterprise level.

3.7 SUMMARY

The objective of this chapter is to introduce the concepts of SOA. The evolution of SOA from structured programming principles to service-oriented principles is discussed. The drivers for SOA and the three dimensions of SOA – reuse, integration and agility – are presented. The subsequent chapters build on the basic concepts described in this chapter to provide insights into architecture, design and development aspects of SOA.

KEY TERMS

Service-Oriented Architecture (SOA) SOA is an architecture style that is based on the concept of coarse-grained, loosely coupled components called services. Services exposed by service provider applications are invoked by service consumer applications via messages.

Service Contract A service contract is an interface that defines the message types used by service providers and service consumers to exchange messages.

Data Contract A data contract is a formal agreement between a service and a client that abstractly describes the data to be exchanged.

Service Registry	Service registry is a directory that contains information about available services. Service consumers look up the service registry to know what services are available.
Enterprise Service Bus (ESB)	An ESB is an architectural pattern that acts as the mediator/broker between the service provider and the service consumer. It forms the communication infrastructure for services to interact with one another across locations, supporting different transports, and across organizational boundaries.
Orchestration	Orchestration is the execution of services based on a pre-defined sequence. The pre-defined sequence corresponds to a workflow. Orchestration controls the process-level integration and automation of services.
Unified Modeling Language (UML)	UML is an industry standard notation for modeling software systems. Modeling involves specification, visualization, construction and documentation of the artifacts of software systems.
Business Process Execution Language (BPEL)	BPEL for Web services is an XML-based language to specify the sequence of execution of services that corresponds to workflow of a business process.
Web Services	Web services is a technology to expose reusable functionality as services. It involves communication of SOAP messages over a communication protocol such as HTTP.
Agility	The ability to change business processes of an organization in response to changing market conditions is representative of the business agility of the organization.

REFERENCES

Bakker L. (2005) *Goodbye Hub-and-Spoke, Hello ESB? Integration Architecture With BizTalk 2004, .NET Developer Journal,* http://dotnet.sys-con.com/read/121831.htm

Bartels, A. and Rymer, J. (2006) *The Future of Enterprise Software,* Forrester Document, June 29, Forrester Research Document, Cambridge, MA.

Evdemon, J. (2005) The Four Tenets of Service Orientation, http://www.bpminstitute.org/articles/article/article/the-four-tenets-of-service-orientation.html

IDC (2006) *Service-Oriented Architecture will Offer a Tremendous Opportunity for Service Providers Through 2010*, IDC Press Release, 03 Apr 2006.

Morrison, S. (2009) *What Do You Think will be the Biggest Trend or Development for SOA in 2010*? eBizQ, http://www.ebizq.net/MT4/mt-cp.cgi?_mode=view& blog_id=43& id=79

MSDN (2007) *Using Data Contracts*, Microsoft, http://msdn2.microsoft.com/en-us/library/ms733127.aspx

Natis, Y. and Shulte, R. (2006) *Advanced SOA for Advanced Enterprise Projects*, Gartner Research Document, ID: G00141940, 13 December 2006.

Nickull, D. (2005) *Service Oriented Architecture*, Whitepaper from Adobe.

OASIS (2007) *OASIS Advances Standards to Simplify SOA Application Development*, http://www.oasis-open.org/news/oasis-news-2007-04-11.php

OMG (2006) *The OMG and Service Oriented Architecture*. http://www.omg.org/attachments/pdf/OMG-and-the-SOA.pdf

Rosenthal, A. (2009) *What Do You Think will be the Biggest Trend or Development for SOA in 2010*? eBizQ, http://www.ebizq.net/MT4/mt-cp.cgi?_mode=view& blog_id=43& id=241

Schulte, R. (2006) *Five Principles of SOA in Business and IT*, Gartner Research Document, ID: G00145180, 18 December 2006.

Schulte, R. and Abrahms, C. (2006) *SOA Overview and Guide to SOA Research*, Gartner Research Document, ID: G00144894, 15 December 2006.

Skonnard, A. (2005) *SOA: More Integration, Less Renovation*, MSDN, http://msdn.microsoft.com/msdnmag/issues/05/02/ServiceStation/default.aspx

SML (2009). *Service Modeling Language*, Version 1.1, W3C Recommendation 12 May 2009.

SOAML (2009) *Service Oriented Architecture Modeling Language (SoaML)*, Specification for the UML Profile and Metamodel for Services (UPMS), OMG Document No: ptc/2009-04-01.

SOA-RAF (2009) *Reference Architecture Foundation for Service Oriented Architecture Version 1.0*, Committee Draft 02 14 October 2009.

SOA-RM (2006) *Reference Model for Service Oriented Architecture 1.0*, OASIS Standard, 12 October 2006.

Thompson, J. (2006) *Service Component Architecture Is a Winner in the Quest to Establish a Common Notation for SOA*, Gartner Research Document, ID: G00137638, 6 March 2006.

W3C (2004) *Web Services Architecture*, W3C Working Group Note 11 February 2004, http://www.w3.org/TR/ws-arch/#service_oriented_architecture

CHAPTER 4

Enterprise-Wide SOA

CONTENTS

LEARNING OBJECTIVES

After reading this chapter, you would be able to:

- Define an enterprise.
- Examine the considerations for enterprise-wide SOA.
- Get insights on Strawman architecture.
- Know the different enterprise SOA layers.
- Study the application development process for service-oriented applications.
- Understand the SOA methodology.

An *enterprise* is an organization consisting of one of more divisions that delivers value to its stakeholders. A large enterprise has several divisions that not only create value by providing products or services but also has forward and backward linkages with other external agencies. SOA provides significant return on investment through reuse, agility and integration when implemented at enterprise level.

This chapter discusses considerations for defining and implementing SOA at the enterprise level, provides Strawman architecture for enterprise-wide SOA and also discusses the SOA methodology for enterprise-wide SOA.

4.1 CONSIDERATIONS FOR ENTERPRISE-WIDE SOA

An enterprise includes interdependent resources (people and technology) that must coordinate their functions and share information in support of a defined vision. SOA is an architectural style that when applied at enterprise level corresponds to enterprise architecture. Thus, all the considerations of enterprise architecture will also be applicable to enterprise-wide SOA.

The following are key considerations for developing enterprise architecture:

1. objectives, drivers and goals of business;
2. business process definition to support business goals;
3. alignment of IT with business processes;
4. scalability of IT;
5. management of change by governance.

In addition to the above-mentioned enterprise architecture considerations, the following dimensions of services model need to also be taken into account:

1. **Reusability:** Reusable coarse-grained nature of a service is fundamental to the services model.

2. **Agility:** Applications based on services model have their business processes externalized in an "orchestrable" manner.
3. **Integration:** Service providers and service consumers are loosely coupled and communication between them is based on a published contract.

4.2 STRAWMAN ARCHITECTURE FOR ENTERPRISE-WIDE SOA

This section presents Strawman architecture for developing enterprise-wide SOA. Strawman architecture is the initial architecture that serves as a starting point for developing the target architecture. It is refined over number of iterations and results in the development of the target architecture. The Strawman architecture presented here could serve as a starting point for developing a SOA-based solution for an enterprise. In this section, discussion is not restricted to a particular technology. A generic view of a service is considered. Figure 4-1 represents Strawman architecture for enterprise-wide SOA.

The dimensions of SOA, namely reuse, integration and agility discussed in Chapter 3, require that coarse-grained reusable functionality be exposed as services, integrated through the principle of loose coupling and orchestrated to implement agile business processes.

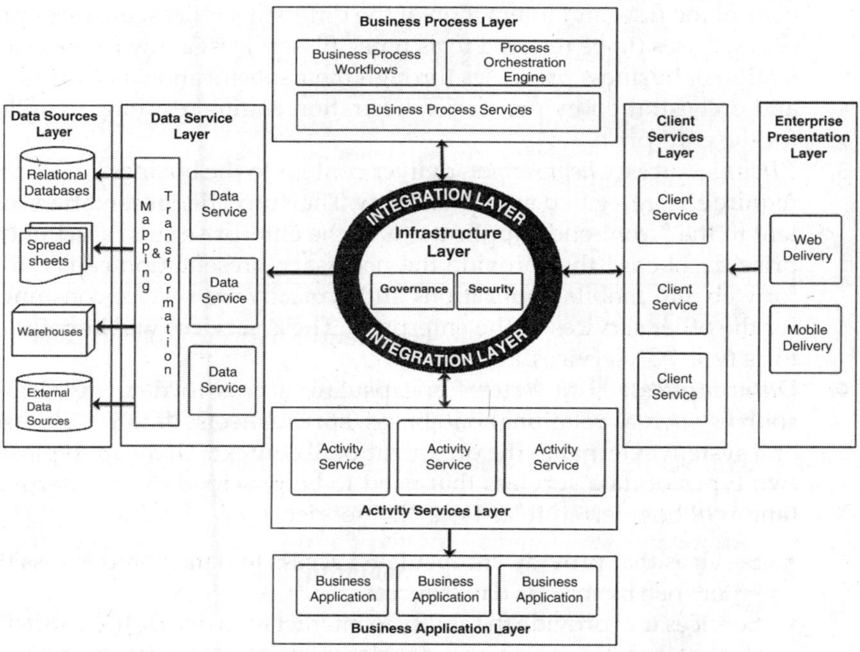

FIGURE 4-1 Strawman architecture for enterprise-wide SOA.

Several types of services have been defined for SOA (Cohen, 2007). The following four types of services have been identified at enterprise level (Kambhampaty and Chandra, 2006):

1. business services or activity services;
2. business process services;
3. client services;
4. data services.

The Strawman architecture shown in Figure 4-1 represents a logical perspective of the four types of services and their relationships.

A description of the services is as follows:

1. ***Activity services or business services:*** The activity services or business services encapsulate functionality exposed as services in various business applications. These services are reusable business level services that can be orchestrated as part of a configured business process. In order to avoid confusion with business process services and to highlight their role as implementing steps or activities of the business process, they will be referred to as *activity services*. These services will be referred to as type "A" services.
2. ***Business process services:*** *Business process services* handle orchestration of business processes implemented as a set of services. These services control the flow and interaction of the different services. Business process services (to be referred to as type "B" services) allow for externalization of business processes through their specification as workflows and orchestration by process orchestration engine resulting in agility for the enterprise.
3. ***Client services:*** *Client services* deliver content to the business users that require an aggregated enterprise view. They provide presentation content to the "front-end" applications of the enterprise such as an enterprise dashboard that provide the necessary presentation capabilities for web and mobile applications and typically are service consumers for the other services in the enterprise. These services will be referred to as type "C" services.
4. ***Data services:*** *Data services* encapsulate access to data in various sources such as relational databases, spreadsheets, data warehouses or a system external to the organizational context. There are typically two types of data services that need to be provided in an enterprise (and will be referred to as type "D" services):

    - Services that provide encapsulated access to data stored across the enterprise in various data sources.
    - Services that provide the ability to interact with data sources outside the enterprise. Design and development of data services involves transformation and mapping of data in data sources before being exposed as services.

A key feature of the architecture is the use of Enterprise Service Bus (ESB) as part of integration layer that enables a smooth communication between the services. An Enterprise Service Bus (ESB) pattern abstracts the mediation and interaction elements needed for communication as a *bus* that is used for integration of services. ESB is often described as a product, especially in the marketing literature of various vendors. But, in a strict sense, ESB is an architectural style. The Strawman architecture for enterprise-wide SOA has the ESB as the heart of communication between applications (Endrei et al., 2004).

Another important aspect of the Strawman architecture is *infrastructure layer* that provides:

1. Service Security – Infrastructure needed to secure services: Solutions that implement *authentication* and *authorization* patterns for security ensure that the credentials of a component (another service or application) invoking a service are verified through the process of authentication and access to the resources are provided through a process of authorization. It is typically based on privileges defined for the invoking component (Rossebo, 2006).
2. Service Governance – Infrastructure needed to govern services: Solutions that exercise control over services in SOA including monitoring service invocations and imposing policies provide service governance (Windley, 2006).

The Strawman architecture presented above brings out three key aspects in development of SOA at enterprise level:

1. identification and development of different types of services (essentially, types A, B, C, D services mentioned earlier);
2. implementation of an integration layer based on the ESB pattern;
3. implementation of service infrastructure that enables service security and service governance.

4.3 ENTERPRISE SOA LAYERS

The services discussed above can be grouped into layers on the basis of the level of abstraction (Arsanjani, 2004). Figure 4-2 shows the layers for enterprise-wide SOA based on the four types of services identified in Strawman architecture.

The activity services, data services and client services expose services that can be orchestrated as part of a business process. Hence, these are grouped as part of the *services layer*. The business applications that implement the functionality of the services (including legacy applications) and the data stores form part of the *application layer*. The content for the aggregated view delivered to business users is rendered by the *enterprise presentation layer*. The business processes are externalized and defined using a language such as Business Process

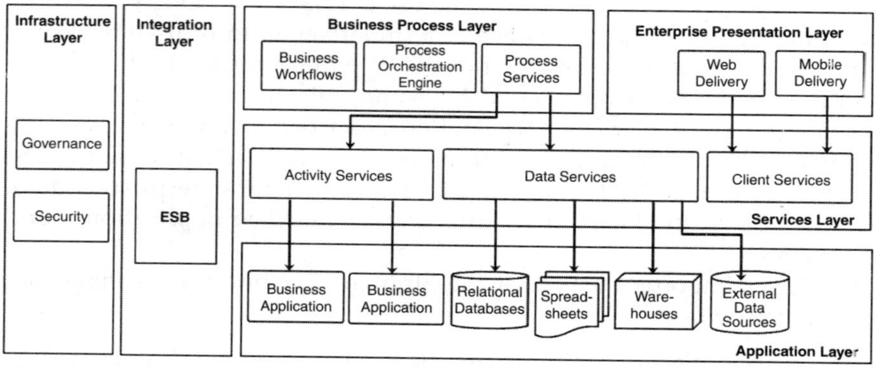

FIGURE 4-2 SOA layers.

Execution Language (BPEL). A process orchestration engine that forms part of a *business process layer* executes the services exposed by the *services layer* as steps of the business process. The *integration layer* provides the ESB capability, and the *infrastructure layer* provides security and governance mechanisms to interact securely with systems external to the enterprise as well as the service monitoring and management capabilities.

4.4 APPLICATION DEVELOPMENT PROCESS

In software engineering, *process* is "sequence of steps required to develop or maintain software" (Humphrey, 1995). A *process model* deals with the *what* of developing software (Visitacion, 2001). *Methodology* is a set of principles, practices and procedures that may be repeatedly applied to develop a specific category of applications. Methodology deals with the *how* of developing software.

With the advent of object-oriented paradigm, Object Oriented Analysis and Design (OOAD) process has been applied to develop object-oriented applications. Object-oriented applications are developed on the basis of the following principles:

1. encapsulation;
2. abstraction;
3. inheritance;
4. interface;
5. polymorphism.

Object-oriented analysis and design process involves modeling real world objects abstracted as classes. The requirements are described as a set of use cases and realized through a process that involves identification of the analysis classes (boundary, control and entity) and their mapping to technology elements that

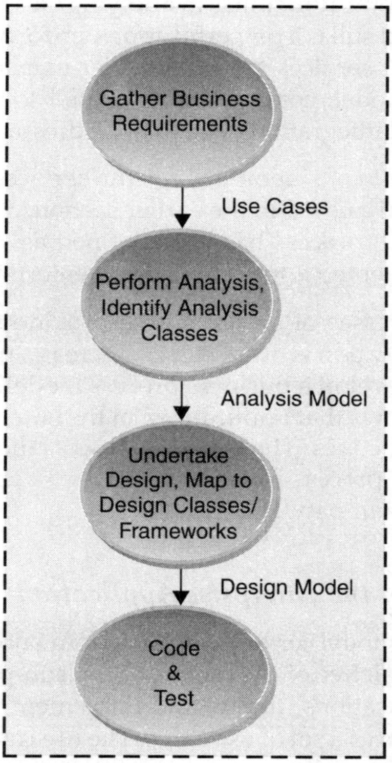

FIGURE 4-3 OOAD process.

constitute the design classes. Classes are fine-grained elements that are tightly coupled. Design classes and related software constructs are implemented using a programming language to develop the required application.

The key steps in OOAD process are shown in Figure 4-3.

While OOAD is a powerful technique that leverages the modeling of objects based on their class hierarchies, it presents some difficulties when applying to service-oriented applications (Zimmermann et al., 2004).

The granularity in OO applications is at class level. Service-oriented applications deal with services at a course level of granularity. While interfaces defined for objects do provide for abstraction and information hiding and in principle can provide loose coupling, the fine-grained nature of the classes and interfaces do not yield the benefits that one could derive from a services model. Further, class hierarchies are based on inheritance which brings strong associations and tight coupling. Service definition on the other hand promotes loose coupling between service providers and consumers. Also, the run-time environment for OO applications assumes object housekeeping services (such as Garbage collection in J2EE applications).

Though there are some difficulties in applying OOAD to address all aspects of service orientation, it still is a powerful approach for addressing some aspects of process required for services model. In order to extend the OOAD process to support services model, considerations related to services model namely reusability, agility and integration need to be addressed in the process.

Taking into account considerations for the services model and the different types of services discussed in the earlier section, a service-oriented analysis and design (SOAD) process has been defined as shown in Figure 4-4 for developing service-oriented applications in an enterprise.

The business processes of an enterprise provide the context in which a service-oriented application is built. Hence, there is a need to first gather business objectives and develop a business process model that identifies business processes and workflows that applications in the enterprise would support to meet the business objectives. The business process model thus generated is a key artefact in SOAD process for service-oriented applications developed in the enterprise (Kambhampaty, 2007).

Service Modeling for the Enterprise Application

The business process model serves as input to four sub-processes identified in Figure 4-4 by the first letter of the names of the sub-processes. It is analyzed to scope out the applications (that would implement the business processes) and their requirements as a set of use cases. The use cases identified determine the scope of each of the applications for the future state from a functional perspective. The activity services, business process services, client services and data services exposed or consumed by the application are identified. A service model is developed that represents the services (based on notation such as UML 2 Profile for Software Services).

It may be noted that composite applications that are built on services through orchestration need business process services to also be defined and implemented at application level. For non-composite applications, business process services are defined at enterprise level that orchestrate services exposed by several applications.

Sub-Process A – Activity Services (or Business Services) Development: The business applications expose activity services (referred to as type "A" services in Strawman architecture) that are developed through this sub-process. It may be noted that any enterprise would have a set of applications supporting the current-state business. Minor or major changes may be needed for applications that support future-state business to not only support the services model but also to meet the objectives of the future-state business. Activity services are identified and specified by means of service and data contracts. Existing applications are analyzed, changes needed to design to expose the required

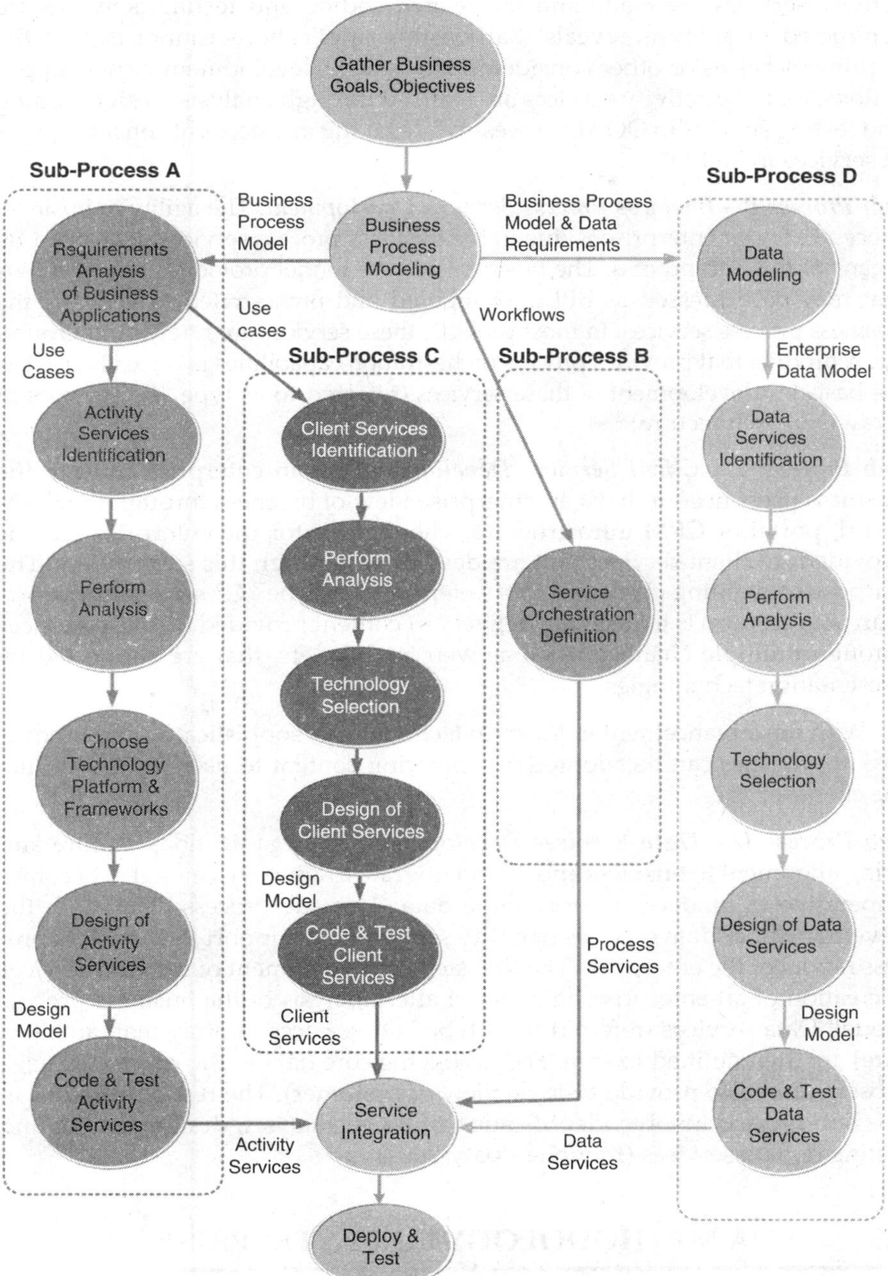

FIGURE 4-4 SOAD process.

activity services are made and the related coding and testing activities are conducted. If analysis reveals that existing applications cannot expose the required services or other considerations require development of new applications, then the activity services are realized through analysis, design, coding and testing steps as in OOAD process while taking into account considerations of services model.

Sub-Process B – Business Process Services Development: The agility in business processes for an enterprise is due to the business process services developed by means of this sub-process. The business process model provides the workflows that may be expressed as BPEL, configured and orchestrated to generate the business process services. In most projects, these services are rarely built ground up. A product that provides process orchestration capabilities is typically used as the basis for development of these services (referred to as type "B" services in Strawman architecture).

Sub-Process C – Client Services Development: In an enterprise context, the business users need to have an enterprise view of business through the dashboard, portal or CRM infrastructure. The content for the enterprise view is provided by client services that are developed through this sub-process. The purpose of defining client services (referred to as type "C" services in Strawman architecture) is to facilitate delivery of content provided by these services through multiple channels such as web, mobile, etc. that are supported by presentation technologies.

With the advancement in Mashup technologies, sophisticated and innovative approaches can be adopted in delivering content to users by leveraging the client services.

Sub-Process D – Data Services Development: As organizations mature and bring alignment to business and IT and migrate to a services model, it becomes imperative to model enterprise-wide data. This sub-process deals with the development of data services or entity services that support the business process model of the enterprise. The first step in development of the data services is creation of an enterprise data model after analysis of the business process model. Data services (referred to as type "D" services in Strawman architecture) are then defined to store and access the core data in the enterprise (e.g., those required to provide a single view of customer). The rest of the steps in this sub-process involve identification of tools, analysis, design, coding and testing of data services (Kambhampaty, 2007).

4.5 SOA METHODOLOGY FOR ENTERPRISE

The SOAD process already discussed provided details at the application level, that is *what* was involved in developing a service-oriented application that exposes or consumes different types of services. A methodology is needed

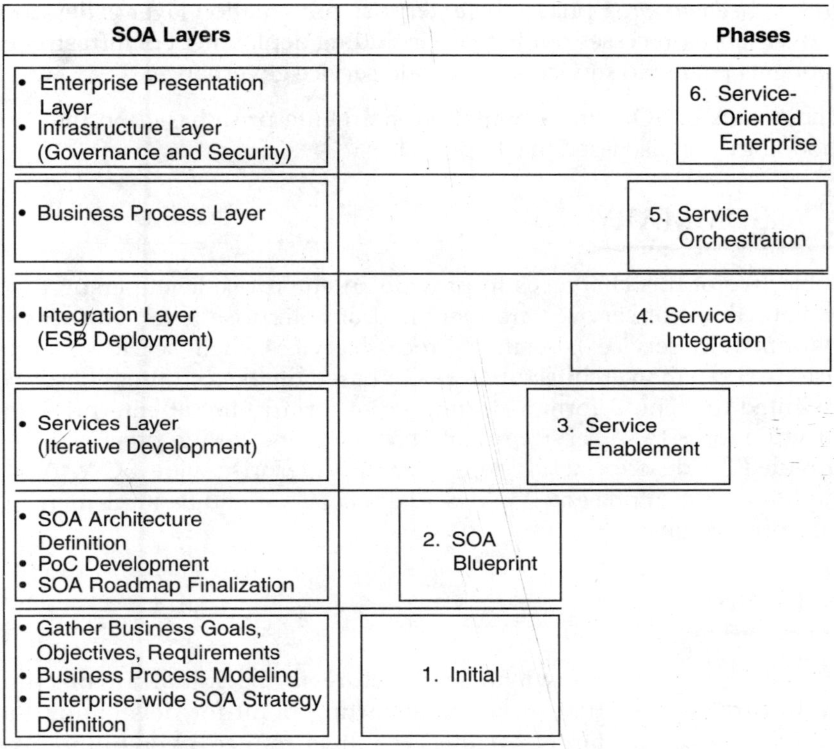

FIGURE 4-5 SOA methodology.

to leverage SOA at enterprise level to implement the SOA layers defined in Section 4.3.

SOA methodology can be described by specifying *how* the different processes need to be implemented. Several approaches such as Spiral and Waterfall can be chosen depending on the business and IT considerations of the enterprise.

SOA methodology based on the iterative approach is shown in Figure 4-5.

SOA methodology includes six overlapping phases to develop the SOA layer identified for the enterprise. The *initial* phase results in a business process model which also ends with the *SOA blueprint* phase during which SOA architecture for the enterprise is defined. The *service enablement* phase involves development of services layer in an iterative manner. The ESB and associated integration layer components are implemented in the *service integration* phase. During the *service orchestration* phase the process services are developed and the services layer (activity, client and data services) developed in the earlier phase is orchestrated with a process execution engine. In the final *service-oriented enterprise* phase, the enterprise presentation layer is developed and governance processes put in place including deployment of infrastructure components related to service security and service governance.

The details of SOA implementation in an enterprise based on the above methodology are discussed in Chapter 11.

4.6 SUMMARY

The objective of this chapter is to provide an enterprise-level perspective of SOA. Four types of services are identified at enterprise level: business services (or activity services), business process services, client services and data services. A Strawman architecture for SOA based on the four types of services is presented that could form a starting point for arriving at enterprise-wide architecture for SOA. A service-oriented analysis and design process (SOAD) is provided to describe *what* steps lead to enterprise-wide SOA. A SOA methodology is also presented to describe *how* SOA could be implemented in an enterprise context.

KEY TERMS

Strawman Architecture — Strawman architecture is the initial architecture that serves as a starting point for developing the target architecture. It is refined over number of iterations and results in the development of the target architecture.

Activity or Business Services — The activity services or business services encapsulate functionality exposed as services in various business applications. These services are reusable business level services that can be orchestrated as part of a configured business process.

Business Process Services — Business process services handle orchestration of business processes implemented as a set of services. These services control the flow and interaction of the different services.

Client Services — Client services deliver content to the business users that require an aggregated enterprise view. They provide presentation content to the "front-end" applications of the enterprise.

Data Services — Data services encapsulate access to data in various sources such as relational databases, spreadsheets, data warehouses or a system external to the organizational context.

Object-Oriented Analysis and Design (OOAD)	OOAD process involves modelling software applications based on real-world objects rather than data or processes.
Service-Oriented Analysis and Design (SOAD)	SOAD process involves modelling software applications based on services.
Process	Process is sequence of steps required to develop or maintain software. A process deals with the what of developing software.
Methodology	Methodology is a set of principles, practices and procedures that may be repeatedly applied to develop a specific category of applications. Methodology deals with the how of developing software.
Architecture Governance	Architecture Governance refers to the processes used to oversee and control the adoption and implementation of architecture.

REFERENCES

Arsanjani, A. (2004) *Service-Oriented Modeling and Architecture*, IBM, http://www.ibm.com/developerworks/webservices/library/ws-soa-design1/

Cohen, S. (2007) Ontology and taxonomy of services in a service-oriented architecture, *The Achitecture Journal*, 11, MSDN.

Endrei, M., Ang, J., Arsanjani, A., Chua, S., Comte, P., et al. (2004) *Patterns: Service- Oriented Architecture and Web Service*, IBM Red Book, http://www.ibm.com/redbooks

Humphrey, W. (1995) *A Discipline for Software Engineering*, Addison-Wesley Publishing Company, Inc., Reading, MA.

Kambhampaty, S. (2007) *Service Oriented Analysis and Design Process for the Enterprise*, 7th WSEAS International Conference on Applied Computer Science Venice, Italy, November 21–23, 2007, WORLD SCIENTIFIC and ENGINEERING ACADEMY and SOCIETY.

Kambhampaty, S. and Chandra, S. (2006) Service oriented architecture for enterprise applications, *WSEAS Transactions on Business and Economics*, **2**(3).

Rossebo, J. and Braek, R. (2006) *Towards a Framework of Authentication and Authorization Patterns for Ensuring Availability in Service Composition*, Proceedings of the First International Conference on Availability, Reliability and Security, IEEE Computer Society.

Visitacion, M. (2001) *Understanding the Difference Between Process and Methodology*, Forrester, Document ID No.: RIB-072001-00146.

Windley, P. (2006) *SOA Governance: Rules of the Game*, InfoWorld.com, 23 January 2006.

Zimmermann, O., Krogdahl, P. and Gee, C. (2004) *Elements of Service-Oriented Analysis and Design*, http://www.ibm.com/developerworks/webservices/library/ws-soad1/

CHAPTER 5

Enterprise Applications

CONTENTS

LEARNING OBJECTIVES

After reading this chapter, you would be able to:

- Define an enterprise application.
- Look at the architectural considerations of enterprise applications.
- Study the solution architecting process for enterprise applications.
- Know what is involved in specifying different levels of architecture: Level 0: High-Level Architecture; Level 1: Baseline Architecture; Level 2: Detailed Architecture.
- Gain insights on solution architecting for enterprise applications based on SOA.

An enterprise consists of one or more divisions that deliver value to stakeholders and includes interdependent resources that coordinate their functions and share information in support of a defined vision (EPA, 2005).

Enterprise software applications (or enterprise applications) satisfy the information needs of an enterprise and provide a strategic advantage to its business. They automate business processes, manage business data and integrate enterprise activities.

On account of the benefits due to reuse, agility and integration and in order to provide competitive and strategic advantage, SOA is increasingly being adopted for enterprise applications. In the context of an organization, enterprise applications expose and consume the four different types of services (activity, business process, client and data services) discussed in Chapter 4.

In this chapter, the architectural considerations for enterprise applications are reviewed and an approach for developing solution architecture for enterprise applications is presented.

5.1 ARCHITECTURAL CONSIDERATIONS

The architecture of an enterprise application corresponds to the solution architecture that fulfils the functional and non-functional requirements. The following are the key architectural considerations of enterprise applications:

1. ***Functional requirements:*** It is important that the *architecturally significant use cases* are addressed in the architecture. A *use case* describes the interaction of users (called actors) with the system. The functionality of systems can, therefore, be expressed in terms of use cases. Architecturally significant use cases have a substantial architectural

coverage in that they affect many architectural elements. Hence, ensuring that architecturally significant use cases are appropriately addressed is key to getting the architecture right.

2. ***Non-functional requirements:***
   - ***Performance:*** An application needs to meet the expected performance levels for being successfully adopted by users of the enterprise. Performance is measured as the response time for a specified number of concurrent user interactions with the online screens of the system and the time taken for batch jobs that run at the end of day (or at the end of the month).
   - ***Scalability:*** Enterprise applications deal with large amounts of data and a number of users. The ability of the application to perform within acceptable limits with changed workload in terms of size of data, or volume of users, or both, is called *scalability*. In order to meet an increased workload, enterprise applications need to be architected such that addition of hardware and software resources (ideally in a linear manner), to the application environment, can maintain the performance characteristic of the application.
   - ***Availability:*** The degree to which users of a system experience degradation, or interruption in service, as a result of failure of hardware or software components of the system is called *availability*. Many enterprise applications are critical to the business and hence need to be architected for high availability. Availability is measured relative to "100% operational" or "never failing" (SearchDataCenter, 2005). One of the benchmarks of high availability is "Five 9s" (99.999%) availability.
   - ***Reliability:*** Reliability is the enterprise applications' ability to withstand failures and recover gracefully from unexpected events. This is achieved by identifying and isolating single points of failure in the architecture and spreading the risk across hardware and software infrastructure. Reliability is expressed in terms of *Mean Time Between Failures* (MTBF) and *Mean Time To Restore* (MTTR).
   - ***Security:*** Every action performed by the user has to be properly authenticated and authorized in most enterprise applications. Additionally, the security model of some enterprise applications requires that security be dependent on the domain of the application and also be based on a hierarchy defined for data items. The security objectives of the application need to taken into account and the security infrastructure for enterprise applications have to be architected and implemented.
3. ***Service-oriented model considerations:*** The architectural considerations for enterprise applications discussed above are equally relevant to applications of different architectural styles including SOA. Additionally, for enterprise application participating in enterprise-wide SOA discussed in Chapter 4, the following need to be considered:

- ***Services exposed or consumed:*** Activity, business process, client or data services that enterprise application exposes or consumes need to be identified.
- ***Granularity of services exposed:*** The granularity of services exposed has to be at the right level for effective integration and service orchestration.
- ***Integration model for services exposed or consumed:*** Enterprise service bus and other patterns for integration are to be considered.
- ***Business process model:*** Business process model of the enterprise and the specific business processes implemented by the enterprise application have to be taken into account.
- ***Enterprise data model:*** Data model for the application has to align with enterprise data models that may be defined at the organization level.
- ***Infrastructure:*** Authentication and authorization patterns for service security and solutions for design-time and run-time governance (including technologies for service registry and repository) are to be considered.

5.2 SOLUTION ARCHITECTURE FOR ENTERPRISE APPLICATIONS

The architecture of an enterprise application corresponds to the solution architecture that fulfils the functional and non-functional requirements (and service model considerations for applications participating in enterprise-wide SOA).

Solution architecture definition is a key part of enterprise application development lifecycle. Project teams in some cases conduct detailed design of enterprise application without taking key aspects of solution architecture into consideration. Consequently, such projects run into issues related to quality attributes such as performance, scalability, etc. on account of non-functional requirements not being addressed adequately. On a different dimension, the current technological advancements have been driving the need for formalization in solution architecture than ever before. This section describes the architecting process that can be employed for solution architecture definition of enterprise applications.

Solution architecture is elaborated in an iterative manner at different stages of the software development cycle on the basis of the perspectives of the stakeholders involved. Figure 5-1 shows three recommended levels of architecture that communicate the solution for a given set of requirements elaborated to the level of detail required by the stakeholders:

1. ***Level 0 – High-level architecture:*** In the initial stages of the project, before requirements are gathered and documented, the architect

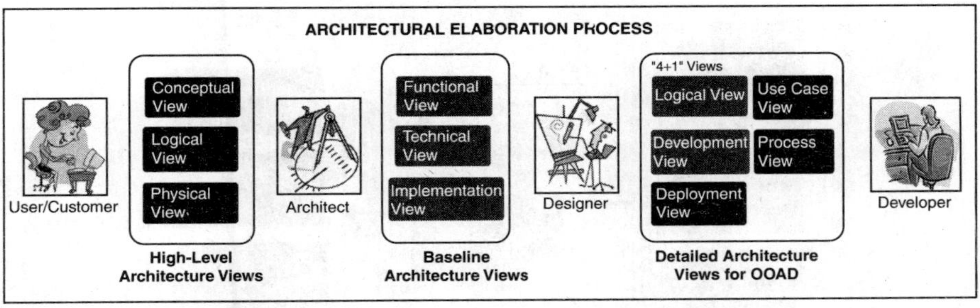

FIGURE 5-1 Architectural elaboration process.

develops a high-level architecture with three views – *conceptual view, logical view and physical view* (Platt, 2002). The objective of this level is to validate the understanding of the scope and the high-level requirements provided by the business users (or customer when the solution development is done by an external organization) and develop a solution to meet the requirements.

2. ***Level 1 – Baseline architecture:*** On completion of requirements analysis phase of a project, the next version of the architecture is developed. This version of the architecture is represented with *functional view, technical view and deployment view*. The objective of this level (MSDN, 2004) is to identify architecturally significant use cases from a functional perspective and provide a solution from a technical perspective based on architectural decisions made after consideration of the various options available for technology platforms, frameworks, products and on analysis of the architecture tradeoffs. This version of the architecture serves as a baseline for a given set of requirements, architecture decisions and tradeoffs.
3. ***Level 2 – Detailed:*** At the start of the design process, baseline architecture is further elaborated and several views are added that can form the basis of the design process. This level provides detailed architectural views based on the methodology to be employed for development of the enterprise application. For Object-Oriented Analysis and Design (OOAD) methodology, the "4+1" views (Krutchen, 1995) consisting of *use case view, logical view, process view, development view* and *deployment view* are one of the most widely used forms of representation of detailed architecture. A tool (such as IBM Rational Software Architect or Borland Together Control Center Edition) is also often employed to model the architectural elements initially and later continue into the design process.

Level 0: High-Level Architecture

The high-level architecture of an enterprise application is typically defined by the architect of the IT department of an organization in discussion with the business users, sponsors and other stakeholders of the organization. When solution

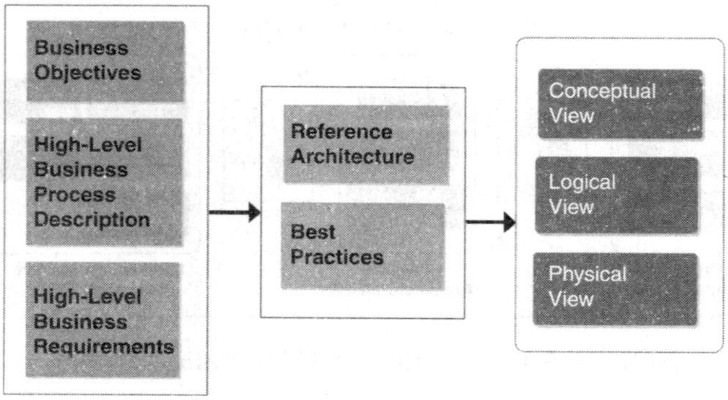

FIGURE 5-2 High-level architecture.

development is done by an external organization, a Request for Proposal (RFP) or discussions with the business users and IT department of the customer organization provide the required inputs which include business objectives, description of high-level business processes and business requirements of the enterprise application. The architect analyzes the inputs and leverages the available reference architectures for the domain and best practices from developing similar applications to represent the architecture with the three views shown in Figure 5-2 – *conceptual, logical and physical views*. The high-level architecture is presented to business users and/or IT department and validated for scope, functionality and suitability to meet business and IT needs.

Conceptual View

Conceptual view is the abstracted business model of the application described in terms familiar to the users (Kazman, 1998). A conceptual view of a Loan Management System (LMS) would look like the view shown in Figure 5-3.

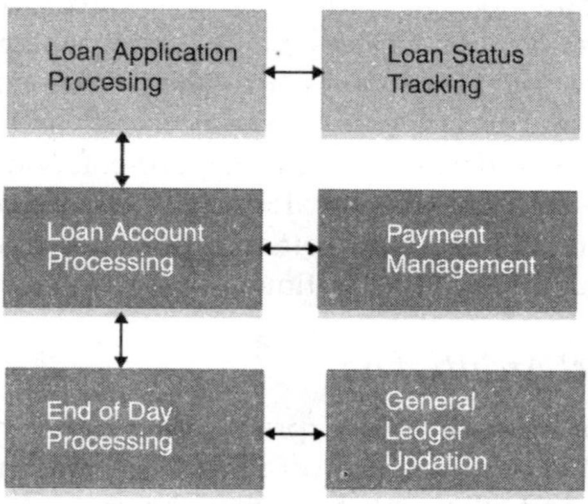

FIGURE 5-3 Conceptual view of LMS.

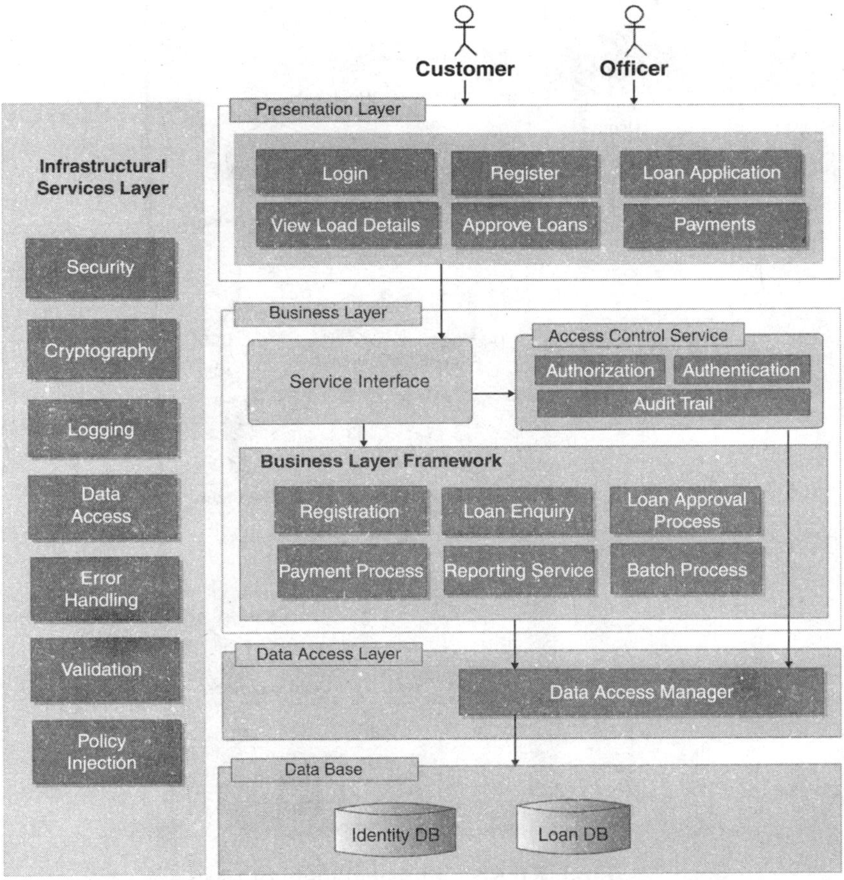

FIGURE 5-4 Logical view of LMS.

Logical View

Logical view shows the structuring of main functional components of the application based on the architectural patterns (such as layering) and their relationships (Platt, 2002). The technical details of how the functional subsystems are implemented are not shown. A logical view of an LMS could look like the one shown in Figure 5-4.

Physical View

Physical view provides details of the implementation components (hardware and software) and their relationships (Platt, 2002). The physical view of high-level architecture may be represented as in Figure 5-5.

The validated high-level architecture allows for broad agreement between the users (and/or IT department) and the architect on the solution for the

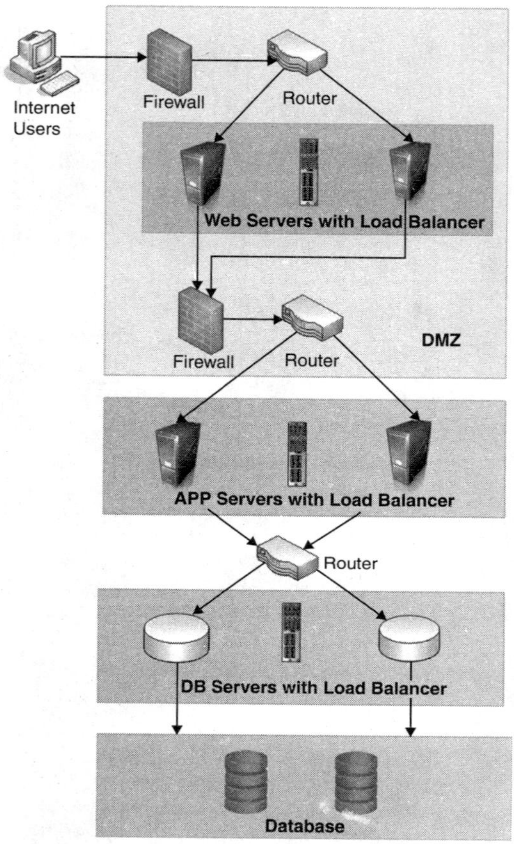

FIGURE 5-5 Physical view of LMS.

scope of enterprise application specified and facilitates effort and cost estimate for development activities involved.

Level 1: Baseline Architecture

During the software development lifecycle, requirements of the application are captured and documented as use cases (with the help of business analysts, where necessary). Domain-intensive enterprise applications require business process model-related inputs to be provided to the solution architect. As discussed in Chapter 4, creation of business process model is an important step for SOA applications. As part of the baseline architecture, the architect analyzes the architecturally significant use cases, decides on suitable technology standards, frameworks and guidelines and represents the architecture using three views shown in Figure 5-6 – *functional view*, *technical view* and *implementation view*.

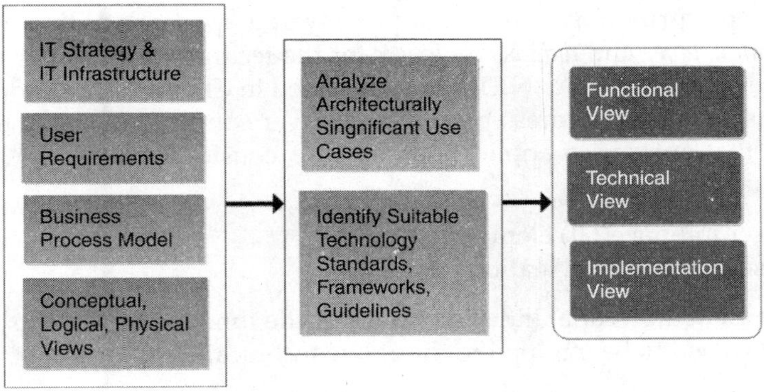

FIGURE 5-6 Baseline architecture.

Functional View

The functional view of an application defines key functional elements that deliver the application's functionality, their responsibilities, interfaces they expose and the interactions between them (Rozanski and Woods, 2005). The functional elements identified in the functional view are then mapped to the technical elements in the technical view. Figure 5-7 provides an example of functional view for an LMS.

Technical View

The technical view describes technical elements of an enterprise application, their interfaces, interaction and interdependence in order to satisfy a specified set of requirements (Kruijk, 2001). The technical view provides the basis for the design and development stages of software development lifecycle.

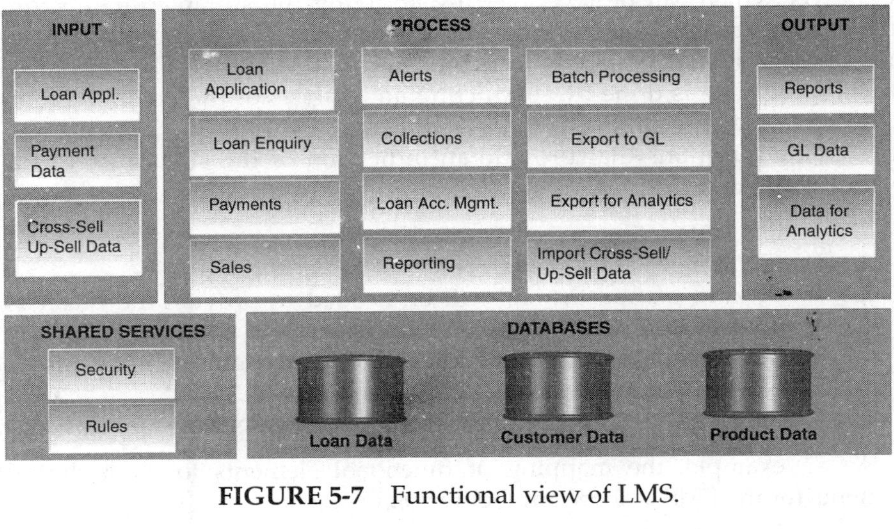

FIGURE 5-7 Functional view of LMS.

Many enterprise applications adopt a layered approach with *presentation layer*, *business layer* and *data access layers* for the technical view. Software platforms such as Java EE and .NET, to be discussed in Chapter 6, provide significant infrastructure to address presentation layer concerns. The key technical elements that enterprise applications need to consider for the presentation layer include:

1. user interface(UI) elements;
2. user interface navigation elements.

The presentation capabilities required for the functional elements in functional view need to be mapped to the above technical elements.

The business layer of the technical view of enterprise application provides a technical solution for the functionality required. The elements in functional view that offer a solution from functional perspective need to be mapped to technical elements in the technical view.

The key technical elements at business layer (of technical view) that are mapped to functional elements (of functional view) include:

1. static data maintenance;
2. transactions;
3. workflows;
4. batch processing;
5. business rules;
6. reporting;
7. integration.

As in the case of presentation layer, the software platforms for enterprise applications such as Java EE and .NET provide several capabilities for business layer which can be leveraged by applying the suitable architecture and design patterns for the respective platforms. The mapping of functional elements in functional view to technical elements in business layer of technical view is done by conducting an analysis of the architecturally significant use cases along with requirements of interfacing systems and data. Some questions that provide an indication of the suitability of the technical elements are:

1. Is static data maintenance required?
2. Would there be any batch processes?
3. What kind of transactions will be needed to provide the business functions?
4. Would there be a need for workflow and rules engine components?
5. Would there be a necessity for messaging?
6. Would there be a need to interface with other enterprise applications?

As an example, the mapping of functional elements to the technical elements for the LMS is shown in Figure 5-8.

Modules \ Technical Elements	Static Data Maintenance	Transactions	Workflows	Batch Process	Business Rules	Reporting	Integration
Loan Application	✓	✓	✓		✓	✓	
Loan Acct. Mgmt.	✓	✓	✓		✓	✓	
Sales	✓	✓	✓		✓	✓	✓
Collections	✓	✓	✓		✓	✓	✓
Batch Process				✓			
Payments	✓	✓	✓		✓	✓	✓
Loan Enquiry	✓					✓	
Alerts		✓			✓	✓	

FIGURE 5-8 Mapping of functional elements to technical elements.

The technical view of enterprise application can then be described in terms of the technical elements and their interactions. For example, Figure 5-9 shows the technical view of the business layer for .NET platform.

The data access layer of the technical view of an enterprise application provides encapsulated access to the data stored in the underlying databases and other data stores. Various sources of data and the enterprise data model are considered in arriving at the application data model and the elements for the data access layer. Object relational mapping elements and the data access mechanisms are key technical elements for the data access layer.

Implementation View

The implementation view of an enterprise application represents the elements from which the solution is built. It also describes how the solution will be developed, deployed, validated, managed and funded (Kruijk, 2001). It is arrived at by mapping elements in the technical view to physical infrastructure such as software products and hardware servers and describing the project-related details on implementing the solution.

The baseline architecture takes into account architecturally significant use cases of an enterprise application and provides a solution to the requirements from functional, technical and implementation perspectives. This architecture when validated by the IT department becomes a baseline for further detailing done in the next level of architecture and the design process in the software development lifecycle.

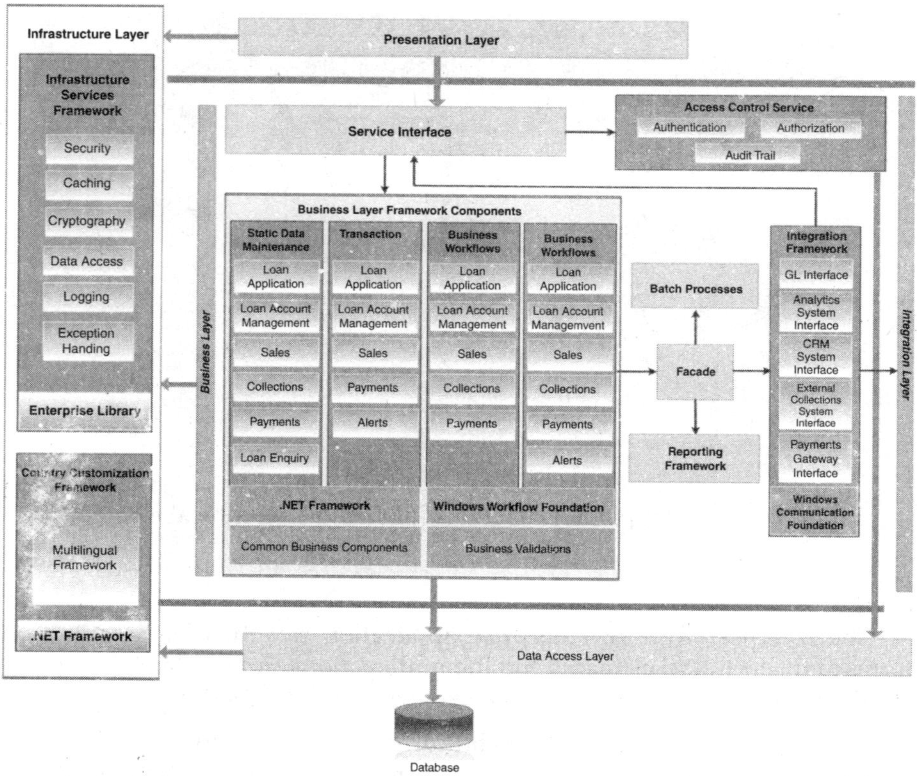

FIGURE 5-9 Technical view of business layer of LMS (.NET).

Detailed Architecture

The views of Level 0 (high-level architecture) and Level 1 (baseline architecture) described above can be employed for enterprise applications developed with different methodologies such as OOAD and Structured Systems Analysis and Design (SSAD). However, as detailed architecture would be an input to analysis and design processes in the following stages of the development cycle, the views for this level are aligned with the methodology adopted. Also, as detailed architecture forms the foundation for design, the views for detailed architecture are similar to the design views and are build on the architecture views, the only difference being that the views for detailed architecture are still abstractions not meant to be programmed by developers while design views are detailed enough and meant to be constructed by the use of development tools. For OOAD methodology, the "4+1" views (Krutchen, 1995) are employed for representing the detailed architecture. Each of the views discussed in the following sub-sections can be modelled using Unified Modelling Language (UML) standardized by Object Management Group (OMG).

Use Case View

Use cases describe user interactions with the application (deployed on a system). Hence, functionality of the system can be described in terms of use cases. The architecturally significant use cases, as indicated earlier, are the key to determining the suitable architecture. Use case view models use cases of an application and can be represented by means of use case diagrams (based on a notation such as UML) that pictorially depict users (actors) of the system and interactions with the application. This view of architecture corresponds to the "+1" of the "4+1" views and validates the other four views, namely logical, process, development and deployment views (Quatrani, 2002).

Logical View

The logical view describes the object model of an application that satisfies the functional requirements described by use cases. The object model is arrived at by analysis of use cases and their realization by means of collaborating classes. In the logical view of detailed architecture, classes are defined for the architecturally significant use cases which are generally at analysis level (Evans, 2004). These analysis classes, during the design phase, are mapped to design classes to develop the design model.

Development View

The development view represents software module organization involving packages and components along with their interconnections in order to structure the physical artefacts of the application. The artefacts include components, build scripts, source files, executables, etc. This view, therefore, describes the artefacts required to assemble and release the application (Muchandi, 2007).

Process View

The process view deals with non-functional requirements such as performance, scalability and throughput and captures the run-time structure of the application. It models how running processes address run-time considerations such as concurrency and synchronization aspects of the architecture. A process is a group of tasks that form an executable unit and, hence, the process view models interactions of tasks and processes of an application. Layers can be identified in this view that can have an impact on hardware needed as well as the cost and quality of service of the application (Sterkin, 2006).

Deployment View

The deployment view describes the physical architecture of the system on which the application is deployed and includes nodes, network topology and other physical infrastructure that forms the environment of the application. The focus of deployment view is on distribution, communication and provision of the deployment environment of the application (Booch, 2004).

5.3 SOLUTION ARCHITECTURE FOR ENTERPRISE APPLICATIONS BASED ON SOA

SOA is one of the architectural styles that can be employed in the architecture of enterprise applications. Hence, the solution architecting process discussed in the earlier section is equally applicable to enterprise applications that participate in enterprise-wide SOA as detailed in Chapter 4. The solutions architecture for the enterprise applications that expose the activity and client services can also be specified using the solution architecting process discussed above.

The service model considerations provided in Section 5.1, however, need to also be addressed in the solution architecture. The impact of these considerations on the solution architecting process is as follows:

1. ***Level 0 – High-level architecture:*** In order that the architecture of enterprise application aligns with the enterprise-wide SOA, business process model would be created and would form an input to high-level architecture definition activities. The reference architecture and the best practices considered by the architect are those of services model for arriving at the conceptual, logical and physical views.
2. ***Level 1 – Baseline architecture:*** The services exposed and consumed by an application are identified and patterns for SOA considered for defining the functional, technical and implementation views of Baseline architecture. For example, the Enterprise Service Bus is a key pattern for integration of services and this pattern is included as part of an integration layer defined for the application.
3. ***Level 2 – Detailed architecture:*** While the 4+1 views used for OOAD can also be used for the detailed architecture, the logical view is extended to reflect the services model. A UML 2 Profile for software services is an example of representing the services model (Johnston, 2005).

In the chapters so far, SOA concepts have been presented and the architecting of SOA at enterprise level and application level has been discussed. The next chapter identifies the software platforms for enterprise applications that support SOA for implementing the architecture.

5.4 SUMMARY

The objective of this chapter is to introduce enterprise applications to set the stage for discussing service-oriented applications in subsequent chapters.

Enterprise applications are defined and the architectural considerations for enterprise applications are described. A solution architecting process for enterprise applications is discussed that involves defining three views – conceptual, logical and physical – as Level 0 high-level architecture in the initial stages of a project. This is followed by defining three other views – functional, technical and implementation – as Level 1 baseline architecture after elaboration of requirements in the project. At the start of design process, architecture is further elaborated as Level 2 detailed architecture.

KEY TERMS

Non-Functional Requirements (or Qualities) Non-functional requirements are constraints on various attributes of a system. These represent the qualities of the system. Examples of non-functional requirements include performance, scalability, availability, reliability and security.

Conceptual View (of Architecture) Conceptual view is the abstracted business model of the application described in terms familiar to the users.

Logical View Logical view shows the structuring of main functional components of the application based on the architectural patterns (such as layering) and their relationships.

Physical View Physical view provides details of the implementation components (hardware and software) and their relationships.

Functional View The functional view of an application defines key functional elements that deliver the application's functionality, their responsibilities, interfaces they expose and the interactions between them.

Technical View The technical view describes technical elements of an enterprise application, their interfaces, interaction and interdependence in order to satisfy a specified set of requirements.

Implementation View The implementation view of an enterprise application represents the elements from which the solution is built. It also describes how the solution will be developed, deployed, validated, managed and funded.

"4+1" View Model The "4+1" view model describes software architecture using five concurrent views, each of which addresses a specific set of concerns.

REFERENCES

Booch, G. (2004) *Software Architecture*, IBM, www.booch.com/architecture/blog/artifacts/Software%20Architecture.ppt

EPA (Environmental Protection Agency) (2005) *Enterprise Architecture Policy*, Classification No.: 2120.3, CIO POLICY TRANSMITTAL 06-001.

Evans, G. (2004) *Getting from Use Cases to Code, Part 1: Use-Case Analysis*, IBM, http://www.ibm.com/developerworks/rational/library/5383.html

Kazman, R. (1998) Representing software architecture, *The Architect, SEI Interactive*, **1**(3).

Kruijk, R. (2001) *The Meaning of the Business Case*, Presentation from Landelijk Architectuur Congres 2001, http://www.serc.nl/lac/LAC-2001/5-case/stream_05.html

Krutchen, P. (1995) The 4+1 view model of architecture, *IEEE Software*, **12**(6), 42–50.

Johnston, S. (2005) *UML 2.0 Profile for Software Services*, IBM, http://www.ibm.com/developerworks/rational/library/05/419_soa/

MSDN (2004) *Using Patterns to Design the Baseline Architecture*, MSDN, Microsoft, http://msdn2.microsoft.com/en-us/library/ms978704.aspx

Muchandi, V. (2007) *Applying 4+1 View Architecture with UML 2*, Sparx Systems, http://www.sparxsystems.com.au/downloads/whitepapers/FCGSS_US_WP_Applying_4+1_w_UML2.pdf

Platt, M. (2002) *Microsoft Architecture Overview*, MSDN, Microsoft, http://msdn2.microsoft.com/en-us/library/ms978007.aspx

Quatrani, T. (2002) *Visual Modeling with Rational Rose 2002 and UML*, Addison Wesley Professional, Boston, MA

Rozanski, N. and Woods, E. (2005) *Software Systems Architecture: Working With Stakeholders Using Viewpoints and Perspectives*, Addison-Wesley, Boston, MA

SearchDataCenter (2005) *High Availability*, SearchDataCenter.com, http://searchdatacenter.techtarget.com/sDefinition/0,,sid80_gci761219,00.html

Sterkin, A. (2006) *Layered Architecture Revised*, ESA '06 – The 2006 International Conference on Embedded Systems & Applications, Nevada, US.

Software Platforms for Enterprise Applications

CHAPTER 6

CONTENTS

LEARNING OBJECTIVES

After reading this chapter, you would be able to:

- Discuss the software platforms for enterprise applications.
- Review the packaged enterprise applications: ERP; CRM; SCM.
- Know the best principles in architecting solutions for enterprise application platforms: Java EE Platform; Microsoft .NET Platform.
- Gain in-depth understanding of Java EE and .NET platforms from architecture perspective.
- Study reference model and indicative technical architecture for enterprise applications developed for Java EE and .NET platforms.

Enterprise applications need hardware infrastructure and software frameworks to run. A software platform for enterprise applications provides the framework to develop and deploy them. It includes a run-time environment or in some cases a *container* that provides a set of services to run programs written with a programming language. Programs can avail the services by confirming to the programming model of the run-time environment (or container).

Software platforms for enterprise applications can often support multiple hardware platforms. The portability of the run-time environment (or container) also allows for portability of enterprise application to multiple hardware platforms with minimal or no changes.

This chapter discusses the software platforms for enterprise applications. Enterprise applications, as indicated in Chapter 5, satisfy the information needs of the enterprise and automate business processes, manage business data and integrate enterprise activities.

With increased focus on business competitiveness, one of the strategies that organizations employ for IT platforms is to buy what they can and build what they must. Two types of platforms accordingly support enterprise applications:

1. packaged application platforms;
2. enterprise application platforms.

6.1 PACKAGED APPLICATION PLATFORMS

Packaged application platforms provide pre-built capability for a specific domain that can be customized to meet the requirements of the enterprise. The following are packaged enterprise application platforms (Mertz et al., 2007):

1. Enterprise Resource Planning (ERP);
2. Supply Chain Management (SCM);
3. Customer Relationship Management (CRM).

Packaged applications form the backbone of IT infrastructure of an enterprise when the nature of business of the enterprise is such that the core of business processes can be implemented efficiently by their customization. For example, a retail store may IT enable its core business processes by implementing an ERP application suite. It may be noted that products for a specific industry vertical (such as Core Banking product for Banking vertical) also are packaged applications and can serve as platform for the enterprise.

Enterprise Resource Planning (ERP)

ERP application suite is a platform that provides an enterprise view of business (Jones, 2004) and includes software infrastructure that is modular, integrated and with a unified database to meet the requirements of seamless business processes. Many of the modules in ERP application suites such as manufacturing, HR management, financials and asset management are related to back-office functions (while not necessarily all). The SAP Netweaver platform and Oracle E-Business Suite are two widely used packaged applications for ERP.

Customer Relationship Management (CRM)

CRM application platform enables a single view of customer across the applications in an enterprise. CRM application suites have modules for marketing, customer sales and support which are typically front-office functions in an organization. They include functions for support of processes for organization's sales or service representative, communication with customers and analysis of customer data for a broad range of purposes. A Software as a Service (SaaS) model of delivery of services of the platform is also being offered by several vendors. Salesforce.com, Oracle OnDemand, Microsoft Dynamics and SAP CRM are some of the vendors of the CRM platforms (Thompson et al., 2007).

Supply Chain Management (SCM)

SCM application platform provides capabilities to integrate the processes of the trading partner in order to optimize product flows, information flows and finance flows among the enterprises. This results in a concept of an extended enterprise for sharing data with suppliers, manufacturers and end customers of an organization. The objective of SCM applications is to reduce time-to-market, optimize costs and effectively manage resources for the organization and its supply chain partners. SCM platform includes two types of applications, one to determine the best way to fill order for products and second to track products and finances (SearchCIO, 2006).

6.2 ENTERPRISE APPLICATION PLATFORMS

It may not be possible for all enterprise-level requirements to be met by implementing packaged applications. Even if it were possible, the cost of a packaged solution and its customization may not be viable for organizations. Enterprise application platforms offer an alternative to packaged applications and provide software infrastructure for custom development of enterprise applications to meet the needs of the stakeholders of business and IT of an enterprise. They provide a programming model and a run-time environment (or container) in which the application can be deployed.

The following are key enterprise application platforms (Natis et al., 2006):

1. Java Platform Enterprise Edition (Java EE);
2. .NET Microsoft Application Platform (MSAP);
3. Customer Information Control System (CICS);
4. Common Object Broker Architecture (CORBA).

Of the platforms mentioned above, Java EE and .NET Microsoft application platforms have been predicted to witness increased adoption in future (Duggan et al., 2007) and hence are discussed in further detail in the following sub-sections.

Application Server Platforms

Both Java EE and .NET Microsoft application platforms support distributed processing through component models that allow for application components to be grouped logically into different layers and deployed in different physical configurations to enable distributed processing across number of machines. These platforms support the concept of an *application server* that serves as a container for deploying the enterprise application and provides several common services such as lifecycle management for resources.

In order to efficiently address functional and non-functional requirements, enterprise applications developed for Java EE and .NET Microsoft application platforms are structured with multiple layers each addressing the concern of the layer. The following are some of the best principles that can be applied in the architecture of enterprise applications:

Principle 1: Well-defined application layers

1. A layer is a logical grouping of software elements that address similar concerns (Lhotka, 2005).
2. Concerns of the application is separated into distinct layers – presentation layer, business layer and data access layer.
3. Rationale for layers
   - ***Presentation layer***: User interface (UI) requirements change frequently. Hence, changes need to be localized by the definition of a layer.

- *Business layer:* A separate layer is required to implement the business logic while addressing that non-functional requirements such as performance, scalability, etc.
- *Data access layer*: A layer is specified to provide encapsulated access to data in data stores and localize changes to this layer of application should it be necessary to change the type or scheme of data stores.

Principle 2: Closed layer architecture

1. Each layer communicates only with the layers immediately next to it.
2. Communication between the layers happens via well-defined interfaces.

Principle 3: Configurable plug-in points for screen navigation and application business rules

1. Navigation logic is not hard-coded into the application.
2. Changes to screen navigation and business rules are handled through few changes to code.
3. Screen navigation is handled through metadata.

Principle 4: Separation of validation logic from business logic

1. Validation logic for application is separated from business logic as failure to do so makes the code difficult to maintain.

Principle 5: Encapsulation of access to databases

1. No calls are made directly to the database from presentation layer.
2. Data access layer (DAL) is designed to interact with set of data sources and to coordinate transactions among them.

Principle 6: Cache data on the server and/or client for improved performance

1. Data that changes less frequently is cached on the server and/or client for improved performance.

Principle 7: Failover and redundancy is used for high availability and disaster recovery

1. Cluster configurations address failover and redundancy requirements.
2. Horizontal and vertical clustering of servers is considered for high availability and disaster recovery solutions.

Principle 8: Scalability options

1. Applications have goals for the desired performance for changing workload that could include number of concurrent users and the amount of data that the system would need to store/process. These scalability goals are considered in architecture, design and when developing the application in order that the enterprise application scales as the business it serves grows.

2. Component models that allow for distributed deployment and execution of components are leveraged for scalability.
3. Network load balancing and component load balancing techniques direct end-user service requests to the servers and components that are least busy and therefore are capable of providing the required performance even with increasing workload characteristic.

Principle 9: Deployment of application components in multiple tiers

1. A tier is a physical boundary and represents physical separation of application components (Rotem, 2006).
2. By grouping application components into separately deployable elements called tiers, the components can leverage the physical infrastructure better through greater optimization and utilization while interoperating with one another.
3. Tiers offer performance, scalability, fault tolerance and security when judiciously used and, therefore, application components of enterprise applications are structured as tiers and deployed accordingly (Lhotka, 2005).

Principle 10: Wrapping of calls to third-party products and components

1. Third-party products and components used in applications (e.g., rule engine/workflow engine) may need to be replaced during the lifecycle of application owing to business and technical considerations.
2. A framework-based approach is considered in order to wrap access to third-party products and components.

Principle 11: Encapsulation of communication with external applications

1. Hiding of implementation details of invocation of external applications is essential in order to deal with issues related to communication, encoding and security.
2. A *broker pattern* is used to encapsulate access to a layer other than business layer.
3. In the interest of performance, the number of calls to the legacy systems and other applications are kept at a minimum.

The Java EE and .NET Microsoft application platforms are discussed in the following sub-sections. There are significant number of books and other forms of literature available that discuss in detail the platform technologies as well as the tools for implementing applications. The purpose of the following sub-sections is to cover relevant concepts on the enterprise paltforms before providing detalis on how they can be leveraged for developing SOA-based enterprise applications.

Java Platform Enterprise Edition

> *Java Platform, Enterprise Edition (Java EE) is a set of coordinated technologies and practices that enable solutions for developing, deploying, and managing multi-tier, server-centric applications. Sun Developer Network (SDN, 2007).*

Java EE is, therefore, a platform specification that is implemented by different vendors to provide an application model for enterprise applications. The Java EE application model splits an enterprise application into three fundamental parts (Anagol-Subbarao, 2004) – containers, components and connectors – as shown in Figure 6-1.

Container provides several services to the components and the clients of enterprise application including transaction management and resource pooling. It provides a run-time environment for the components and also through its services provides "plumbing" required for managing the lifecycle of the components. The mediation by the container allows run-time behavior of components to be specified through a descriptor at deployment time. A container is essentially a Java Virtual Machine (JVM) that can load and run Java classes (compiled to intermediate code by the compiler). Each type of container shown in Figure 6-1 can run specific type of components supported by that container in addition to Java objects supported by the Java Platform Standard Edition (Java SE).

Components are designed and programmed to conform to the contract required between the container and the component (as published in the Java EE specification) in order that the services of the container – such as life cycle management of the component – can be leveraged. This significantly reduces housekeeping code that otherwise enterprise applications would need to build for optimizing the creation, pooling and release of components. The application components in Java EE include web components, Enterprise JavaBean (EJB) components, applets and application client components.

Connectors provide integration of the container and components to heterogeneous Enterprise Information Systems (EIS). This aspect of the application model allows for components and container to encapsulate access and communicate with different EIS that conform to a specified Java EE connector architecture in a consistent and seamless manner.

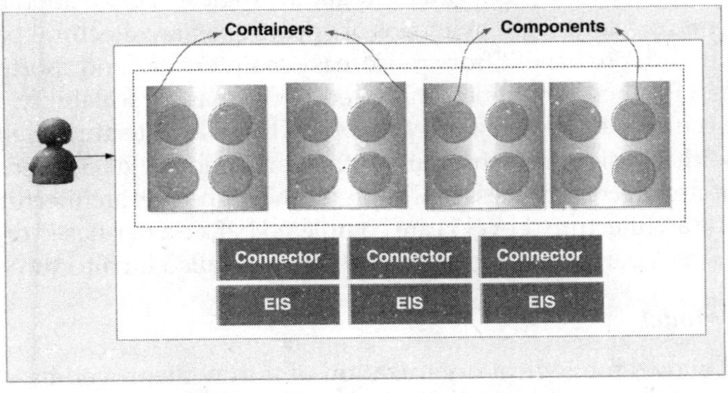

FIGURE 6-1 Java EE application model.

On the basis of the application model shown in Figure 6-1, Java EE specifies the following types of containers:

1. ***Web container:*** A web server contains a web container which provides a run-time environment for web components that include Java Server Pages (JSP), Servlets, JSF applications, filters and web event listeners.
2. ***EJB container:*** The lifecycle of the EJB is managed by the EJB container. EJBs are scalable, transactional and multi-user secure components that implement the business logic for an enterprise application.
3. ***Applet container:*** Applets are client-side graphical user interface components that run in an applet container of a browser. Applets can provide a UI for Java EE applications by leveraging the client-side processing capabilities.
4. ***Application client container:*** Application client programs are Java programs that run in their container on client machines and have access to the server-side Java EE facilities.

The above-mentioned containers provide a platform for application components deployed in them which may access and in turn be accessed by a variety of protocols that containers support. Figure 6-2 represents pictorially the interoperability of components and containers along with the supported protocols.

Applications can be structured to conform to specifications for containers, components and connectors. In a Java EE application, the components are deployed in the following three tiers (Broemmer, 2003):

1. ***Client tier:*** Web browser with the Java Virtual Machine (JVM), the applet container and the application client container constitute the client tier.
2. ***Middle tier:*** Web server and the application server with the web container and EJB container comprise the middle tier.
3. ***Enterprise information tier:*** Databases and other applications that the enterprise application interacts with form the enterprise information tier.

The purpose of the tiers mentioned above is to describe where physically the code runs. Very often, it is important to get the logical organization of architecture elements and code right by means of applying an architectural pattern such as *layering* in order to benefit from reuse, easy maintenance and shorter development cycles. Further benefits in improved performance, scalability, fault tolerance and security can be realized by mapping those architectural elements such as layers with physical infrastructure in the tiers (Lhotka, 2005). Hence, as indicated in the architecting process in Chapter 5, the high-level architecture (Level 0) and baseline architecture (Level 1) are completed before a tier-based organization is arrived at as a part of the deployment view in detailed architecture.

Reference Model

Figure 6-3 shows the logical organization of a thin client web-based Java EE application as layers. It depicts reference model for a layered web-based Java

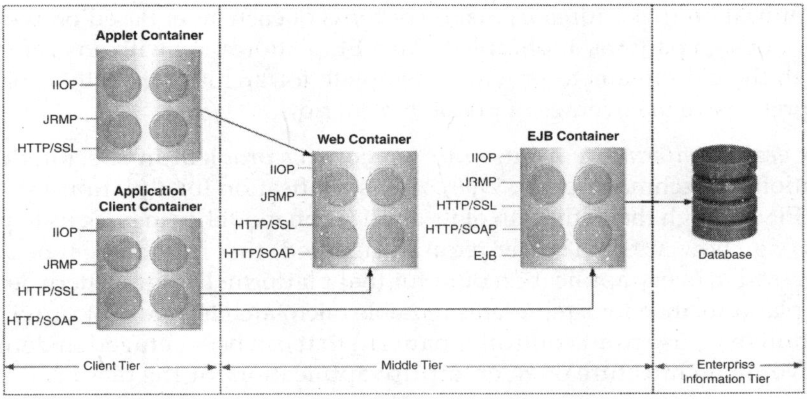

FIGURE 6-2 Container–component interactions.

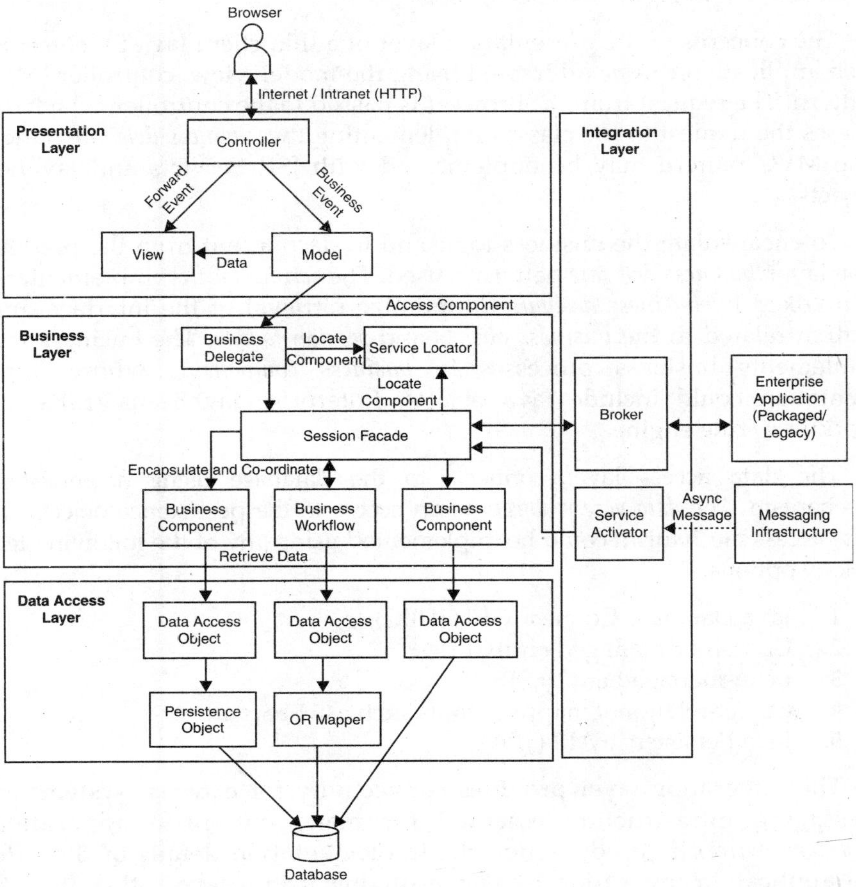

FIGURE 6-3 Reference model of web-based Java EE enterprise application.

EE application that addresses major concerns of each layer based on the concept of design patterns applicable to Java EE platform. As with any reference model, the objective is to provide a template for architecture rather than be comprehensive in coverage of possible scenarios.

A *design pattern* is a solution to a recurring problem in specific design situations (Buschmann et al., 1996). Any specification for a platform such as Java EE, through the definition of its application model, brings focus to problems (e.g., how are HTTP user requests handled) that need to be repeatedly addressed in every application built for that platform. Design pattern defined for a platform, therefore, represents reusable micro-architecture that provides a solution (e.g., use front controller pattern) that can be leveraged in defining the overall architecture of an enterprise application for the platform.

Several design patterns have been identified for Java platform (Alur et al., 2003). Table 6-1 lists some of the key patterns that form the basis for a reference model shown in Figure 6-3 (SDN, 2002).

The concerns of the presentation layer of a thin client Java EE enterprise web application can be addressed using the model–view–controller (MVC) pattern. The request from the browser is passed to the controller, which then passes the request to the classes implementing the *business delegate* pattern. The MVC pattern may be implemented with JSP, Servlets and JavaBean objects.

To encapsulate the business logic and to decouple it from the presentation layer, *business delegate* pattern is used. The *service locator* implementation is invoked by *business delegate* to optimize retrieval of the interface information related to the *business objects* and *session facade*. The business layer implements business processes in *business components* whose implementation could include Java objects, Enterprise JavaBeans (EJBs) and workflow/rule engine.

The data access layer connects to the database using a persistence mechanism. The *data access objects* wrap access to the persistence objects. The data access mechanism could be implemented using any of the following technology options:

1. Java Database Connectivity (JDBC);
2. Container-managed entity EJB;
3. Bean-managed entity EJB;
4. Object-relational mapping tools such as Hibernate;
5. Java Persistence API (JPA).

The integration layer provides connectivity for external systems and messaging infrastructure essential for many enterprise applications. A *broker pattern* is used to hide the implementation details of the external application invocation by encapsulating it in a layer other than the business layer. The Java Connector Architecture (JCA) is a specification

TABLE 6-1 Key patterns for Java EE reference model

Pattern	*Description*
Model–view–controller	Pattern suitable for providing multiple views of data. It separates three types of objects – *models* that maintain data, views that display all or a portion of the data, and controllers that handle events that affect the model or view(s).
Business delegate	Pattern to decouple presentation layer from business layer. The business delegate encapsulates the business layer and hides implementation details such as lookup and EJB interfaces. **Note:** *In the architecture diagrams in this book, business delegate has been shown in business layer in the logical view to be consistent with definitions in [Alur et al., 2003]. The business delegate-related classes are deployed in web tier.*
Service locator	Pattern for service lookup and creation. It abstracts the usage of JNDI, EJB home lookup and creation.
Session facade	Pattern to encapsulate interactions among business objects. Session facade manages business objects and provides course-grained access to clients.
Data access object	Pattern to abstract access to all data stores. It manages the connection with the database and performs operations on data stores.
Broker	Pattern to communicate with remote objects. The broker pattern hides the implementation details of communication with remote objects by encapsulating them in a separate layer.

supported by Java EE specification that allows for encapsulated access to non-Java EE applications. In order to provide asynchronous capabilities, a *service activator* pattern is used in integration layer to trigger processing on the arrival of asynchronous messages from messaging infrastructure. Message-driven bean (MDB) is supported to Java EE in order to support asynchronous processing in the EJB container on the arrival asynchronous JMS messages.

Technical Architecture

The reference model in Figure 6-3 may be implemented by appropriate choice of software elements provided by Java EE platform. This results

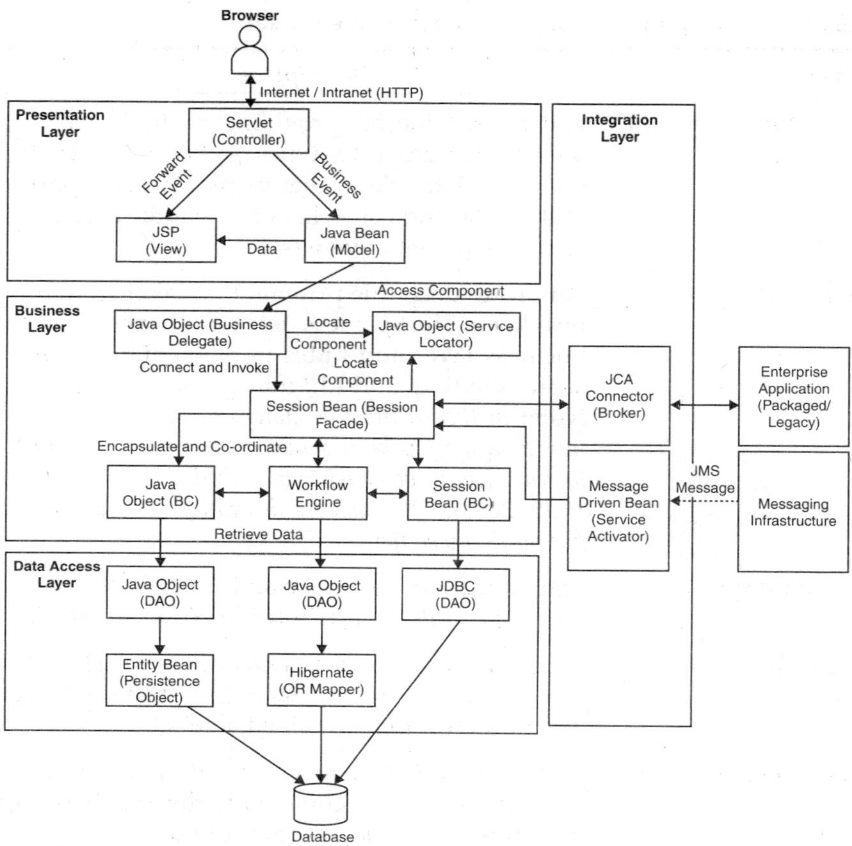

FIGURE 6-4 Technical architecture (indicative) of Java EE enterprise application.

in the reference technical architecture for Java EE platform shown in Figure 6-4. The technical architecture shown is meant to be indicative rather than cover all the possibilities for the Java EE platform. For a given enterprise application, technical architecture can be derived by using the reference technical architecture as a starting point and making changes and enhancements by taking into account the functional and non-functional requirements.

The technical architecture shows the presentation layer with Servlets, JSPs and JavaBeans. While the presentation layer can be developed ground up, there are many advantages of using frameworks such as Struts and JSF for the presentation layer which implement the MVC design pattern and, therefore, may be leveraged for implementing the presentation layer.

Likewise, several enterprise application technologies can be leveraged for the business, data access and integration layers. These include (SDN, 2007):

1. Enterprise JavaBeans (EJB);
2. J2EE Connector Architecture (JCA);
3. JavaBeans Activation Framework (JAF);
4. JavaMail API;
5. Java Message Service API;
6. Java Persistence API;
7. Java Transaction API (JTA).

.NET Microsoft Application Platform

> *The Microsoft enterprise application development platform is a comprehensive platform for building connected systems based on the .NET Framework. Microsoft Developer Network (MSDN, 2005)*

Enterprise applications for the Microsoft application platform are built to run on the .NET framework that is currently available for the Microsoft Windows family of operating system. The .NET framework makes available API for the class libraries that provide several capabilities for enterprise applications such as the user interface, data access, security, transactions, etc.

The Microsoft application platform provides the following capabilities that form the foundation for a .NET enterprise application:

1. ***Windows Server Family:*** Operating system support for enterprise application.
2. ***Common Language Run-time (CLR):*** Run-time environment for the components of the application.
3. ***.NET Framework Libraries:*** API for developing the following enterprise applications:
   - *ASP .NET and WPF:* user interface development;
   - *ADO .NET:* data retrieval;
   - *WCF, WF:* business service and workflow development.
4. ***Core Products:*** Supporting products for enterprise information tier:
   - *SQL Server:* database;
   - *BizTalk:* process orchestration and integration;
   - *Share Point Portal:* portal infrastructure;
   - *Host Integration Server:* legacy integration.

Figure 6-5 shows the above-mentioned capabilities as concentric circles. The enterprise application (shown in the outermost circle) leverages the capabilities of each of the circles (inner).

Windows OS

Microsoft family of operating systems supports the .NET framework and CLR essential for an enterprise application. While in theory CLR can be ported to

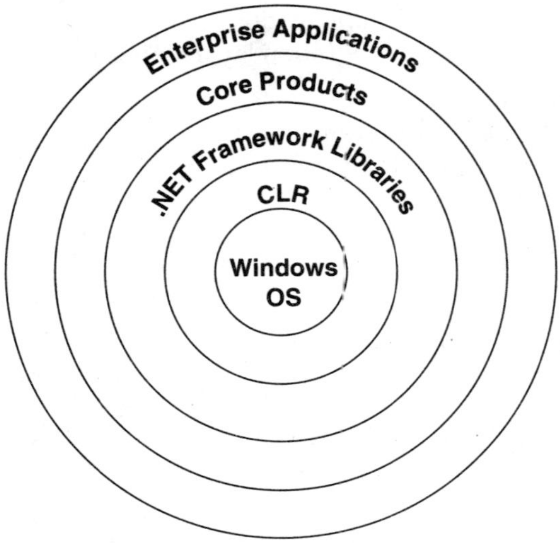

FIGURE 6-5 .NET Microsoft application platform.

other operating systems, only Windows family of operating systems supports it as of now. The open source Mono project is an effort to provide the .NET framework and CLR on the Unix family of operating systems.

Common Language Run-time (CLR)

The CLR (which acts in a fashion similar to the container in the Java EE platform) provides an environment for .NET components built using .NET framework to run. While portability across different types of operating systems has been the goal of the different versions of Java EE, support of multiple programming languages has been the goal for Microsoft platforms. The CLR allows for support of multiple languages by compilers that convert the programming language code (e.g., C#, VB) in a file to an intermediate language called Microsoft Intermediate Language (MSIL) in the Portable Executable (PE) file format as shown in Figure 6-6. Assemblies are the basis for the deployment and versioning features of .NET. An assembly is a collection of one or more files – PE files, resource files, HTML pages, GIFs that implement types and resources. The components of an assembly are described in a manifest. A manifest is a block of data that enumerates the assembly's files, and controls what types and resources are exposed outside of the assembly (Richter, 2000).

The MSIL so generated is converted to native code of the CPU of the platform by Just-In-Time (JIT) compiler for the underlying hardware platform at run-time when the CLR loads the classes in the assembly. The CLR implements a formal specification for how object classes are defined called the Common

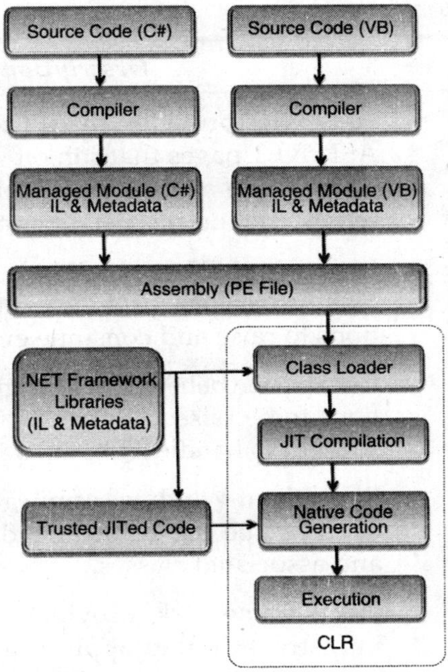

FIGURE 6-6 CLR and code.

Type System (CTS). CTS specifies rules governing type inheritance, virtual functions, etc. and the language compiler maps the type definitions of the language of the program to CTS. .NET applications, components and controls are built on the types defined by .NET framework.

.NET Framework Libraries

The .NET framework provides a number of libraries for enterprise application development (MSDN, 2007). Table 6-2 lists the .NET Framework libraries commonly used in enterprise application development.

TABLE 6-2 .NET framework libraries

Library	*Description*
.NET Framework Class Library	The .NET framework provides several types and to accelerate the development process. Several fundamental types such as integer, float, etc. are defined in the core library.

(continued)

TABLE 6-2 (*Continued*)

Library	*Description*
ASP .NET	ASP .NET provides an API to create and render ASP .NET pages that run on web server.
ADO .NET	ADO .NET is a set of classes that allow insert, update, retrieve and delete operations on data in data stores.
Events	Events in .NET are based on the delegate model. The framework provides capability to applications to raise and consume events.
Exceptions	Unexpected behavior of a program can cause exceptions to be raised. The .NET framework provides support to handle exceptions in applications.
Windows Forms	Rich Client Windows applications may be developed by the use of the Windows forms controls and associated classes.
XML Web Services	.NET framework provides XML web services infrastructure that applications can use to build web services-based applications.

Core Microsoft Products

Most enterprise applications for the Microsoft platform use one or more of the products listed in Table 6-3 to meet the requirements.

TABLE 6-3 Core products for Microsoft application platform

Product	*Description*
SQL Server	The SQL Server product provides traditional database support for OLTP applications as well as analysis services for OLAP applications. SQL Server is scalable as a database based on the shared-nothing architecture.
BizTalk	BizTalk provides transformation and routing capabilities in addition to integration services for enterprise applications. Several adapters are available for ERP and other packaged enterprise applications to enable integration.
SharePoint portal	Enterprise portals can be developed using SharePoint portal product. Integration of Microsoft

(*continued*)

TABLE 6-3 (*Continued*)

Product	*Description*
	Office with SharePoint services (MOSS) has resulted in more sophisticated Microsoft Office front-ends for SharePoint server.
Host Integration Server	Host Integration server provides integration of .NET enterprise applications with mainframe systems.

Reference Model

The logical organization of a .NET enterprise application in presentation, business and data access layers is shown in Figure 6-7. It represents a reference model for a layered web-based .NET application that addresses the concerns of each layer based on the concept of design patterns applicable to .NET platform. As with any reference model, the objective is to provide a template for architecture rather than be comprehensive in coverage of possible scenarios.

Several design patterns have been identified for .NET platform (Trowbridge et al., 2003). Table 6-4 lists some of the key patterns that form the basis for a reference model shown in Figure 6-7.

The presentation layer shown in the reference model includes the MVC pattern to address the user interface concerns of the enterprise application. Other

TABLE 6-4 Key patterns for .NET reference model

Pattern	*Description*
Model–view–controller	Pattern suitable for providing multiple views of data. Separates three types of objects – *models* that maintains data, *views* that displays all or a portion of the data, and *controller* that handles events that affect the model or view.
Service interface	Pattern to decouple presentation layer from business layer while exposing functionality of business layer as services. The service interface supports and encapsulates network protocol used for communication between service consumer and the service provider.
Broker	Pattern to communicate with remote objects. The broker pattern hides the implementation details of communication with remote objects by encapsulating them in a separate layer.

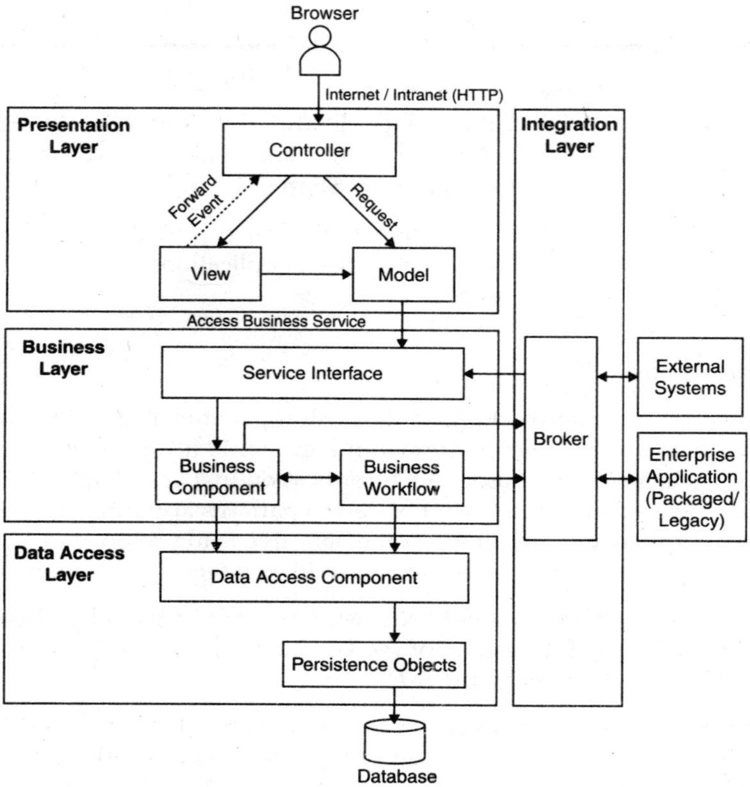

FIGURE 6-7 Reference model of .NET enterprise application.

patterns such as *model–view–presenter* and *page controller* can also be applied to address the concerns of presentation layer. ASP .NET, with the concept of *code behind*, provides most of the support needed for handling HTTP requests from users and implementing the MVC pattern.

The *service interface* pattern encapsulates the functionality provided by the business layer. It supports multiple transports such as Web Services, MSMQ and .NET Remoting and hence the same functionality can be exposed to different types of clients by the use of *service interface* pattern. Windows Communication Foundation (WCF) can provide the capability required to implement the *service interface* pattern. Business components and workflows implement the business functionality of the enterprise application. BizTalk and Windows Foundation (WF) are two options to implement workflows required in an enterprise application.

The *data access components* encapsulate access to the databases. ADO .NET model provides support for different operations on databases and can be used by *data access components* for efficient access of data.

As in the case of the Java EE enterprise application, the integration layer in .NET application provides connectivity for external systems. A *broker* pattern is used for the same purpose as in a Java EE application, which is to hide the implementation details of the external application invocation by encapsulating it in a layer other than the business layer. The Microsoft application platform has products such as BizTalk and Host Integration server that can be used to implement the *broker* pattern and provide connectivity to external applications.

Technical Architecture

The reference model in Figure 6-7 may be implemented by the appropriate choice of software elements provided by .NET platform. This results in the reference technical architecture for .NET platform shown in Figure 6-8. The technical architecture shown, as in the case of Java EE platform, is meant to be indicative rather than covering all the possibilities for the .NET platform. For a given enterprise application, technical architecture can be derived by using the reference technical architecture as a starting point and making changes and enhancements by taking into account the functional and non-functional requirements.

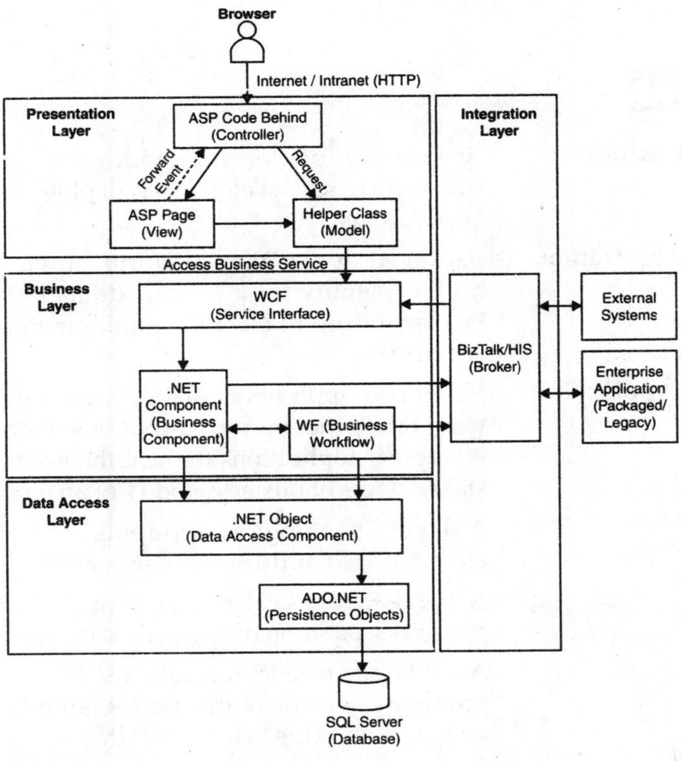

FIGURE 6-8 Technical architecture (indicative) of .NET enterprise application.

The technical architecture shows the different layers built using ASP .NET, ADO .NET, WCF and WF. While these layers can be developed ground up with the API mentioned, there are many benefits in using libraries and software factories such as Enterprise Library and Web Client Software Factory provided by Microsoft Patterns and Practices Group.

The next chapter discusses SOA-based enterprise applications.

6.3 SUMMARY

The objective of this chapter is to discuss the software platforms for enterprise applications. These platforms are also leveraged by service-oriented enterprise applications and hence the concepts presented here will be extended in subsequent chapters for the services model. Two types of application platforms have been identified: packaged application platforms and enterprise application platforms. The enterprise application platforms, Java EE and Microsoft Net are discussed in detail. The reference models and indicative technical architectures for these platforms based on the solution architecting process discussed are also presented.

KEY TERMS

Software Platform — A software platform provides the software framework to develop and deploy software applications.

Packaged Application Platform — Packaged application platform provides pre-built capability for a specific domain that can be customized to meet the requirements of the enterprise.

Enterprise Application Platform — Enterprise application platform provides software infrastructure for custom development of enterprise applications to meet the needs of the stakeholders of business and IT of an enterprise.

Layer — A layer is a logical grouping of software elements that address similar concerns.

Tier — A tier is a physical boundary and represents physical separation of application components.

Container — A container provides a set of services to run programs written with a programming language. Programs can avail the services by conforming to the programming model of the run-time environment (or container).

Java EE	Java Platform, Enterprise Edition (Java EE) is a set of coordinated technologies and practices that enable solutions for developing, deploying, and managing multi-tier, server-centric applications.
Design Pattern	A design pattern is a solution to a recurring problem in specific design situations.
Java Virtual Machine (JVM)	A Java Virtual Machine (JVM) is a set of software programs and data structures that provide a run-time environment for Java programs.
Common Language Run-time (CLR)	A CLR is a set of software programs and data structures that provide a run-time environment for the components of a .NET application.

REFERENCES

Alur, D., Crupi, D. and Malks, D. (2003) *Core J2ee Patterns: Best Practices and Design Strategies*, 2nd edn, Prentice Hall/Sun Microsystems Press, New Jersey.

Broemmer, D. (2003) *J2EE Best Practices*, 1st edn, John Wiley & Sons, Ltd., Chichester.

Buschmann, F., Meunier, R., Rohnert, H., Sommerlad, P. and Stal, M. (1996) *Pattern-Oriented Software Architecture – A System of Patterns*, John Wiley & Sons, Ltd., Chichester.

Duggan, J., Stang, D., Iyengar, P., Murphy, T., Young, A., et al. (2007) *Hype Cycle for Application Development, 2007*, Gartner Research Publication, ID No.: G00147982.

Jones, K. (2004) *Enterprise Resource Planning Primer*, Aberdeen Group, http://www.microsoft.com/dynamics/product/erp_primer.mspx

Lhotka, R. (2005) *Should all Apps be N-tier?*, http://www.lhotka.net

MSDN (2005) *Building Connected Systems: The .NET Framework and the Microsoft Enterprise Application Development Platform*, http://msdn2.microsoft.com/en-us/library/ms973223.aspx

— (2007) *.NET Framework Developer's Guide – Quick Technology Finder*, http://msdn2.microsoft.com/en-us/library/63bf39c2(VS.80).aspx

Mertz, S., Eschinger, C. and Pang, C. (2007) *Key Issues for Business Processes and Application Software Markets*, Gartner Research Publication, ID No.: G00145738.

Natis, Y., Pezzini, M., Iijima, K. and Barnes, M. (2006) *Magic Quadrant for Enterprise Application Servers, 2Q06,* Gartner Research Publication, ID No.: G00141872.

Richter, J. (2000) *Microsoft .NET Framework Delivers the Platform for an Integrated, Service-Oriented Web,* MSDN, http://msdn.microsoft.com/msdnmag/issues/0900/framework/

Rotem, A. (2006) *Tier Is a Natural Boundary,* http://www.rgoarchitects.com

SearchCIO (2006) *Supply Chain Management,* SearchCIO.com, http://searchcio.techtarget.com/sDefinition/0,,sid19_gci214546,00.html

SDN (2002) *Core J2EE Patterns: Patterns Index Page,* Sun Developer Network, http://java.sun.com/blueprints/corej2eepatterns/Patterns/index.html

— (2007) *Java EE Technologies at a Glance,* Sun Developer Network, http://java.sun.com/javaee/technologies/

Thompson, E., Maoz, M., Dunne, M. and Collins, K. (2007) *What's Hot in CRM Applications in 2007,* Gartner Research Publication, ID No.: G00146319.

Trowbridge, D., Macini, D., Quick, D., Hohpe, G., Newkirk, J., et al. (2003) *Enterprise Solution Patterns Using Microsoft .NET,* Microsoft Publication, ISBN No.: 0-7356-1839-9.

Service-Oriented Enterprise Applications

7

CHAPTER

CONTENTS

LEARNING OBJECTIVES

After reading this chapter, you would be able to:

- Understand the considerations for service-oriented enterprise applications.
- Know the SOA patterns for: Service enablement; Service integration; Service orchestration.
- Study the pattern-based reference model and indicative technical architecture for: Service-oriented Java EE enterprise application; Service-oriented .NET enterprise application.
- Define a composite application.
- Study the different SOA Programming Models: Service Component Architecture (SCA); Windows Communication Foundation (WCF).

Service-oriented applications expose and consume services. In Chapter 4, SOA at enterprise level and methodology for implementing the same were discussed. The methodology involves development of enterprise applications that conform to service-oriented model explained in Chapter 3.

This chapter focuses on SOA-based enterprise applications. It builds on the concepts related to enterprise applications provided in Chapter 5, the reference models for different platforms in Chapter 6 and extends them to support service orientation.

7.1 CONSIDERATIONS FOR SERVICE-ORIENTED ENTERPRISE APPLICATIONS

In Section 5.1, Chapter 5, the following considerations of service-oriented model for enterprise applications were summarized. They can be grouped under three categories:

1. service enablement;
2. service integration;
3. service orchestration;
4. service infrastructure.

Service Enablement

The factors involved in determining the services that can be exposed by an enterprise application have a bearing on the extent to which services are *reused*, one of the drivers of SOA. Hence, these considerations include:

1. ***Identification of services exposed or consumed:*** Activity, business process, client or data services that enterprise application exposes or consumes need to be identified.

2. ***Right level of granularity of services exposed:*** The granularity of services exposed has to be at the right level for effective integration and service orchestration.
3. ***Selection of technologies for service enablement:*** Technologies such as web services need to be considered.

Service Integration

For service providers and consumers to effectively communicate with one another, the concern of *integration*, another driver to SOA, needs to be addressed by

1. Identifying patterns for integration (integration model) of services exposed or consumed.
2. Selecting technologies that implement the patterns for integration: Several technology providers offer products that implement integration patterns. A careful selection of products can ensure the trade-offs are addressed appropriately.

Service Orchestration

The third driver for SOA, agility, requires orchestration of business processes based on the services defined. The following need to be considered to implement orchestration in enterprise applications:

1. ***Business process model:*** Business process model of the enterprise and the specific business processes implemented by the enterprise application have to be taken into account.
2. ***Workflows:*** The human tasks based workflows and long-running workflows involved in business processes that the application implements determines the suitability of workflow engine or orchestration engine for their implementation.
3. ***Enterprise data model:*** Data model for the application has to align with enterprise data model that may be defined at the organization level.

Service Infrastructure

Security is one of the key non-functional requirements for any application model and this is true for service-oriented applications as well. To ensure security in service-oriented applications:

1. The nature of authentication, authorization and other security mechanisms have to be identified.
2. Products and solutions that support the patterns have to be implemented.

In order that the services that are exposed/consumed fulfill the service level requirements, the following need to be considered:

1. design-time service governance through use of service registry and repository;
2. run-time service governance through service level monitoring and policy enforcement.

7.2 PATTERNS FOR SOA

The considerations for service-oriented enterprise applications may be addressed from an architecture perspective through the use of patterns.

Patterns for Service Enablement

Patterns for service enablement may be applied to expose the functionality as a service and also to consume remote services. These patterns include (Fowler, 2003) the following:

1. ***Service layer:*** It encapsulates application's business logic and controlling transactions and co-ordinates responses with interfacing layers.
2. ***Service proxy:*** It provides consumers with an interface to the service.
3. ***Service gateway:*** It encapsulates the low-level details of communicating with a service (Trowbridge et al., 2003).

Patterns for Service Integration

Service integration patterns constitute the solution for the problem of integrating service providers and service consumers. The major patterns for service integration are (Arsanjani, 2005):

1. ***Enterprise Service Bus:*** It provides service communication, mediation, transformation and integration.
2. ***Service Adapter:*** It provides a mechanism that allows systems that are not service-oriented to participate in SOA.

Patterns for Service Orchestration

Service orchestration may be employed to orchestrate services exposed within an application context or across applications. The following are the key patterns for service orchestration (Manolescu and Lublinsky, 2005):

1. ***Orchestration Language:*** It is a pattern to specify activities of business processes through a process definition language.
2. ***Orchestration Engine:*** It is a pattern to co-ordinate execution of activities of business processes (specified through an Orchestration Language). Orchestration may be defined as stateful execution of a sequence of activities of a business process. When each activity is implemented as a service, orchestration involves a sequence of invocation of services.

3. ***Compensating Action:*** It is a pattern to cancel the effects of selected actions within an orchestration.

Patterns for Service Infrastructure

Service security patterns ensure that the credentials and permissions of service Consumer (calling party) are checked during service invocations. Key patterns for service security include (Rossebø, et al., 2006):

1. ***Authentication:*** Authentication patterns are of two types:
   - ***Unilateral One-Pass Authentication:*** The authentication process involves establishing the identity of one of the parties, that is, the calling party.
   - ***Mutual Two-Party Authentication:*** In this case, both the calling and called parties establish the identity of each other.
2. ***Authorization:*** Authorization patterns are also of two types:
   - ***User Pull:*** The calling party performs the function of invoking an access server to get authenticated and authorized. An access server holds both authorization and authentication information. The calling party is authenticated by the access server and authorization information is provided by the access server to the calling party. The calling party provides the authorization information to a service invoked.
   - ***Server Pull:*** The service performs the function of authentication and authorization. When the calling party accesses the service, the access server is queried by the called service and the calling party is authenticated and authorized.

Service Governance patterns enable design-time and run-time governance. There are several low-level patterns that may be considered for service governance (Erl, 2008). From a service-oriented application perspective, the following are the key patterns (Soam, 2008):

1. ***The Validation Pattern:*** This is a design-time governance pattern. The services that are developed in an enterprise will have to conform to established guidelines for effective use across the enterprise. The introduction of the service, its modifications over the life-time until being retired have to be managed based on set of policies and procedures in the enterprise. The validation pattern addresses governance related to design-time aspects of the service. It can be implemented using a service registry that maintains a catalog of services and manages their lifecycle and a service repository that holds policies, rules and restrictions that may applied at the time of use of the services.
2. ***The Management Pattern:*** This is a run-time governance pattern. The monitoring of execution of services and enforcement of policies ensures that service-level requirements in terms of performance, throughput and availability are met. The management pattern addresses these run-time concerns of governance. It may be implemented by the use of service management tools in conjunction with service registry and repository.

7.3 PATTERN-BASED ARCHITECTURE FOR SERVICE-ORIENTED ENTERPRISE APPLICATIONS

The patterns for SOA presented in the previous section may be applied to enterprise applications. This results in service-oriented enterprise applications.

Reference Model of Service-Oriented Java EE Enterprise Application

Figure 7-1 shows the logical organization of a thin client web-based Java EE application as layers. It depicts reference model for a layered web-based service-oriented Java EE application that addresses major concerns of each layer based on the concept of design patterns applicable to Java EE platform. As with any reference model, the objective here is to provide a template for architecture rather than be comprehensive in coverage of possible scenarios.

As discussed in Chapter 6, the concerns of the presentation layer of a thin client Java EE Enterprise application can be addressed using the model–view–controller (MVC) pattern. The request from the browser is passed to the controller, which

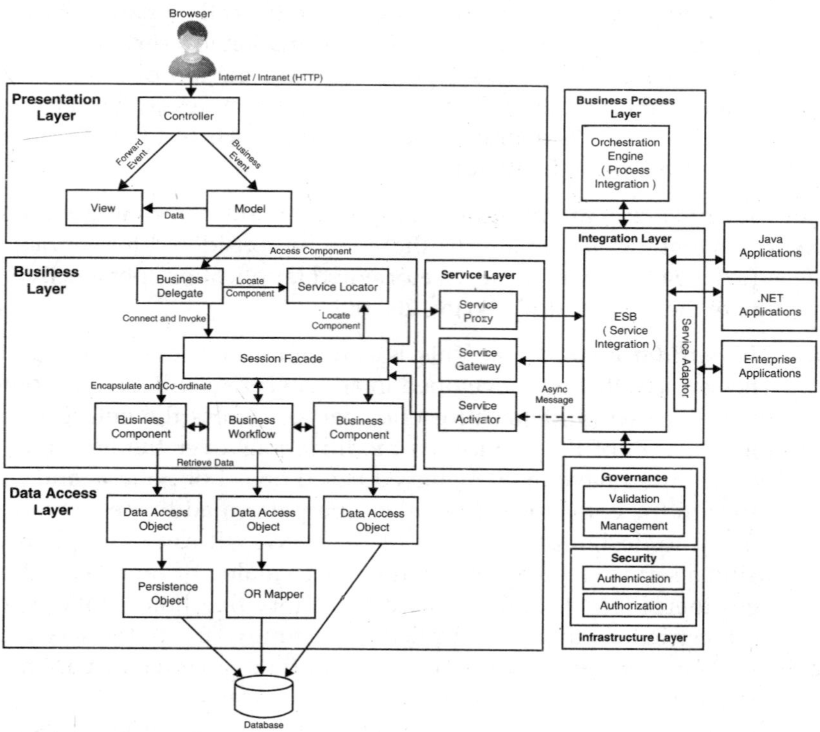

FIGURE 7-1 Reference model of service-oriented Java EE enterprise application.

then passes the request to the classes implementing the *business delegate* pattern. The MVC pattern may be implemented with JSP, Servlets and JavaBean objects.

In order to optimize performance of the enterprise application, the *business delegate* pattern is retained as the pattern to encapsulate the business logic and to decouple it from the presentation layer. The *service locator* implementation is invoked by *business delegate* to optimize retrieval of the interface information related to the *business objects* and *session façade*. The business layer implements business processes in *business components* whose implementation could include Java objects, Enterprise JavaBeans (EJBs) and workflow/rule engine internal to the application.

The data access layer connects to database using a persistence mechanism. The *data access objects* wrap access the persistence objects. The data access mechanism could be implemented using any of the following technology options:

1. Java Database Connectivity (JDBC);
2. Container-managed entity (EJB CMP);
3. Bean-managed entity (EJB BMP);
4. Object-relational mapping tools (e.g., Hibernate);
5. Java Persistence API (JPA).

A service layer is introduced in the reference model of a service-oriented enterprise application on the basis of the *service layer* SOA pattern described earlier to separate the concerns of service orientation from those of the business layer. The *service gateway* pattern has been brought in as part of the service layer to address the need for external applications to access services (e.g., activity services) exposed by the enterprise application. This pattern helps to decouple the processing required to satisfy the requirements laid out by the enterprise application related to security and communication. Service gateway interacts with the service exposed by the enterprise application. Another pattern, *service proxy*, has also been introduced as part of the service layer in order to represent each external service with a proxy object that the business layer uses to access the external service. The *service proxy* implements an interface that handles parameter passing, calling the actual service and returning the results. Additional concerns such as security and communication may also be handled by the *service proxy* class.

The integration layer provides connectivity for external systems and messaging infrastructure essential for the service-oriented enterprise applications. An *enterprise service bus* (ESB) pattern is used for service communication, mediation, transformation, and integration. The ESB products from technology providers have several capabilities to transform data and protocols for different service providers and consumers. The *orchestration engine* pattern is used for Business Process layer to orchestrate externalized business processes and workflows that are described using an *orchestration language* such as Business Process Execution Language (BPEL).

The infrastructure layer addresses concerns of service security and governance. Identity of service consumers and service providers is established by the use of *authentication* pattern (unilateral or mutual) and the service invocations are permitted by the implementation of the *authorization* pattern (user pull or server pull). The *validation* pattern is used for design-time governance for publishing services exposed by service provider applications, managing different versions of services, retiring when not needed by the enterprise and also to specify the policies and procedures for the use of services published in the enterprise. The *management* pattern enables run-time governance of services through monitoring of service execution and policy enforcement to ensure that the service level requirements are met.

Technical Architecture

The reference model in Figure 7-1 may be implemented by appropriate choice of software elements provided by Java EE platform. This results in the reference technical architecture for service-oriented Java EE enterprise application shown in Figure 7-2. The technical architecture shown is meant to be indicative

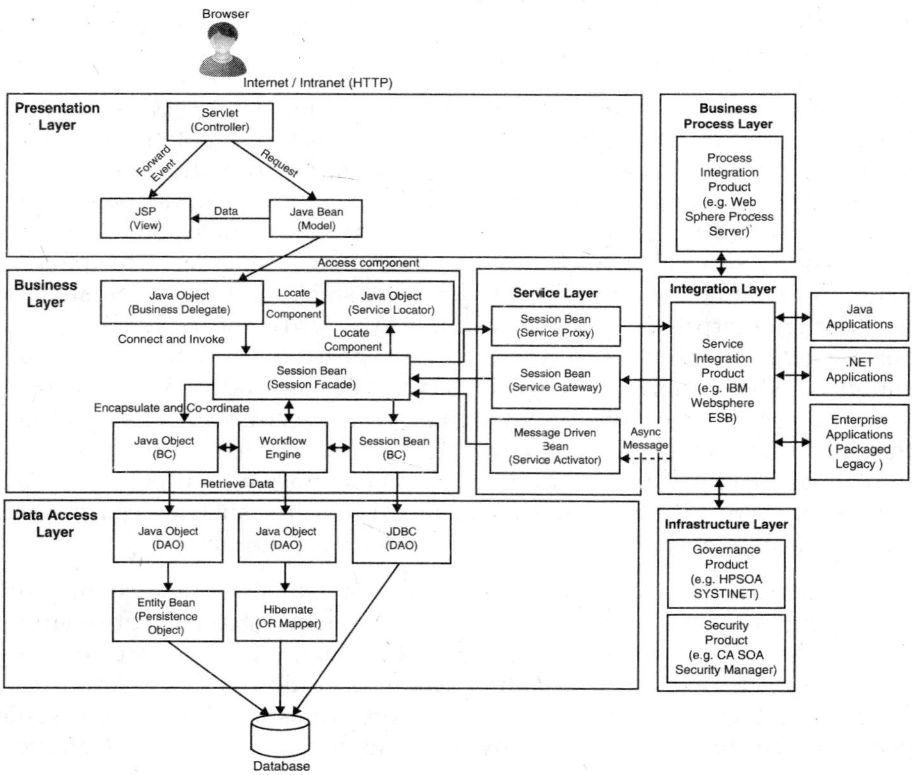

FIGURE 7-2 Technical architecture (indicative) of service-oriented Java EE application.

rather than cover all the possibilities for the Java EE platform. For a given service-oriented enterprise application, technical architecture can be derived by using the reference technical architecture as a starting point and making changes and enhancements by taking into account functional and non-functional requirements.

The technical architecture shows the presentation layer with Servlets, JSPs and JavaBeans. While the presentation layer can be developed ground up, there are many advantages in using frameworks such as Struts and JSF for the presentation layer which implement the MVC design pattern and, therefore, may be leveraged for implementing the presentation layer.

The patterns in the business layer are implemented with Enterprise JavaBeans (EJBs) and Java objects that are deployed in the EJB container. In order that performance is optimal, the patterns in the service layer are also implemented with EJBs and Java objects and deployed in the EJB container.

The pattern for integration layer, namely the Enterprise Service Bus (ESB), is often implemented with products for service integration and process integration. The ESB provides integration of services by being a mediator between service providers and service consumers and undertakes the following processes:

1. transforms message formats;
2. routes messages;
3. augments message content and converts transport protocols;
4. notifies registered message listeners about specific message requests.

Products that implement the ESB are available from:

1. Application Server Vendors (e.g., IBM WebSphere ESB, Microsoft BizTalk);
2. ERP vendors (e.g., SAP XI);
3. Middleware vendors (e.g., Cape Clear ESB, Sonic ESB);
4. Open Source (e.g., WSO2, ServiceMix, Mule).

The orchestration engine in Business Process layer enables process integration through orchestrating cross-application services. Business process orchestration (also referred to as business process management) allows for externalization of those individual processes that were traditionally hard-wired in individual applications. In doing so, it has not only been possible to make the processes configurable through BPEL that most providers of orchestration engines support, but also define business processes that can be realized through invocation of services across multiple applications. Additionally, the orchestration engines allow such business processes, including user interaction, to be "long running" in that they may run for days, weeks or months. For this reason, these business processes are also referred to as workflows. Business process orchestration (or management) therefore enables a configuration-based approach to automate and streamline business processes for an organization and this brings agility to the enterprise.

The infrastructure layer ensures service security and enables service governance. Authentication/authorization patterns may be implemented by specific products that implement identity management and access management (e.g., IBM Tivoli Identity Management and Tivoli Access Management). Identity management solutions already implemented in organizations for enterprise applications (e.g., Netigrity Site Minder or Microsoft Active Directory) may also be integrated and leveraged for this purpose. Service registry and service repository solutions implement validation pattern and several products may be considered for implementing the same (e.g., IBM WebSphere Registry & Repostory, WSO2 Governance Registry, etc.). Specialized Governance Tools have also become available that provide comprehensive design-time and run-time Governance (e.g., Amberpoint Governance system, HP SOA Systinet).

Reference Model of Service-Oriented .NET Enterprise Application

Figure 7-3 shows the logical organization of a thin client .NET application as layers. It depicts reference model for a layered web-based service-oriented

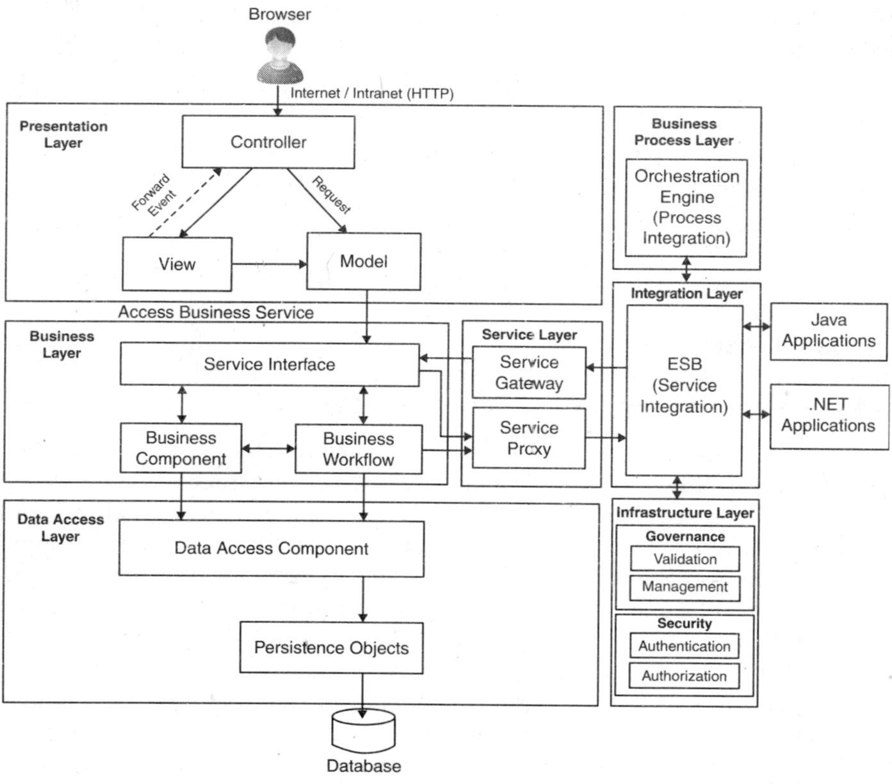

FIGURE 7-3 Reference model of service-oriented .NET enterprise application.

.NET application that addresses major concerns of each layer on the basis of the concept of design patterns applicable to .NET platform. As with any reference model, the objective is to provide a template for architecture rather than be comprehensive in coverage of possible scenarios.

As discussed in Chapter 6, the concerns of presentation layer shown in the reference model include the MVC pattern to address the user interface concerns of the enterprise application. Other patterns such as *model-view-presenter* and *page controller* can also be applied to address the concerns of presentation layer. ASP.NET, with the concept of *code behind*, provides most of the support needed for handling HTTP requests from users and implementing the MVC pattern.

The *service interface* pattern encapsulates the functionality provided by the business layer. The service interface pattern supports multiple transports such as Web Services, MSMQ and .NET Remoting and hence the same functionality can be exposed to different types of clients by the use of *service interface* pattern. Windows Communication Foundation (WCF) can provide the capability required to implement the *service interface* pattern. Business components and workflow / rule engines implement the business functionality of the enterprise application. Windows Workflow Foundation (WF) is an option for implementing human tasks based workflows internal to the application.

The *data access components* encapsulate access to the databases. ADO.NET model provides support for different operations on databases and can be used by *data access components* for efficient access of data.

The following description of service layer and integration layer is common to Java EE and .NET service-oriented enterprise applications and hence repeated here for the sake of completeness.

A service layer is introduced in the reference model of a service-oriented enterprise application based on the *service layer* SOA pattern described earlier to separate the concerns of the service orientation from those of the business layer. The *service gateway* pattern has been brought in as a part of the service layer to address the need for external applications to access services (e.g., activity services) exposed by enterprise application. This pattern helps to decouple the processing required to satisfy the requirements laid out by the enterprise application related to security and communication. Service gateway interacts with the service exposed by the enterprise application. Another pattern, *service proxy*, has been introduced as part of the service layer in order to represent each external service with a proxy object that the business layer uses to access the external service. The *service proxy* implements an interface that handles parameter passing, calling the actual service and returning results. Additional concerns such as security and communication may also be handled by the *service proxy* class.

The integration layer provides connectivity for external systems and messaging infrastructure essential for the service oriented enterprise applications. An *enterprise service bus* (ESB) pattern is used for service communication, mediation, transformation, and integration. The ESB products from technology providers have several capabilities to transform data and protocols for different service providers and consumers. The *orchestration engine* is used for Business Process layer to orchestrate externalized business processes and workflows that are described using an *orchestration language* such as BPEL.

The infrastructure layer, as in the case of Java EE application, addresses concerns of service security and governance. Identity of service consumers and service providers is established by the use of *authentication* pattern (unilateral or mutual) and the service invocations are permitted by the implementation of the *authorization* pattern (user pull or server pull). The *validation* pattern is used for design-time governance for publishing services exposed by service provider applications, managing different versions of services, retiring when not needed by the enterprise and also to specify the policies and procedures for the use of services published in the enterprise. The *management* pattern enables run-time governance of services through monitoring of service execution and policy enforcement to ensure that the service-level requirements are met.

Technical Architecture

The reference model in Figure 7-3 may be implemented by appropriate choice of software elements provided by .NET platform. This results in the reference technical architecture for service-oriented .NET enterprise application shown in Figure 7-4. The technical architecture shown is meant to be indicative rather than covering all the possibilities for the .NET platform. For a given service-oriented enterprise application, technical architecture can be derived by using the reference technical architecture as a starting point and making changes and enhancements by taking into account the functional and non-functional requirements.

The technical architecture shows the different layers built with ASP.NET, ADO.NET, WCF and WF. While these layers can be developed ground up with the API mentioned, there are many benefits in using libraries and software factories such as Enterprise Library and Web Client Software Factory provided by Microsoft Patterns and Practices Group.

As in the case of service-oriented Java EE enterprise application, the pattern for integration layer, namely the ESB, is often implemented with products for service integration and process integration. Microsoft BizTalk provides the capabilities for service and process integration. The ESB provides integration of services by being a mediator between service providers and service consumers. It does the following:

1. transforms message formats;
2. routes messages;
3. augments message content and converts transport protocols;
4. notifies registered message listeners about specific message requests.

Microsoft Patterns and Practices Group has provided guidance on implementing an ESB with BizTalk (CodePlex, 2007).

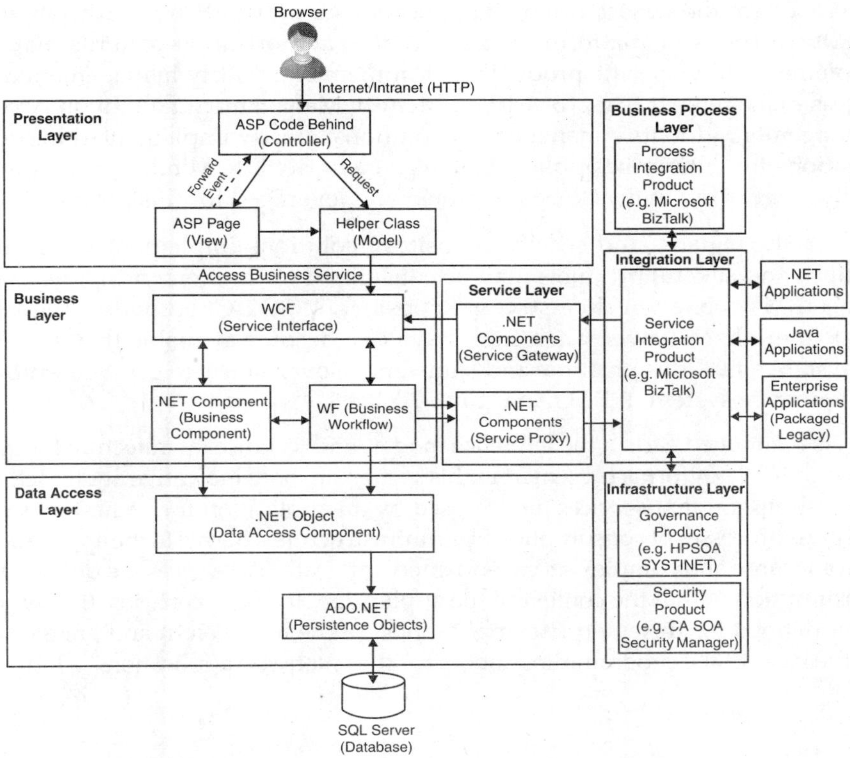

FIGURE 7-4 Technical architecture (indicative) of service-oriented .NET application.

The orchestration engine in Business Process layer, as in the case of Java EE application, enables process integration through orchestrating cross-application services. Business process orchestration (also referred to as business process management) allows for externalization of those individual processes that were traditionally hard-wired in each of the applications. In doing so, it has not only been possible to make the processes configurable through BPEL that most providers of orchestration engines support, but also define business processes that can be realized through invocation of services across multiple applications. Additionally, the orchestration engines allow such business processes – including user interaction – to be "long running" in that they may run for days, weeks or months. For this reason, these business processes are also referred to as workflows. Business process orchestration (or management), therefore enables a configuration based approach to automation and streamlining of business processes for an organization and this brings agility to the enterprise. One of the options to implement long-running workflows is to use the BPEL based orchestration engine in BizTalk.

The infrastructure layer is usually implemented at an enterprise level and the service security and service governance patterns and technologies discussed for the service-oriented applications for Java EE are also applicable for Microsoft .NET platform. Authentication/authorization patterns may be implemented by specific products that implement identity management and access management (e.g., IBM Tivoli Identity Management and Tivoli Access Management). Identity management solutions already implemented in organizations for enterprise applications (e.g., Netigrity Site Minder or Microsoft Active Directory) may also be integrated and leveraged for this purpose.

Service registry and service repository solutions implement validation pattern and several products may be considered for implementing the same (e.g., IBM WebSphere Registry & Repostory, WSO2 Governance Registry, etc.). Specialized Governance Tools have also become available that provide comprehensive design-time and run-time Governance (e.g., Amberpoint Governance system, HP SOA Systinet).

As mentioned earlier, the reference models and technical architecture for Java EE and .NET platforms presented in this section are only indicative and based on the assumption that services are exposed by an application for orchestration of business processes or consumption by an infrastructure external to the application. In some large and complex service-oriented applications, services are defined for consumption within the context of the application. In such scenarios, the service layer defined for the enterprise applications can be lightweight and architected on the basis of the programming model for the enterprise application.

7.4 COMPOSITE APPLICATIONS

A logical next step to developing applications that expose and consume services is to develop an application that is built by combining multiple services. Such an application is called a composite application. A composite application can be developed by aggregation of other services or orchestration of a stateful sequence of service invocations. Composite application is both a form of integration as well an application type. Examples of composite applications include portal solutions that involve *mashup* of aggregated content received from a number of services and workflow solutions to enable business process management. WS-CAF is a web services standard for composite applications.

Each of the four types of services discussed in Chapter 4, namely, *activity, business process, client* and *data* services may be implemented as composite applications. Composite application development involves the following (Frye, 2005):

1. identification of services of right granularity that can be basis for building larger services;
2. configurable mechanisms for composition of services;

3. metadata repository for reusability;
4. assembly of services.

As composite applications are based on the principles of SOA, approaches to implement the same are referred to as SOA programming models.

7.5 SOA PROGRAMMING MODELS

Implementation of a composite application based on the principles of SOA includes the following (Matsumura, 2005):

1. ***Configuration***: This can be achieved through declarative programming techniques.
2. ***Composition:*** The techniques to combine services through aggregation and orchestration enable composition.
3. ***Customization:*** It is the ability to modify or enhance capability of a service without change to the service interface definitions.

The following programming models are available for developing composite applications (Lublinsky, 2006):

1. Service Component Architecture (SCA);
2. Windows Communication Foundation (WCF).

Service Component Architecture (SCA)

SCA is a set of specifications which describe a model for building applications based on assembly of service components (or services). SCA abstracts a service without tightly coupling with the details of the implementation. SCA also defines Service Data Object (SDO) to represent business data and to provide uniform access regardless of the underlying data storage/model. A key aspect of SCA is that it lives in the integration layer (Barcia and Brent, 2005) as shown in Figure 7-5.

The basic artefact in SCA is the *module*, which can be deployed in an SCA run-time environment. SCA run-time is a framework (e.g., Apache Tuscanny) that provides run-time support for components such as BPEL orchestration engine, service registry, etc. The scope of SCA run-time corresponds to the *SCA Domain*. A *module* within an *SCA Domain* specifies services which can be accessed remotely. *Module* holds one or more components that contain the business functionality provided by the module. SCA components may be implemented using different technologies such as EJBs, Java objects, BPEL and Spring Beans. SCA components can invoke applications outside SCA run-time (specified declaratively as *imports*) or alternatively be invoked by non-SCA clients (specified declaratively as *exports*). At development time, the SCA components can be composed by defining *references* and using *wires*. The run-time characteristics (e.g., asynchronous/synchronous invocation) of

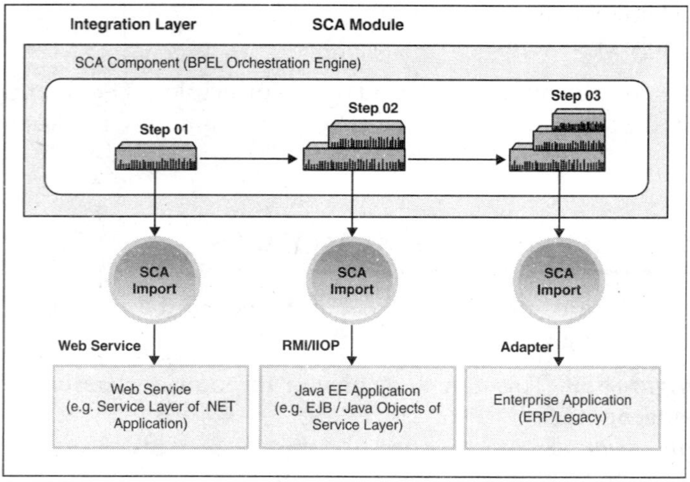

FIGURE 7-5 SCA programming model.

the components can also be specified. SCA run-time environment implements the run-time behavior on the basis of the characteristics specified.

Thus, the integration layer for service-oriented application may be implemented using the SCA programming model.

Windows Communication Foundation (WCF)

WCF is a unified programming model and run-time for developing service-oriented applications for the Microsoft platform. WCF is part of .NET framework and allows functionality of applications to be exposed as services over multiple transports – Web services, .NET Remoting, Messaging, WSE and Enterprise Services.

A service exposed by WCF provides a collection of *endpoints*. An *endpoint* is a mechanism for the client to communicate with the service. Each endpoint is identified by an *address* at which the service is accessed, the *binding* protocol to be used for communication and a *contract* that specifies the operations supported. A client calling a service provides the URI of the service as an address, specifies the binding protocol and the operation in the service contract as shown in the Figure 7-6.

WCF provides the following infrastructure needed for composite applications such as SCA:

1. Any class can be exposed as a service with WCF.
2. Attributes can be specified to define service interfaces. Web Services (WS-*) specifications are supported to provide secure, reliable and transactional communication using SOAP.

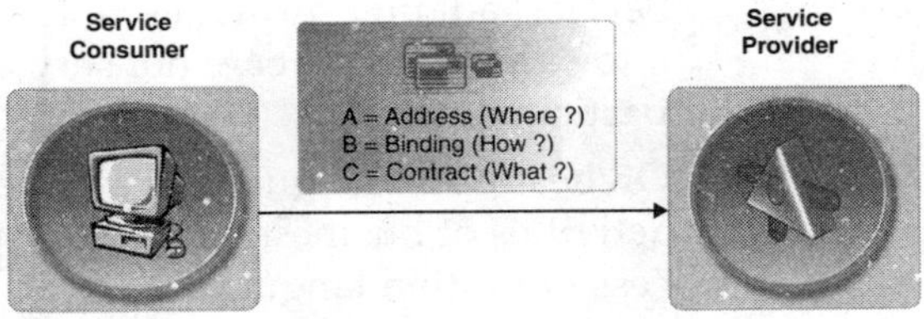

FIGURE 7-6 WCF endpoint.

3. Session-oriented communication (with state maintained throughout a series of calls), traditional RPC-type communication and one/two interactions are also supported by WCF.

However, unlike SCA, WCF does not provide an approach to assemble services whose binding can be specified at run-time. In WCF, it is necessary to specify binding and endpoints that will be used at development time.

The next chapter presents techniques for analysis and design of services.

7.6 SUMMARY

The objective of this chapter is to present the architectural aspects of service-oriented enterprise applications. The considerations of service-oriented enterprise applications under the three categories – service enablement, service integration and service orchestration – were discussed. The patterns for SOA for the three categories are identified and the reference models and indicative technical architectures of service-oriented enterprise applications for Java EE and .NET platforms are described. Composite applications built with services and the SOA programming models of SCA and WCF are also explained.

KEY TERMS

Service Layer A service layer is a set of software components that encapsulates application's business logic and controlling transactions and co-ordinates responses with interfacing layers.

Service Proxy A service proxy provides consumers with an interface to a service.

Service Gateway A service gateway abstracts access to the functionality of a system (or application) to a single interface.

Service Adapter	Service adapter provides a mechanism that allows systems that are not service-oriented to participate in SOA.
Orchestration Language	Orchestration language is a pattern to specify activities of business processes through a process definition language.
Orchestration Engine	Orchestration engine is a pattern to co-ordinate execution of activities of business processes (specified through an Orchestration Language).
Compensating Action	Compensating action is a pattern to cancel the effects of selected actions within an orchestration.
Composite Application	Composite application is an application that is built by combining multiple services through aggregation or orchestration.
Service Component Architecture (SCA)	SCA is a set of specifications which describe a model for building applications based on assembly of service components (or services).
Windows Communication Foundation (WCF)	WCF is a unified programming model and runtime for developing service-oriented applications for the Microsoft platform. WCF is part of .NET framework and allows functionality of applications to be exposed as services over multiple transports – Web services, .NET Remoting, Messaging, WSE and Enterprise Services.

REFERENCES

Arsanjani, A. (2005) *Toward a Pattern Language for Service-Oriented Architecture and Integration, Part 1: Build a Service Eco-system,* IBM, http://www.ibm.com/developerworks/webservices/library/ws-soa-soi/index.html?ca=drs-

Barcia, R., and Brent, J. (2005) *IBM WebSphere Developer Technical Journal: Building SOA solutions with the Service Component Architecture – Part 2, Assembling SCA Components,* IBM, http://www.ibm.com/developerworks/websphere/techjournal/0512 barcia/0512 barcia.html

Codeplex (2007) *ESB Guidance,* Microsoft Patterns & Practices, 2006 – 2007, http://www.codeplex.com/esb

Fowler, M. (2003) *Patterns for Enterprise Application Architecture,* Addison-Wesley, Boston, MA.

Frye, C. (2005) *The Role of Composite Applications in an SOA,* http://searchsoa.techtarget.com/qna/0,289202,sid26 gci1109080,00.html

Lublinsky, B. (2006) *SOA Programming Models,* InfoQ, http://www.infoq.com/articles/SOA-programming-models

Manolescu, D. and Lublinsky, B. (2005) *Service Orchestration Patterns: Graduating from State of the Practice to State of the Art,* Companion to the 20th annual ACM SIGPLAN conference on Object-oriented programming, systems, languages, and applications OOPSLA '05, San Diego, CA.

Matsumura, M. (2005) *The Three 'C's of SOA Programming,* Loosely Coupled, http://www.looselycoupled.com/opinion/2005/matsu-3cs-dev1004.html

Rossebø, J. and Bræk, R. (2006) A Policy-driven Approach to Dynamic Composition of Authentication and Authorization Patterns and Services, *Journal of Computers,* Vol. 1, No. 8, December 2006.

Soam, R. (2008) *Delivering on the Promise of SOA Through Effective SOA Governance,* http://stepauto.com/images/7%20-%20Ravindra%20Soam,%20Jigar%20Bhansali_Software%20AG.pdf

Trowbridge, D., Macini, D., Quick, D., Hohpe, G., Newkirk, J., et al. (2003) *Enterprise Solution Patterns Using Microsoft .NET,* Microsoft Publication, ISBN No.: 0-7356-1839-9.

Service-Oriented Analysis and Design

8

CHAPTER

CONTENTS

LEARNING OBJECTIVES

After reading this chapter, you would be able to:

- Get into the details of Service-Oriented Analysis and Design.
- Identify the need for design models.
- Know the principles of service design.
- Gain insights on the design of activity services, business process services, client services and data services.
- Review the design of service contract and data contract of a service.
- Conduct an in-depth study of the design of business process orchestration.

The architectural aspects discussed in earlier chapters described *what* was needed in terms of architectural constructs (e.g., layers and components) to meet the functional and non-functional requirements of an enterprise application. The next step in the software development lifecycle is design that specifies the elements that need to be programmed and *how* they come together to meet the requirements of the enterprise application. For service-oriented applications, a service-oriented analysis and design process (SOAD) has been described in Chapter 4. This chapter elaborates the analysis and design steps involved for the different business services – activity, business process, client and data services.

8.1 NEED FOR MODELS

The design of an enterprise application involves identifying and defining a number of elements. A pictorial representation of the design of an application not only makes it easy to communicate the design details but also allows depiction of relationships between the elements. A *model* is a pictorial representation of a specific kind of elements based on an established notation. When the model represents the design elements, it is referred to as the design model.

The Unified Modelling Language (UML) from Object management Group (OMG, 2006) is a widely accepted notation and is supported by number of tool vendors. The current, UML 2.0 specification, describes 13 types of diagrams under three categories:

1. ***Structure diagrams:*** class diagram, object diagram, component diagram, composite structure diagram, package diagram and deployment diagram.
2. ***Behavior diagrams:*** use case diagram, activity diagram and state machine diagram.

3. ***Interaction diagrams:*** sequence diagram, communication diagram, timing diagram and interaction overview diagram.

Of the different types of diagrams mentioned above, a few are widely used to represent the design of enterprise applications. These include:

1. class diagram;
2. activity diagram;
3. sequence diagram;
4. communication diagram.

Using the provision of UML to extend the definition of standard UML elements through the concept of profile, several attempt have been made to provide a notation to model services of which the following are noteworthy.

1. A UML 2 Profile for Software Services (Johnston, 2005).
2. SOAML Profile from OMG (SOAML, 2009).

The design model to describe the software services can be based on such profiles.

8.2 PRINCIPLES OF SERVICE DESIGN

The principles of service design are guidelines for effective design of services that emanate from the dimensions of SOA described in Chapter 3 and may be categorized accordingly.

Reuse

One of the key objectives of service-oriented model is reuse. The following principles enable higher degree of reuse:

1. ***Well-chosen granularity (Artus, 2006):*** Services are coarse-grained that expose functionality to be consumed by number of other services or applications. A rule of thumb in designing services for reusability is its potential reuse in three or more services or applications in an enterprise context.
2. ***Abstraction:*** Service interfaces abstract underlying implementation. All interactions are based on service contract, data contract and associated policies.
3. ***High cohesion:*** Service interfaces are defined to be cohesive. All operations on related functionality are grouped together.
4. ***Autonomy (Evdemon, 2005):*** Service autonomy is the degree of control of a service over its environment and the required resources. Service boundaries, which define the scope of a service, are explicit and services interact through explicit message-passing over well-defined boundaries.

Integration

Loose coupling: It involves defining elements such that there is minimum dependency on each other. This is made possible in service design by restricting all interactions between service providers and service consumers to be based strictly on service interfaces defined. No assumptions are made by service providers regarding service consumers (except that they conform to service interface definition for interactions) and vice versa.

Agility

1. ***Statelessness:*** Service implementations do not store conversational state for service invocations. This allows for business processes to be externalized and implemented as a set of orchestrable stateless services.
2. ***Composability (Erl, 2007):*** Definition of services facilitates combining of services to build new services through aggregation or orchestration. Adoption of this design principle enables a "building block" approach to design of applications.
3. ***Discoverability:*** Metadata that describes the capability and limitations of the service is defined for access by service consumers. Service registry is implemented for dynamic discovery of services by consumers.

8.3 DESIGN OF ACTIVITY SERVICES (OR BUSINESS SERVICES)

As indicated in Chapter 4, the initial steps in the service-oriented analysis and design process include gaining an understanding of the business goals and objectives of the enterprise and defining a business process model for the future state of business in line with business goals and objectives.

The activity services encapsulate access to functionality exposed as services by various business applications. Activity services are reusable business-level services that can be orchestrated as part of a configured business process.

The design of activity services based on the SOAD process described in Chapter 4 is shown in Figure 8-1. The scope of applications that expose or consume activity services may be to implement portions of the business processes defined in the business process model. This may involve enhancing of existing applications to support the services model (bottom-up) or developing service-oriented applications through forward engineering (top-down).

The analysis of requirements of an application results in documented set of use cases. The services exposed or consumed by the application are identified (based on their reusability and suitability for invocation as part of orchestrable workflow process) and specified in terms of *service contracts* and *data contracts*. The *service contract* defines the service exposed along with the operations that can be invoked. For receiving and sending the data from/to the service, a *data contract* is defined to specify the format in which the data is exchanged.

When activity services are designed through forward engineering, analysis classes are identified as a first step in services design. A decision on technology

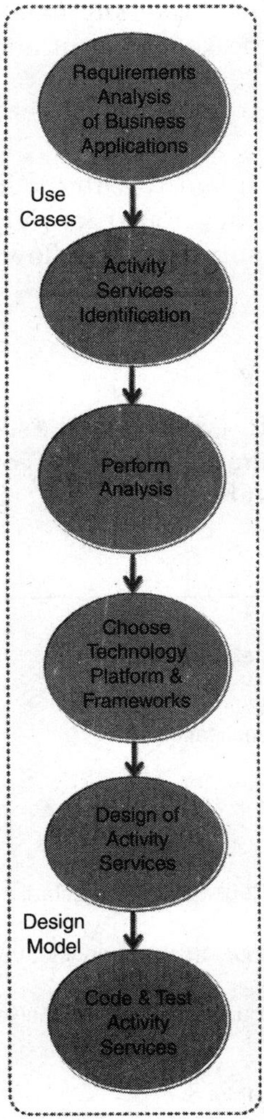

FIGURE 8-1 Design of activity services.

platform is made taking into consideration capabilities of the enterprise application platforms, technology strategies of the organization, available skill set and cost of development and maintenance. Available reusable frameworks (such as Spring/Struts for Java EE and Enterprise Library/Software factories for .NET) are also considered for improved productivity and quality.

The identified analysis classes are then mapped to design classes and represented through class diagrams, sequence diagrams and communication diagrams often by the use of a round trip engineering tool (such as IBM Rational Software Architect).

The design model so defined can help to communicate the design detail to developers and can also be kept current and consistent with round trip engineering tools.

Illustration

The above process may be explained with the help of an example. Consider a Loan Management System developed for .NET platform (developed with Microsoft WCF and C#) that supports the following use cases:

1. Register User;
2. Request Loan;
3. View Loan Status.

A service called *LoanService* is defined. The service contract for *LoanService* is *IMyLoan* defined with operation contracts corresponding to the methods of the *LoanService* as shown in Figure 8-2.

```
using System;
using System.ServiceModel;
using DataLayer;
using MessageDefinitions;
using System.Runtime.Serialization;
[ServiceContract()]
public interface IMyLoan
{
   [OperationContract]
   RegistrationResponse RegisterUser(RegistrationRequest Regreq);
   [OperationContract]
   LoanResponse LoanRequest(LoanRequest Lnreq);
   [OperationContract]
   LoanStatusResponse LoanStatus(LoanStatusRequest Lnstatusreq);
}
public class LoanService : IMyLoan
{
   public RegistrationResponse RegisterUser(RegistrationRequest Regreq)
   {
      //Implementation
   }
   public LoanResponse LoanRequest(LoanRequest Lnreq)
   {
      //Implementation
   }
   public LoanStatusResponse LoanStatus(LoanStatusRequest Lnstatusreq)
   {
      //Implementation
   }
}
```

FIGURE 8-2 Service contract specification.

The *ServiceContract* attribute defines the service interface and the *OperationContract* attribute specifies methods of the service. A service contract specification is converted by a development tool to a Web Services Definition Language (WSDL) definition. A WSDL definition file has the following two parts:

1. A technology-independent abstract description that describes the service interface (*portType*), its methods (*operations*) and their input–output parameters (*messages*).
2. A concrete description for *binding* the communication protocol with the *port* (endpoint) of the *service*.

The abstract description for the service contract for *LoanService* is shown in Figure 8-3(a) whereas the concrete description for the service contract for *LoanService* is shown in Figure 8-3(b).

The data contract for exchanging data with the *LoanRequest* operation of *LoanService* may be specified using Microsoft WCF as shown in Figure 8-4. The data contract is generated as separate XSD files which are referenced in WSDL file and used for input/output messages.

Using a development tool (e.g., Visual Studio), WSDL with service and data contracts may be created for .NET platform. While the technologies for developing services and syntax for specifying the contract may be different for other platforms such as Java EE, the WSDL file generated is technology-neutral and can be used by service consumers on any platform. There are several key aspects that are worth careful consideration. First, the service contract

```
- <wsdl:portType name="IMyLoan">
- <wsdl:operation name="RegisterUSer">
  <wsdl:input wsaw:Action="http://tempuri.org/IMyLoan/RegisterUSer"
message="tns:IMyLoan_RegisterUSer_InputMessage"/>
  <wsdl:outputwsaw:Action="http://tempuri.org/IMyLoan/RegisterUSerResponse"
message="tns:IMyLoan_RegisterUSer_OutputMessage"/>
  </wsdl:operation>
- <wsdl:operation name="LoanRequest">
  <wsdl:input wsaw:Action="http://tempuri.org/IMyLoan/LoanRequest"
message="tns:IMyLoan_LoanRequest_InputMessage"/>
  <wsdl:outputwsaw:Action="http://tempuri.org/IMyLoan/LoanRequestResponse"
message="tns:IMyLoan_LoanRequest_OutputMessage"/>
  </wsdl:operation>
- <wsdl:operation name="LoanStatus">
  <wsdl:input wsaw:Action="http://tempuri.org/IMyLoan/LoanStatus"
message="tns:IMyLoan_LoanStatus_InputMessage"/>
  <wsdl:outputwsaw:Action="http://tempuri.org/IMyLoan/LoanStatusResponse"
message="tns:IMyLoan_LoanStatus_OutputMessage"/>
  </wsdl:operation>
  </wsdl:portType>
```

(a)

FIGURE 8-3 *(continued)*

```
- <wsdl:binding name="WSHttpBinding_IMyLoan" type="tns:IMyLoan">
  <wsp:PolicyReference URI="#WSHttpBinding_IMyLoan_policy" />
  <soap12:binding transport="http://schemas.xmlsoap.org/soap/http" />
- <wsdl:operation name="RegisterUser">
  <soap12:operation soapAction="http://tempuri.org/IMyLoan/RegisterUser" style="document" />
- <wsdl:input>
  <wsp:PolicyReference URI="#WSHttpBinding_IMyLoan_RegisterUser_Input_policy" />
  <soap12:body use="literal" />
  </wsdl:input>
- <wsdl:output>
  <wsp:PolicyReference URI="#WSHttpBInding_IMyLoan_RegisterUser_output_policy" />
  <soap12:body use+"literal" />
  </wsdl:output>
  </wsdl:operation>

- <wsdl:operation name="LoanRequest">
  <soap12:operation soapAction="http://tempuri.org/IMyLoan/LoanRequest" style="document" />
- <wsdl:input>
  <wsp:PolicyReference URI="#WSHttpBinding_IMyLoan_LoanRequest_Input_Policy" />
  <soap12:body use="literal" />
  </wsdl:input>
- <wsdl:output>
  <wsp:PolicyReference URI="#WSHttpBinding_IMyLoan_LoanRequest_output_policy" />
  <soap12:body use="literal" />
  </wsdl:output>
  </wsdl:operation>

- <wsdl:operation name="LoanStatus">
  <soap12:operation soapAction="http://tempuri.org/IMyLoan/LoanStatus" style="document" />
- <wsdl:input>
  <wsp:PolicyReference URI="#WSHttpBinding_IMyLoan_LoanStatus_Input_policy" />
  <soap12:body/use="literal" />
  </wsdl:input>
- <wsdl:output>
  <wsp:PolicyReference URI="#WSHttpBinding_IMyLoan_LoanStatus_output_policy" />
  <soap12:body use="literal" />
  </wsdl:output>
  </wsdl:operation>
</wsdl:binding>
- <wsdl:service name="LoanService">
- <wsdl:port name="WSHttpBinding_IMyLoan" binding="tns:WSHttpBinding_IMyLoan">
  <soap12:address location="http://hts-tagsrv01.corp.tempuri.ad/WCFService/Service.svc" />
- <wsa10:EndpointReference>
  <wsa10:Address>http://hts-tagsrv01.corp.tempuri.ad/WCFService/Service.svc</wsa10:Address>
- <Identity xmlns="http://schemas.xmlsoap.org/ws/2006/02/addressingidentity">
  <Spn>host/hts-tagsrv01.corp.tempuri.ad</Spn>
  </Identity>
  </wsa10:EndpointReference>
  </wsdl:port>
</wsdl:service>
```

(b)

FIGURE 8-3 WSDL (a) abstract part; (b) concrete part.

which specifies the interface is different from the implementation. This means that the implementation of a service can change over time but so long as the contract remains the same, the calling applications will not be affected and

```
using System;
using Sustem. Runtime. Serialization;

namespace Message Definitions
{
  [Data Contract]
  public class LoanRequest
  {
    [DataMember]
    public string LoanType;

    [DataMember] public int Duration;

    [DataMember]
    public long LoanAmount;

    [DataMember]
    public string ModeofPayment;
  }

}
```

FIGURE 8-4 Data contract specification.

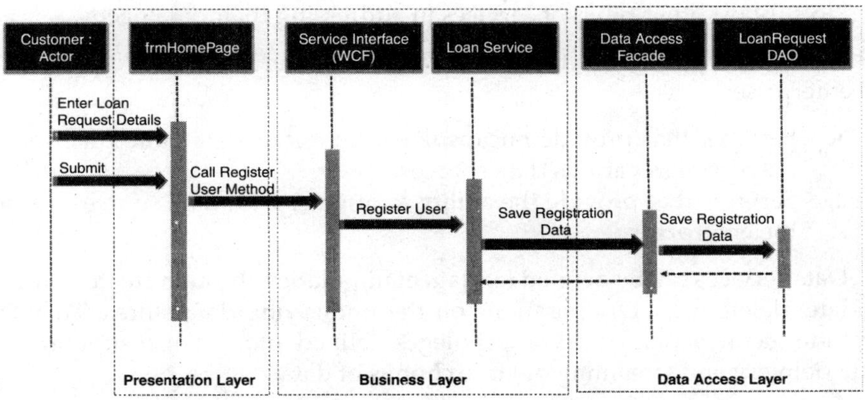

FIGURE 8-5 Sequence diagram.

hence do not need to make changes. Second, the service may be delivered over multiple transport protocols by binding to the appropriate protocol (such as Web Services, .NET Remoting, etc. in .NET). Finally, the address of the service may be published for consumer applications to invoke the service.

The design of *Loan Service* involves identification of candidate analysis classes and mapping them to design classes taking into account capabilities of WCF and .NET platform. The sequence diagram for the *RegisterUser* use case implemented for .NET platform is shown in Figure 8-5. It is assumed that a user registers with the system through the implementation of the *RegisterUser* use case before requesting a loan. Requests from the user are handled by objects in presentation, business and data access layers. A request for registration from the user is submitted through the page with the required presentation elements to the service interface through the invocation of WSDL of the associated web service. The implementation of the *RegisterUser* operation of the *LoanService* results in registration data being logged to the database.

8.4 DESIGN OF DATA SERVICES

One of the critical success factors for SOA is effective data integration. The data services decouple the data consumers from the underlying data stores providing a consistent view of data across the enterprise. The data services are typically technology-oriented and more fine-grained than the activity services and promote consistency, flexibility and reuse thus forming the building blocks for data integration.

The first step in design and development of data services is to analyze the business process model of the enterprise and using knowledge of the domain, develop an enterprise data model as depicted in Figure 8-6. Such a strategic view of data enables determination of common data requirements across different business processes. Data services can accordingly be identified to support other types of services in addressing their data needs.

There are typically two types of data services that need to be supported in an enterprise:

1. Services that provide encapsulated access to data stored across the enterprise in various data sources.
2. Services that provide the ability to interact with data sources outside the enterprise.

Data services can be defined for data manipulation through create, retrieve, update, delete (CRUD) operations on the underlying data stores. They can provide secure access based on privileges defined and can also support bulk data delivery and streaming of large chunks of data.

Not all types of data are suitable to be exposed and consumed as services. A good example of data service is one that provides access to master data related to customers of the organization. Exposing transaction data as a service may result in additional overhead on account of the services model and can affect performance.

A number of tools to extract, transform and load (ETL) data and to manage metadata are available from technology providers (e.g., Metamatrix). Data services may be designed on the basis of the capabilities of these tools to provide access to distributed data and to manage format and semantic differences between data sources. The identified data services are specified in terms of *service contracts* and *data contracts* as in the case of activity services.

A set of well-designed data services provides a single view of key data items such as customer across the enterprise and eliminates a number of issues

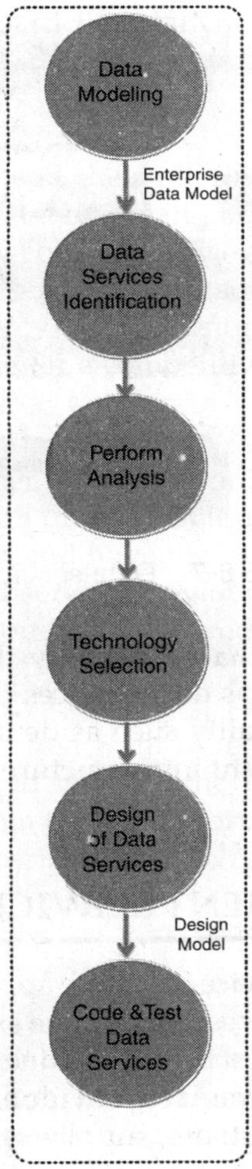

FIGURE 8-6 Design of data services.

related to duplication and synchronization of data across the applications that may otherwise be needed in an enterprise. Figure 8-7 shows the logical model for data services layer.

The data services layer connects data in different types of sources (both internal and external to the enterprise) available in number of formats. The physical data models in sources are mapped and transformed as a part of a data service management infrastructure to integrated data objects in a canonical form in order to abstract data in the data sources. It provides federated view of data and mediation among data sources to separate consumers from implementation of data. This is typically done by creating metadata

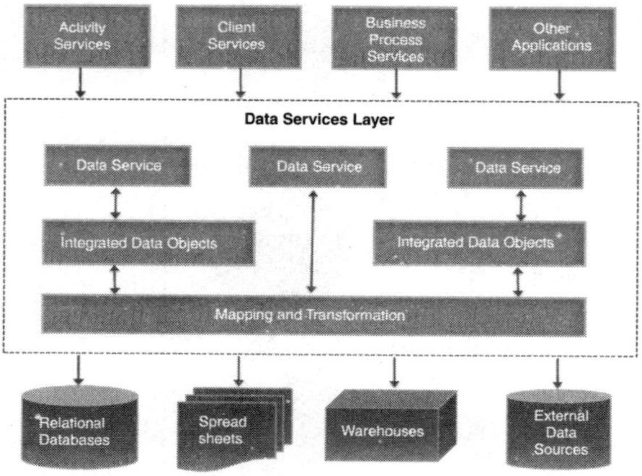

FIGURE 8-7 Data services layer.

for models of data sources that is used by the data service management infrastructure to expose data as data services (Friedman and Muzilla, 2006). Data quality-related functionality such as de-duping is also often provided by the data service management infrastructure in delivering data services in an enterprise context.

8.5 DESIGN OF CLIENT SERVICES

In an enterprise context, service-oriented applications expose or consume activity services and data services. Further, the externalized business processes defined as workflows are orchestrated by business process services. In addition to these services, there is also a need to provide enterprise-level content related to the business users (or its partners/suppliers).

Client services deliver content to the business users that require an aggregated enterprise view. They provide presentation content to the "front-end" applications of the enterprise such as portal, dashboard or CRM applications that provide the necessary presentation capabilities and typically are service consumers for the other services in the enterprise.

As in the case of data services, not all content related to business is suitable to be exposed and consumed as client services. Presentation capabilities for capture and display of large volumes of transaction data are best done by applications architected and designed to meet the quality objectives of performance and scalability. Client services provide significant value when user interaction can trigger workflows to fulfil the user requests. The content required to enable user interaction and to provide continuous status of user requests is provided by client services.

Several sophisticated collaboration tools are available for delivering content aggregated by client services to the users. These include tools that support web-based user interaction such as portals, content management systems and mobile device support.

The emergence of Web 2.0 technologies especially Ajax and REST has resulted in new tools (such as JackBe Presto) that provide the infrastructure for aggregation of content through enterprise mashup using information from service-enabled applications across the enterprise.

The design of client services involves the following steps shown in Figure 8-8:

1. The first step is identification of requirements of users who need enterprise-level aggregated content.
2. Analysis of requirements results in determination of use cases that need to be supported by client services.

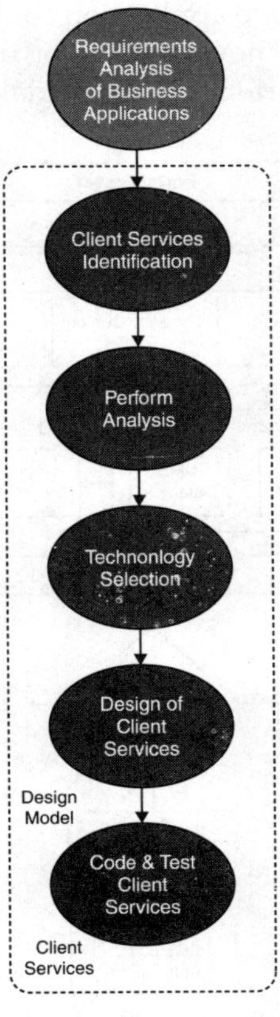

FIGURE 8-8 Design of client services.

3. The next step is identification of client services implementing which will result in enterprise-level information being made available to collaboration tools such as portals and mobile infrastructure for delivery to users.
4. This is followed by the step involving analysis of client services to determine the sources of information that are aggregated by client services.
5. The technology infrastructure selection is made next to include identification of protocols for integration and tools that bind sources of information to allow aggregation of information through techniques such as mashup.
6. The identified client services are specified in terms of service contracts and data contracts as in the case of activity services.

Figure 8-9 shows client services aggregating data from a number of sources of information to provide an enterprise-level view of an organization's performance.

The client services aggregate application content (e.g., accounts receivable data), dynamic content (e.g., news, events or updates about the enterprise) and static content (e.g., quarterly investor data) from number of sources.

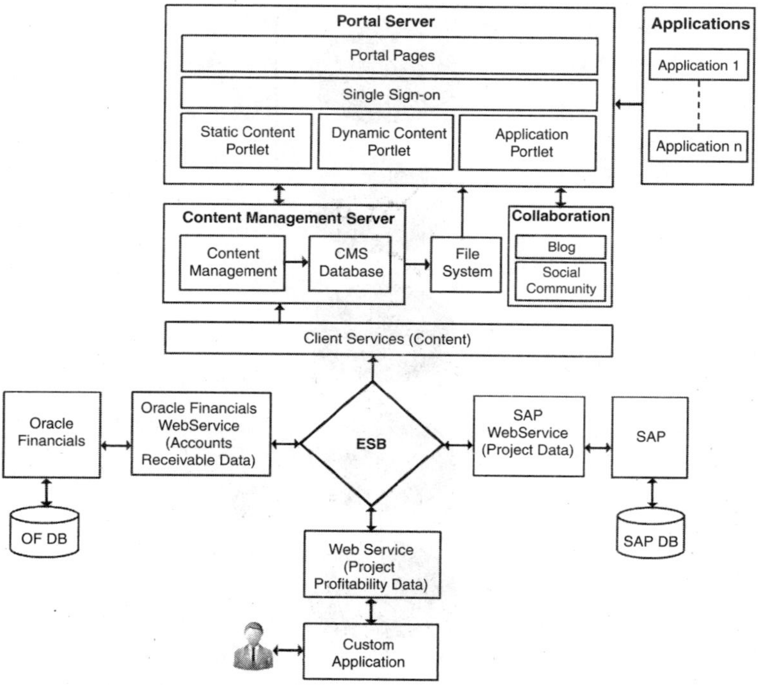

FIGURE 8-9 Client services layer.

The client services are consumed by a web content management system (e.g., Interwoven, Drupal) for content creation in an enterprise context.

A web content management system provides capabilities to author, approve, publish content. The content so published may be disseminated by an enterprise portal (such as IBM WebSphere Portal, Alfresco, etc.) with portlets for static content, dynamic content and applications while providing security features such as single sign-on. Figure 8-9 also shows a metadata driven portal framework for easy maintainability and scalability of the solution. The content created and published to the Portal server is either rendered directly as web (HTML) content or as a link to a file in the filesystem.

8.6 DESIGN OF BUSINESS PROCESS SERVICES

As indicated in Chapter 4, business process services allow for externalization of business processes in an orchestrable fashion resulting in agility for an enterprise.

In order to externalize business processes, these services should provide the capability to define the steps that constitute the business process as a flow of service interactions. This allows for definition of interaction protocol for each service corresponding to a step of the business process in addition to ordering the steps as per the flow of the business process. The language for specifying the choreographed service interactions is the Web Services Business Process Execution Language (WS-BPEL) known in short as BPEL.

BPEL is a XML-based language that combines the benefits of hierarchical languages such as XLANG and graph-oriented languages such as WSFL. A Business process service based on BPEL can be invoked as a web service and also invokes web services exposed by other providers (called *partners)* as part of orchestration.

BPEL is designed to work in an agile environment where business processes may need to change frequently. This is achieved through decoupling of the business process definition from the services that implement the business process. In order to incorporate changes in business processes, the steps of the business process flow may be changed in a configurable manner and bound to new or modified services to implement the changes.

The run-time environment for BPEL is a process orchestration engine. Most process orchestration engines come with visual tools for specifying the business processes. These tools generate BPEL that is executed by the process orchestration engine. Visual tools (such as those from ActiveBPEL) provided by the process orchestration engine are often used to design the business process pictorially.

Illustration – Loan Approval Business Process

Figure 8-10 shows a loan approval process. In this scenario, a bank customer initiates the loan approval process by requesting a loan. This results in a notification being sent to a loan officer who makes a decision to approve or reject the loan.

If the loan officer rejects the loan request, a notification is sent to the bank customer about the same. Alternatively, if the loan officer approves the loan

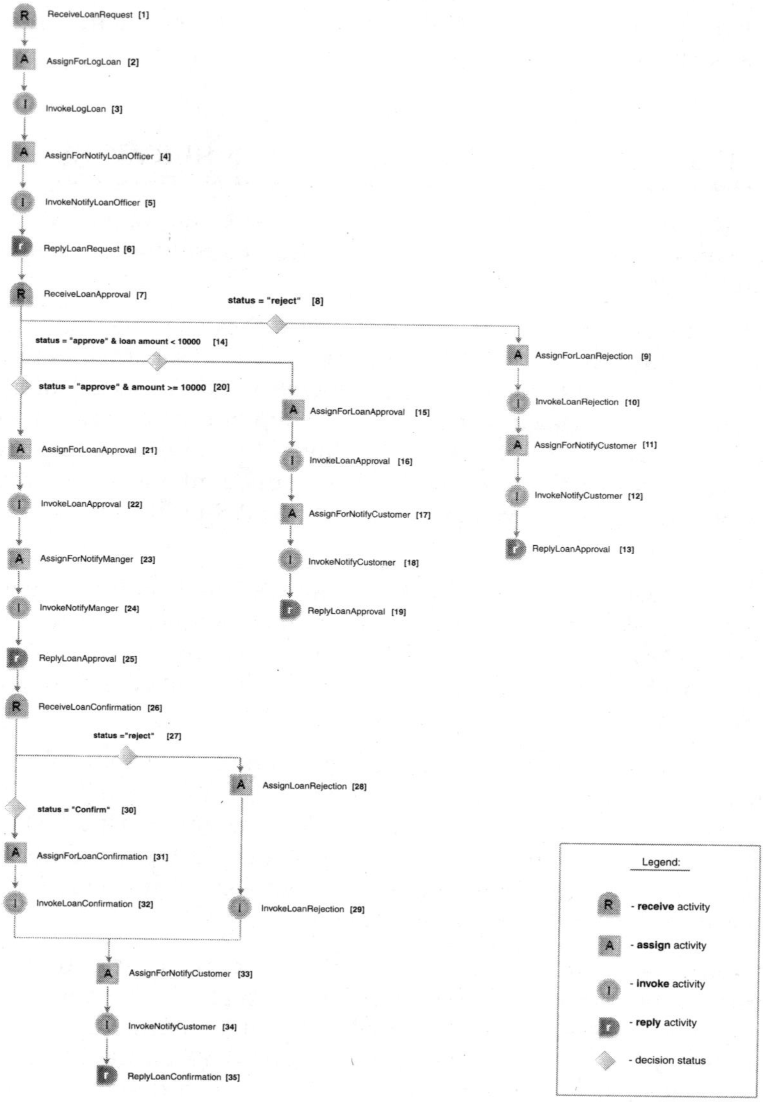

FIGURE 8-10 Loan approval process.

then the system checks if the loan amount is more than 10,000 (in any currency, for instance dollars) or not.

In case the loan amount is less than 10,000 (say in dollars) then a notification is sent to the bank customer about the approval of the loan. If the loan amount is more than 10,000 (say in dollars) then a confirmation is required from a manager and he/she is notified. Manager makes the final decision on loan approval and notifications are sent accordingly.

While the design of business process services is usually done through visual tools provided by the process orchestration engine, it is important to understand the structure of BPEL and the associated concepts to gain insights into how process orchestration works.

The BPEL code for loan approval process depicted pictorially in Figure 8-10 is shown in Annexure B. A BPEL business process is implemented using constructs called *activities* (Graham et al., 2004). There are two types of activities, namely, *basic* and *structured*. *Basic activities* are key building blocks of a business process (Table 8-1). Structured activities are graph-oriented and algebraic complex constructs (Table 8-2).

TABLE 8-1 Basic activities

Activity	*Description*
receive	A BPEL process begins with a receive activity which receives an input message.
invoke	Invoke activity is used to invoke a web service operation from a BPEL process.
assign	In a BPEL process, assign activity can be used for data manipulation of variables.
reply	Reply activity in BPEL process is similar to a return statement in a method call. All receive activities in the loan approval example contain a matching reply.
terminate	It terminates the entire process.
throw	Exception handling in BPEL process is addressed through throw activity.
wait	Waits either for a period of time or until a specified point in time.
empty	Equivalent to a "no-op" instruction in a BPEL process.
compensate	Provides compensation for a successfully completed set of activities.

TABLE 8-2 Structured activities

Activity	*Description*
while	Used to implement loops in BPEL processes.
switch	Allows selection of one branch at a decision.
step.pick	Enables selection of a specific branch when the corresponding message arrives or when timeout occurs.
sequence	Describes a set of activities that are executed sequentially.
flow	Collection of activities that can be executed in parallel (links used to define execution order).
scope	Used to define nested activities, correlation sets, fault handlers, compensation handlers and event handlers.

The following is the detailed explanation of each step of loan approval process shown in Figure 8-10 and the corresponding BPEL code (Annexure B).

Explanation of Loan Approval Process

The loan approval is defined as a long-running transaction. The process is triggered with the user request for a loan and ends when the approval cycle is completed. The order of execution of activities for different steps of the loan approval BPEL process is depicted in Table 8-3.

TABLE 8-3 Long-running loan approval process

Customer requests for a loan	ReceiveLoanRequest [1], AssignForLogLoan [2], InvokeLogLoan [3], AssignForNotifyLoanOfficer [4], InvokeNotifyLoanOfficer [5], ReplyLoanRequest [6]	Branch 1: Long-running process is triggered and the process logs the loan request, sends a notification to the loan officer and the process waits for the loan officer intervention on approval or rejection.
Loan Officer Rejects	ReceiveLoanApproval [7], Transition Condition Status="reject" [8], AssignForLoanRejection [9], InvokeLoanRejection [10], AssignForNotifyCustomer	Branch 2: The process instance is continued from Branch 1 and records the loan rejection, notifies the customer about rejection and the process ends here.

(continued)

TABLE 8-3 (*Continued*)

	[11], InvokeNotifyCustomer [12], ReplyLoanApproval [13]: END OF THE PROCESS	
Loan Officer Approves (Amount < 10000)	ReceiveLoanApproval [7], Transition Condition Status="approve" [14], AssignForLoan Approval [15], InvokeLoanApproval [16], AssignForNotifyCustomer [17], InvokeNotifyCustomer [18], ReplyLoanApproval [19]: END OF THE PROCESS	Branch 3: The process instance is continued from Branch 1. Loan is approved, customer is notified and the process ends here.
Loan Officer Approves (Amount >= 10000)	ReceiveLoanApproval [7], Transition Condition Status="approve" [14], AssignForLoan Approval [21], InvokeLoanApproval [22], AssignForNotifyManager [23], InvokeNotifyManager [24], ReplyLoanApproval [25], ReceiveLoan Confirmation [26]	Branch 4: The process instance is continued from Branch 1. The loan is approved, the manager is notified and the process, awaits the manager's intervention on either confirmation or rejection.
Manager Rejects	ReceiveLoanConfirmation [26], Transition Condition Status="reject" [27], AssignForLoanRejection [28], InvokeLoanRejection [29], AssignForNotifyCustomer [33], InvokeNotifyCustomer [34], ReplyLoanConfirmation [35]: END OF THE PROCESS	Branch 5: The process instance is continued from Branch 4. The loan rejection is recorded, the customer is notified about rejection and the process ends here.
Manager Approves	ReceiveLoan Confirmation [26], Transition Condition Status="confirm" [30], AssignForLoanConfirmation [31], Invoke-LoanConfirmation [32], AssignForNotifyCustomer [33], InvokeNotifyCustomer [34], ReplyLoanConfirmation [35]: END OF THE PROCESS	Branch 6: The process instance is continued from Branch 4. The loan is approved, the customer is notified and the process ends here.

ReceiveLoanRequest [1]: A BPEL process begins with a receive activity which receives an input message. In the loan approval process example, the process commences with **ReceiveLoanRequest** activity which receives input from a bank customer.

BPEL code:

```
<bpel:receive createInstance="yes" name="ReceiveLoanRequest" operation="log" pa
rtnerLink="LoanProcessLPT" portType="ns1:LoanProcess" variable="logRequest">
</bpel:receive>
```

All receive activities in loan approval example contain a matching **reply**. *createInstance* property in above tells the process engine that this receive activity will create the process instance.

AssignForLogLoan [2]:

In a BPEL process, **assign** activity can be used to assign data from one variable to another variable. This activity is used to assign the data from the input message of the **ReceiveLoanRequest** activity to the input message of the invoke activity for logging loan data by **InvokeLogLoan** which is explained later in this section.

BPEL code:

```
<bpel:assign name="AssignForLogLoan ">
<bpel:copy>
  <bpel:from part="loanNo" variable="logRequest"/>
  <bpel:to part="loanNo" variable="logLoanRequest"/>
</bpel:copy>
<bpel:copy>
<bpel:from part="loanAmount" variable="logRequest"/>
<bpel:to part="loanAmount" variable= "logLoanRequest"/>
</bpel:copy>
...
</bpel:assign>
```

InvokeLogLoan [3]:

Invoke activity is used to invoke a web service operation from a BPEL process. This activity is used to invoke *logLoan* operation on *LoanService* web service which will log the loan request into the database.

BPEL code:

```
<bpel:invoke inputVariable="logLoanRequest" name="InvokeLogLoan"
operation="logLoan" outputVariable="logLoanResponse" partnerLink="
LoanServiceLPT" portType="ns2:LoanService">
</bpel:invoke>
```

AssignForNotifyLoanOfficer [4]:

This is the **assign** activity which copies the required data to the input message of the **InvokeNotifyLoanOfficer.**

BPEL code:

```
<bpel:assign name="AssignForNotifyLoanOfficer">
<bpel:copy>
  <bpel:from part="loanNo" variable="logRequest"/>
  <bpel:to part="loanNo" variable="notifyRequest"/>
</bpel:copy>
<bpel:copy>
  <bpel:from part="fixedRate" variable="logRequest"/>
  <bpel:to part="fixedRate" variable="notifyRequest"/>
</bpel:copy>
...
</bpel:assign>
```

InvokeNotifyLoanOfficer [5]:

This **invoke** activities invokes **notify** operation on *LoanService* which sends a notification to the loan officer.

BPEL code:

```
<bpel:invoke inputVariable="notifyRequest" name="InvokeNotifyLoanOfficer"
operation="notify" outputVariable="notifyResponse" partnerLink="LoanServic
eLPT" portType="ns2:LoanService">
</bpel:invoke>
```

ReplyLoanRequest [6]:

Reply activity in BPEL process is similar to a return statement in a method call. **ReplyLoanRequest** activity is the matching **reply** activity for **ReceiveLoanRequest** activity.

BPEL code:

```
<bpel:reply name="ReplyLoanRequest" operation="log" partnerLink="Loan
ProcessLPT" portType="ns1:LoanProcess" variable="logResponse">
</bpel:reply>
```

ReceiveLoanApproval [7]:

This is executed when the loan officer approves or rejects the loan.

BPEL code:

```
<bpel:receive name="ReceiveLoanApproval" operation="approveOrReject"
partnerLink="LoanProcessLPT"
portType="ns1:LoanProcess" variable="approveOrRejectRequest">
</bpel:receive>
```

Transition Condition Status="reject" [8]:

A transition condition is used when the flow has to be based on conditions. There can be multiple numbers of paths following an activity with different transition conditions. When the loan officer rejects the loan, the transition condition status is "reject" and this leads to a flow as shown in Figure 8-10.

BPEL code:

```
<bpel:transitionCondition>$approveOrRejectRequest.status = "reject"</bpel:
transitionCondition>
```

AssignForLoanRejection [9]:

This is the **assign** activity which copies the required data to the input message of the **InvokeLoanRejection.**

BPEL code:

```
<bpel:assign name="AssignForLoanRejection">
<bpel:copy>
  <bpel:from part="loanNo" variable="approveOrRejectRequest"/>
  <bpel:to part="loanNo" variable="rejectLoanRequest"/>
</bpel:copy>
<bpel:copy>
  <bpel:from part="fixedRate" variable="approveOrRejectRequest"/>
  <bpel:to part="fixedRate" variable="rejectLoanRequest"/>
</bpel:copy>
...
</bpel:assign>
```

InvokeLoanRejection [10]:

This activity invokes *rejectLoan* operation on *LoanService.*

BPEL code:

```
<bpel:invoke inputVariable="rejectLoanRequest" name="InvokeLoanRejection"
operation="rejectLoan" outputVariable="rejectLoanResponse" partnerLink=
"LoanServiceLPT" portType="ns2:LoanService"> </bpel:invoke>
```

AssignForNotifyCustomer [11]:

This is the **assign** activity which copies the required data to input message of the **InvokeNotifyCustomer.**

BPEL code:

```
<bpel:assign name="AssignForNotifyCustomer">
<bpel:copy>
<bpel:from part="loanNo" variable="approveOrRejectRequest"/>
<bpel:to part="loanNo" variable="notifyRequest"/>
</bpel:copy>
<bpel:copy>
<bpel:from part="fixedRate" variable="approveOrRejectRequest"/>
<bpel:to part="fixedRate" variable="notifyRequest"/>
</bpel:copy>
...
</bpel:assign>
```

InvokeNotifyCustomer [12]:

This activity invokes **notify** operation on *LoanService.*

BPEL code:

```
<bpel:invoke inputVariable="notifyRequest" name="InvokeNotifyCustomer"
operation="notify" outputVariable="notifyResponse" partnerLink="LoanService
LPT" portType="ns2:LoanService">
</bpel:invoke>
```

ReplyLoanApproval [13]:

This **reply** activity is the matching Reply activity for **ReceiveLoanApproval** activity.

BPEL code:

```
<bpel:reply name="ReplyLoanApproval" operation="approveOrReject" partner
Link="LoanProcessLPT" portType="ns1:LoanProcess" variable="approveOr
RejectResponse">
</bpel:reply>
```

Transition Condition Status="approve" and loan amount < 10000 [14]:

When the loan officer approves the loan and the loan amount is less than 10000, it leads to the loan approval flow as shown in Figure 8-10.

BPEL code:

```
<bpel:transitionCondition>$approveOrRejectRequest.status = "approve" and
$approveOrRejectRequest.loanAmount ; 10000</bpel:transitionCondition>
```

AssignForLoanApproval [15]:

This is the **assign** activity which copies the required data to the input message of the **InvokeLoanApproval.**

BPEL code:

```
<bpel:assign name="AssignForLoanApproval">
<bpel:copy>
  <bpel:from part="loanNo" variable="approveOrRejectRequest"/>
  <bpel:to part="loanNo" variable="approveLoanRequest"/>
</bpel:copy>
<bpel:copy>
  <bpel:from part="fixedRate" variable="approveOrRejectRequest"/>
  <bpel:to part="fixedRate" variable="approveLoanRequest"/>
</bpel:copy>
...
</bpel:assign>
```

InvokeLoanApproval [16]:

This activity invokes *approveLoan* operation on *LoanService*.

BPEL code:

```
<bpel:invoke inputVariable="approveLoanRequest" name="InvokeLoanApproval"
operation="approveLoan" outputVariable="approveLoanResponse" partnerLink="
LoanServiceLPT" portType="ns2:LoanService">
</bpel:invoke>
```

AssignForNotifyCustomer [17]:

This is the **assign** activity which copies the required data to the input message of the **InvokeNotifyCustomer.**

BPEL code:

```
<bpel:assign name="AssignForNotifyCustomer">
<bpel:copy>
  <bpel:from part="loanNo" variable="approveOrRejectRequest"/>
  <bpel:to part="loanNo" variable="notifyRequest"/>
</bpel:copy>
<bpel:copy>
  <bpel:from part="fixedRate" variable="approveOrRejectRequest"/>
  <bpel:to part="fixedRate" variable="notifyRequest"/>
</bpel:copy>
......
</bpel:assign>
```

InvokeNotifyCustomer [18]:

This activity invokes **notify** operation on *LoanService*.

BPEL code:

```
<bpel:invoke inputVariable="notifyRequest" name="InvokeNotifyCustomer"
operation="notify" outputVariable="notifyResponse" partnerLink="LoanService
LPT" portType="ns2:LoanService">
</bpel:invoke>
```

ReplyLoanApproval [19]:

This **reply** activity is the matching activity for **ReceiveLoanApproval** activity. There can be multiple matching reply activities for a receive activity because of different paths as a result of different transition conditions.

BPEL code:

```
<bpel:reply name="ReplyLoanApproval" operation="approveOrReject" partner
Link="LoanProcessLPT" portType="ns1:LoanProcess" variable="approveOrReje
ct Response">
</bpel:reply>
```

Transition Condition Status = "approve" and loan amount >= "10000" [20]:

When the loan amount is more than 10000 and when the loan officer approves the loan, it leads to the loan manager confirmation flow as shown in Figure 8-10.

BPEL code:

```
<bpel:transitionCondition>$approveOrRejectRequest.status = "approve" and
$approveOrRejectRequest.loanAmount &gt;= 10000</bpel:transitionCondition>
```

AssignForLoanApproval [21]:

This is the **assign** activity which copies the required data to the input message of the **InvokeLoanApproval.**

BPEL code:

```
<bpel:assign name="AssignForLoanApproval">
<bpel:copy>
   <bpel:from part="loanNo" variable="approveOrRejectRequest"/>
   <bpel:to part="loanNo" variable="approveLoanRequest"/>
</bpel:copy>
<bpel:copy>
   <bpel:from part="fixedRate" variable="approveOrRejectRequest"/>
   <bpel:to part="fixedRate" variable="approveLoanRequest"/>
</bpel:copy>
. . . . .
</bpel:assign>
```

InvokeLoanApproval [22]:

This activity invokes ***approveLoan*** operation on ***LoanService***.

BPEL code:

```
<bpel:invoke inputVariable="approveLoanRequest" name="InvokeLoanApproval"
operation="approveLoan" outputVariable="approveLoanResponse" partnerLink=
"LoanServiceLPT" portType="ns2:LoanService">
</bpel:invoke>
```

AssignForNotifyManager [23]:

This **assign** activity copies the required data to the input message of the **InvokeNotifyManager.**

BPEL code:

```
<bpel:assign name="AssignForNotifyManager">
<bpel:copy>
   <bpel:from part="loanNo" variable="approveOrRejectRequest"/>
   <bpel:to part="loanNo" variable="notifyRequest"/>
</bpel:copy>
```

```
<bpel:copy>
  <bpel:from part="fixedRate" variable="approveOrRejectRequest"/>
  <bpel:to part="fixedRate" variable="notifyRequest"/>
</bpel:copy>
....
</bpel:assign>
```

InvokeNotifyManager [24]:

This activity invokes **notify** operation on *LoanService*. This notifies the manager that there is a request waiting for approval.

BPEL code:

```
<bpel:invoke inputVariable="notifyRequest" name="InvokeNotifyManager"
operation="notify" outputVariable="notifyResponse" partnerLink="LoanService
LPT" portType="ns2:LoanService">
</bpel:invoke>
```

ReplyLoanApproval [25]:

This activity is the matching reply activity for **ReceiveLoanApproval** activity.

BPEL code:

```
<bpel:reply name="ReplyLoanApproval" operation="approveOrReject" partner
Link="LoanProcessLPT" portType="ns1:LoanProcess" variable="approveOr
RejectResponse">
</bpel:reply>
```

ReceiveLoanConfirmation [26]:

This is executed when the manager confirms or rejects the loan.

BPEL code:

```
<bpel:receive name="ReceiveLoanConfirmation" operation="confirmOrReject"
partnerLink="LoanProcessLPT" portType="ns1:LoanProcess" variable="confirm
OrRejectRequest">
</bpel:receive>
```

Transition Condition Status="reject" [27]:

When the loan manager rejects the loan, it leads to loan rejection flow as shown in Figure 8-10.

BPEL code:

```
<bpel:transitionCondition>$confirmOrRejectRequest.status = "reject"</bpel:
transitionCondition>
```

AssignForLoanRejection [28]:

This is the **assign** activity which copies the required data to the input message of the **InvokeLoanRejection.**

BPEL code:

```
<bpel:assign name="AssignForLoanRejection">
<bpel:copy>
  <bpel:from part="loanNo" variable="confirmOrRejectRequest"/>
  <bpel:to part="loanNo" variable="rejectLoanRequest"/>
</bpel:copy>
<bpel:copy>
  <bpel:from part="fixedRate" variable="confirmOrRejectRequest"/>
  <bpel:to part="fixedRate" variable="rejectLoanRequest"/>
</bpel:copy>
. . . .
</bpel:assign>
```

InvokeLoanRejection [29]:

This activity invokes *rejectLoan* operation on *LoanService.*

BPEL code:

```
<bpel:invoke inputVariable="rejectLoanRequest" name="InvokeLoanRejection"
  operation="rejectLoan" outputVariable="rejectLoanResponse" partnerLink=
"LoanServiceLPT" portType="ns2:LoanService">
</bpel:invoke>
```

Transition Condition Status="confirm" [30]:

This transition condition is used when the manager approves the loan and this leads to a flow as shown in Figure 8-10.

BPEL code:

```
<bpel:transitionCondition>$confirmOrRejectRequest.status = "confirm"</bpel:
transitionCondition>
```

AssignForLoanConfirmation [31]:

This is the **assign** activity which copies the required data to the input message of the **InvokeLoanConfirmation.**

BPEL code:

```
<bpel:assign name="AssignForLoanConfirmation">
<bpel:copy>
   <bpel:from part="loanNo" variable="confirmOrRejectRequest"/>
   <bpel:to part="loanNo" variable="confirmLoanRequest"/>
</bpel:copy>
<bpel:copy>
   <bpel:from part="fixedRate" variable="confirmOrRejectRequest"/>
   <bpel:to part="fixedRate" variable="confirmLoanRequest"/>
</bpel:copy>
.....
</bpel:assign>
```

InvokeLoanConfirmation [32]:

This activity invokes ***confirmLoan*** operation on ***LoanService.***

BPEL code:

```
<bpel:invoke inputVariable="confirmLoanRequest" name="InvokeLoanConfir
mation" operation="confirmLoan" outputVariable="confirmLoanResponse" par
tnerLink="LoanServiceLPT" portType="ns2:LoanService">
</bpel:invoke>
```

AssignForNotifyCustomer [33]:

This is the **assign** activity which copies the required data to the input message of the **InvokeNotifyCustomer.**

BPEL code:

```
<bpel:assign name="AssignForNotifyCustomer">
<bpel:copy>
   <bpel:from part="loanNo" variable="confirmOrRejectRequest"/>
   <bpel:to part="loanNo" variable="notifyRequest"/>
</bpel:copy>
<bpel:copy>
   <bpel:from part="fixedRate" variable="confirmOrRejectRequest"/>
   <bpel:to part="fixedRate" variable="notifyRequest"/>
</bpel:copy>
......
</bpel:assign>
```

InvokeNotifyCustomer [34]:

This activity invokes **notify** operation on *LoanService.*

BPEL code:

```
<bpel:invoke inputVariable="notifyRequest" name="InvokeNotifyCustomer"
operation="notify" outputVariable="notifyResponse" partnerLink="LoanService
LPT" portType="ns2:LoanService">
</bpel:invoke>
```

ReplyLoanConfirmation [35]:

This activity is the matching reply activity for **ReceiveLoanConfirmation** activity.

BPEL code:

```
<bpel:reply name="ReplyLoanConfirmation" operation="confirmOrReject" partner
Link="LoanProcessLPT" portType="ns1:LoanProcess" variable="confirmOrRejec
tResponse">
</bpel:reply>
```

Correlation of Receive Activities:

In the loan approval example, bank customer initiates the process instance and the loan officer and manager interact with the same process instance for approvals or rejections. Correlation Id is used in BPEL process to correlate all the *receive* activities so that they operate on the same process instance.

BPEL code:

Step 1: Define correlation set

```
<bpel:correlationSets>
<bpel:correlationSet name="CS1" properties="ns1:loanNo"/>
</bpel:correlationSets>
```

Step 2: Attach correlation set to the **receive** activity which initiates the process

In the loan approval example, the **ReceiveLoanRequest** activity initiates the process. Note that the initiate property should be set to "yes".

```
<bpel:receive createInstance="yes" name="ReceiveLoanRequest" operation="log"
 partnerLink="LoanProcessLPT"
portType="ns1:LoanProcess" variable="logRequest">
```

```
<bpel:correlations>
  <bpel:correlation initiate="yes" set="CS1"/>
</bpel:correlations>
</bpel:receive>
```

Step 3: Attach the correlation set to the other **receive** activities which interact with the process

Note that for all other receive activities initiate property should be set to "join".

BPEL code:

```
<bpel:receivename="ReceiveLoanApproval"operation="approveOrReject"partner
Link="LoanProcessLPT"
portType="ns1:LoanProcess" variable="approveOrRejectRequest">
<bpel:correlations>
  <bpel:correlation initiate="join" set="CS1"/>
</bpel:correlations>
</bpel:receive>
```

Linking Activities:

The sample BPEL code used to link various activities to make the flow is as follows.

```
<bpel:targets>
  <bpel:target linkName="L20"/>
  <bpel:target linkName="L21"/>
</bpel:targets>
<bpel:sources>
  <bpel:source linkName="L28"/>
</bpel:sources>
```

The target link denotes the target activity in which this link name is configured as the source link.

Reference to Services

To be able to invoke any service from a BPEL process, an **import** statement for the WSDL of the service is needed so that the service can be referenced.

BPEL code (for import of proxy service WSDL):

```
<bpel:import importType="http://schemas.xmlsoap.org/wsdl/" location=
"WSDL/LoanProxy.wsdl" namespace="http://localhost:8080/axis/services/
LoanService"/>
```

8.7 SUMMARY

The objective of this chapter is to provide an insight into the service design. The principles of service design were identified and designs of the four types of services – activity services, business process services, client services and data services – are explained. Using a loan management system as an example, code for service contract, data contract and WSDL are provided. Extending the same example, the definition of externalized loan approval process is described; the BPEL code is explained in detail for providing insight into business process orchestration.

The next chapter discusses the implementation aspects of service-oriented applications.

KEY TERMS

Granularity Granularity is a measure of the size of the services that make up a service-oriented system.

Abstraction The principle of hiding the functionality of a service by the use of service contract is abstraction.

Cohesion Cohesion is the measure of grouping of elements with similar responsibilities. Service interfaces are defined to be highly cohesive. All operations on related functionality are grouped together.

Autonomy Service autonomy is the degree of control of a service over its environment and the required resources.

Loose Coupling Loose coupling is a principle of defining software elements such that there is minimum dependency on each other.

Statelessness The principle of not holding state information in a component or a service is called statelessness.

Composability Composability is the measure of combining services to build new services through aggregation or orchestration.

REFERENCES

Artus, D. (2006) *SOA Realization: Service Design Principles*, IBM, http://www.ibm.com/developerworks/webservices/library/ws-soa-design/

Erl, T. (2007) *SOA Principles of Service Design*, 1st edn, Prentice Hall PTR, New Jersey.

Evdemon, J. (2005) *Principles of Service Design: Service Patterns and Anti-Patterns*, Microsoft, http://msdn2.microsoft.com/en-us/library/ms954638.aspx

Friedman, T. and Muzilla, C. (2006) *Where Data Meets SOA: Data Services*, ebiz Webinar, http://www.ebizq.net/webinars/6953.html

Graham, S., Davis, D., Simeonov, S., Daniels, G., Brittenham, P., et al. (2004) *Building Web Services with Java: Making Sense of XML, SOAP, WSDL, and UDDI*, 2nd edn, Sams Publishing, Indianapolis.

Johnston, S. (2005) *UML 2.0 Profile for Software Services*, IBM, http://www.ibm.com/developerworks/rational/library/05/419 soa/

OMG (2006) *The OMG and Service Oriented Architecture*, http://www.omg.org/attachments/pdf/OMG-and-the-SOA.pdf

SOAML (2009) Service Oriented Architecture Modeling Language (SoaML), Specification for the UML Profile and Metamodel for Services (UPMS), OMG Document No: ptc/2009-04-01.

Technologies for SOA

9 CHAPTER

CONTENTS

LEARNING OBJECTIVES

After reading this chapter, you would be able to:

- Learn about the technologies for service enablement: RESTful Web Services, SOAP Web Services; JAX WS for Java EE Platform; XML Web Services for .NET Platform.
- Service enablement of relational databases.
- Study the technologies for service integration: Service integration with ESB.
- Examine the technologies for service orchestration.

Implementation of enterprise-wide SOA involves identification of technologies for service enablement, integration and orchestration and development of SOA layers identified in Chapter 4 with the chosen technologies.

Two types of technologies can be considered for enterprise-wide SOA:

1. ***Generic technologies:*** The following types of technologies are referred to here as generic technologies:
   - platform-supported technologies;
   - standards-based technologies.
2. ***Vendor-specific technologies:*** Tools from vendors that support generic technologies but offer additional capabilities for improved productivity and quality are referred to here as vendor-specific technologies. (The vendor-specific technologies mentioned in this chapter are meant to be indicative and not a comprehensive source of all the available tools.)

This chapter presents generic and vendor-specific technologies for service enablement, integration and orchestration.

9.1 TECHNOLOGIES FOR SERVICE ENABLEMENT

Service enablement, as discussed in Chapter 4, involves exposing coarse-grained functionalities as services that are invoked by service consumers. Hence, the technologies for service enablement include those that allow service providers to expose services and service consumers to invoke the exposed services.

The generic technologies for service enablement include:

1. RESTful Web services.
2. SOAP Web services.

RESTful Web Services

REST stands for REpresentative State Transfer. A term coined by Roy Fielding, REST is an architectural style that may be used for service enablement (Fielding, 2000).

The ubiquitous nature of Internet based on Hypertext Transfer Protocol (HTTP) has made it feasible to exchange data efficiently over it. Also, policies of organizations allow HTTP protocol to be permitted over firewalls for access to the Internet. HTTP, thus, presents a transport mechanism for service invocations. The conversational nature of HTTP can be extended to enable interactions between service consumers and service providers.

In RESTful web services (or RESTful web API), service consumers (clients) initiate requests to service providers (servers) which process requests and return appropriate responses. Service consumers can either be transitioning between application states or be "at rest". A service consumer sends requests using four methods provided by HTTP (namely GET, POST, PUT and DELETE) when it is ready to transition to a new state. The format of data supported by a RESTful web service is MIME (e.g., JSON, XML). When one or more requests are outstanding, the service consumer is considered to be transitioning states. The service "transfers" the state of the service consumer through the response it provides. The representation of each state of service consumer contains a resource (typically a document identified by a Uniform Resource identifier) that may be used when the service consumer subsequently chooses to initiate a state transition (Wikipedia, 2010).

RESTful web services offer lower overhead in interactions between service providers and service consumers when compared with SOAP web services discussed in the next sub-section.

Several vendor-specific tools are available for service enablement of which the key technologies are listed in Table 9-1.

SOAP Web Services

A key technology that is platform- and vendor-neutral and widely supported to expose identified functionality as a *service* is SOAP *web services*. W3C defines web service as "a software system designed to support interoperable machine-to-machine interaction over a network." It has an interface described in a machine-processable format (specifically WSDL). Other systems interact with the Web service in a manner prescribed by its description using SOAP messages, typically conveyed using HTTP with an XML serialization in conjunction with other Web-related standards" (W3C, 2004).

In accordance with the W3C definition, the term "web service" is used in this book to mean SOAP web service. (The term "RESTful web service" is explicitly used when REST based approach is used to implement a web service.)

TABLE 9-1 Tools for web service development

Tools/Products → *Vendors* ↓	*Web Service Development Tools*	*Vendor Website Reference*
Apache	Axis CXF Embarcadero JBuilder	http://ws.apache.org/axis http://cxf.apache.org/ http://www.embarcadero.com/products/jbuilder
IBM	RAD for WAS WSAD	http://www-306.ibm.com/software/awdtools/developer/ http://www.ibm.com/developerworks/library/i-wsad/application/index.html
Microsoft	Visual Studio.NET Web Service Software Factory	http://msdn2.microsoft.com/en-us/vstudio/default.aspx http://msdn.microsoft.com/en-us/library/aa480534.aspx
Metro	JAX-WS, JAXB	https://metro.dev.java.net
Oracle	JDeveloper	http://www.oracle.com/technology/products/jdev
Proxisoft	Netrifex	http://proxisoft.com

In simple terms, web services involve communication of XML over a transport protocol such as HTTP or SMTP.

Web services have two objectives:

1. To enable interoperability between heterogeneous systems. This is achieved through exchange of data based on a technology-neutral XML which is a canonical format.
2. To provide a standard approach to define service interfaces independent of technology. The Web Services Definition Language (WSDL) based on XML provides such a standard format.

The main components of web services as indicated in Chapter 3 are:

1. *Service provider:* Exposing of functionality as web service by service-provider application.
2. *Service registry:* Publishing of service description for service consumers to discover and consume.
3. *Service consumer:* Invoking of the web service by service consumer.

Web services is one of the implementation technologies for SOA. The open standards supported by Web services are (McGovern et al., 2003):

1. XML for data interchange;
2. HTTP, FTP and SMTP for transport;
3. SOAP for messaging;
4. WSDL for interface description language;
5. UDDI for registry.

XML (eXtensible Markup Language)

XML is text-based extensible markup language without fixed tags (unlike HTML where specific tags are used to specify presentation aspects). An XML document is always structured with tags defining the items that it holds and so XML parsers can be used to retrieve the data from it. Since an XML document is structured, a schema can be specified for it with the XML Schema Definition (XSD) language. XSD is used to specify rules that XML documents for a given purpose need to comply with, and thus, can be used to validate XML documents to conform to the rules. In the case of a web service, data is exchanged as XML with XSD specifying the data contract for the data exchanged between the service provider and consumer. In order to remove ambiguity of tags used, XML namespaces are used in XML data.

SOAP (Simple Object Access Protocol)

During a web service call, an XML message with application data is wrapped in a SOAP envelope, that is, a header and trailer is added to the application data that describes the message structures passed. The SOAP envelope has a mandatory body section that describes the functions to be called and the parameters that are passed to the service and an optional header for additional processing information related to QoS and processing restrictions (Woods and Mattern, 2006). The service thus called strips the application data off the SOAP envelope.

Figure 9-1 depicts pictorially the use of different technologies during a web service call. The data in service consumer application, say Java EE, is serialized as per the data contract of the service provider to XML on the service consumer side. The SOAP envelope and HTTP headers are then added and the data is transferred over HTTP. The service provider receives the HTTP data, removes the HTTP header and SOAP envelope, extracts the XML data and deserializes the data on the basis of the technology of service-provider application (e.g., Java EE).

Security is an important concern for web services as XML is essentially a text. There are two levels of security that may be applied to securing XML data exchanged:

1. wire-level security;
2. message-level security.

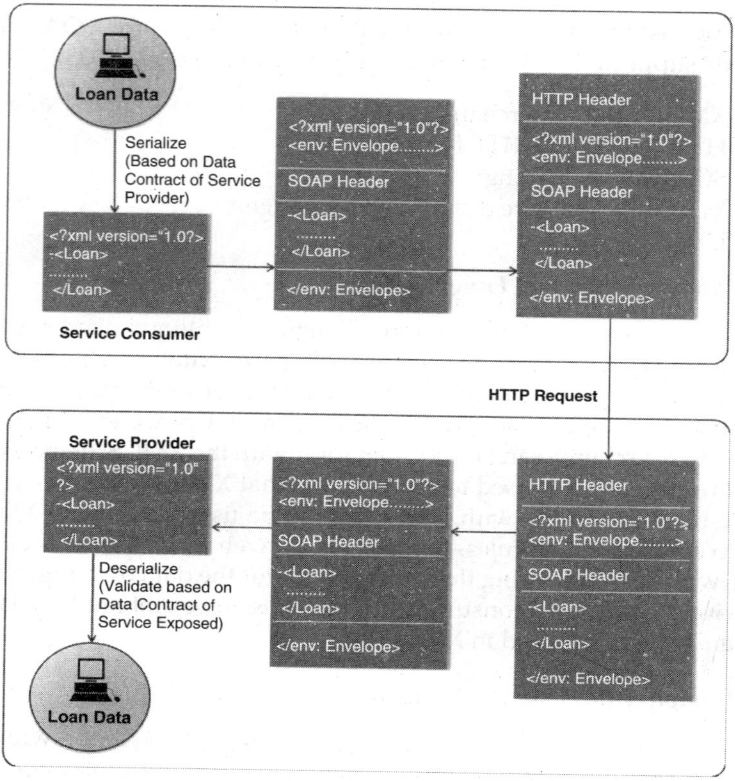

FIGURE 9-1 Technologies in a web service call.

While the former may be achieved by enabling HTTPS at web server level, the latter requires a closer look.

Message-level security involves security of data in SOAP messages. *WS-Security* provides a standard approach to encryption and use of digital signature headers in SOAP messages. WS-Security is one of the several standards for web services security. Three of the other important standards are:

1. WS-Reliable Messaging for reliability of web services;
2. WS-AT for transaction support;
3. WS-Policy and WS-PolicyAttachment for policies of a web service (e.g., security, QoS, etc.).

Web Services Definition Language (WSDL)

Any description of a web service can involve two aspects – functional and nonfunctional. Functional description provides details of *how* the service is invoked while the non-functional description describes *why* a client invokes the service and *who* the service provider is.

The non-functional description for the most part is providing additional details to describe the service on aspects such as security policy (Graham et al., 2004). On the other hand, the functional description of a web service includes *how* the service is invoked by specifying the point of contact for a service called as the *service endpoint* or just *endpoint*. A web service is invoked on the basis of the *interface* supported by the service at the *address* provided by the endpoint and using the communication protocol specified as *binding*. WSDL is the description language for specifying these details for web services.

Accordingly, the WSDL has XML elements to describe the following:

1. Non-functional description
   - policy.
2. Functional description
   - abstract interface;
   - concrete implementation.

The layout of a WSDL file is shown pictorially in Figure 9-2. Most of the XML elements for non-functional description are tags related to the WS Policy. The functional description has two types of XML elements:

1. The *abstract interface*-related XML elements that include description of custom data *types, messages* and *portTypes*.
2. The *concrete implementation-related* XML elements that include XML tags for *bindings* to specify the communication protocol to be used and *address* specified using Uniform Resource Identifier (URI) of the endpoint.

Table 9-1 lists key vendor-specific tools available for service enablement.

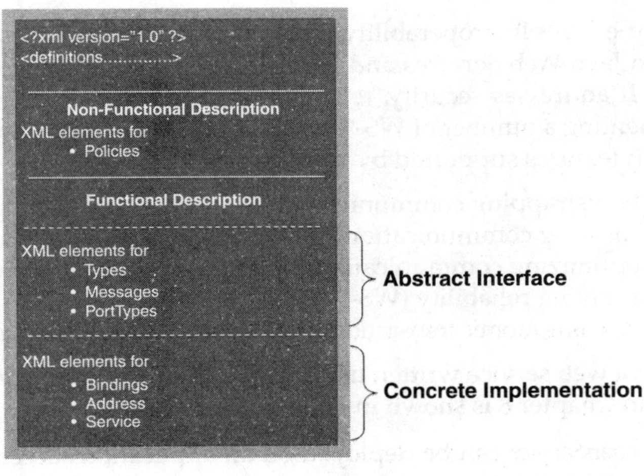

FIGURE 9-2 Layout of WSDL.

Platform and Relational Database Support for Web Services

The enterprise application platforms and relational databases provide significant support to web services. This section provides details of web service enablement capabilities at platform and database level.

JAX-WS for Java EE Platform

Web service development on Java EE platform is supported using a set of technologies collectively referred to as *Metro*. The Metro stack consists of *JAX-WS, JAXB* and *WSIT* technologies.

JAX-WS stands for Java API for XML web services and was formerly known as JAX RPC. JAX-WS is built to make web service development easier than the earlier JAX RPC by providing a library of annotations; a toolkit of Ant tasks and command-line utilities that hide the complexity of the underlying XML message protocol (Smart, 2006). As in the Microsoft WCF for the .NET platform, the developer uses annotations to define methods either in an interface or directly in an implementation class. The service consumer application creates a proxy object and then invokes methods on this proxy. Neither the service-provider application nor the service-consumer application is required to generate or parse SOAP messages. The JAX-WS API takes care of this automatically.

JAXB is an acronym for Java API for XML binding. It enables generation of Java classes from XML schemas with the help of a JAXB binding compiler or vice versa. XML schema may be provided as input to the JAXB binding compiler to generate Java classes and interfaces that are based on the rules defined in the input XML schema. Alternatively, XML documents may be created from Java classes with JAXB (Vohra, 2004). Java applications need to read, process and output XML data when dealing with web services and JAXB reduces the effort and complexity in doing so.

Web Services Interoperability Technology (WSIT) provides interoperability between Java Web Services and Microsoft's Wndows Communication Foundation. It addresses security, reliable messaging and atomic transactions by implementing a number of WS-*specifications. From a functional perspective, the main features supported by WSIT are (SDN WSIT, 2007):

1. bootstrapping communication (WS-MetaDataExchange);
2. securing communication (WS-SecurityPolicy, WS-Security, WS-Trust);
3. optimizing communication (MTOM, WS-SecureConversation);
4. enabling reliability (WS-ReliableMessaging);
5. enabling atomic transactions (WS-Coordination, WS-AtomicTransactions).

A Java web service written using JAX-WS for the *LoanService* example discussed in Chapter 8 is shown in Figure 9-3.

The *LoanService* can be deployed on an application server and the WSDL can be extracted by querying the service (http://<url>?wsdl) as shown in Figures 9-4(a) and 9-4(b).

```
package com;

import javax.jws.WebMethod;
import javax.jws.WebService;

@WebService(serviceName="LoanServiceWSDL", name="LoanSetvice")
public class LoanService {

    @WebMethod()
    public boolean regislerUser(User user) {
      return true;
    }
    @WebMethod()
    public boolean loanRequest(Loan loan) {
      return true;
    }

    @WebMethod()
    public String loanStatus(Loan Instatusreq) {
      return null;
    }
}
```

FIGURE 9-3 Java web service (*LoanService*) based on Java-WS.

The initial portion of the abstract part of WSDL shows the namespace declarations followed by the data contract whose schema is described by the xsd file *LoanServiceWSDL_schema1.xsd* (not shown). This is followed by tags for messages and service contract. The concrete portion of the WSDL shows the bindings. It may be noted that the support for web services in both Java EE and .NET platform (to be discussed next) is substantial for most of the "plumbing" code for a web service is generated automatically.

XML Web Services for .NET Platform

Web services are core to the philosophy of Microsoft .NET platform. Hence, there is significant support for web services on .NET platform. There are mainly three ways by which web services may be exposed by .NET applications:

1. ***Microsoft WCF:*** An example of exposing functionality as a web service using Microsoft WCF was provided in Chapter 8.
2. ***Basic .NET*** platform capabilities. A .NET web service written using .NET platform capabilities for the *LoanService* web service is shown in Figure 9-5. A development tool (e.g., Microsoft Visual Studio) creates a service on compilation that can be deployed in the web server (e.g., IIS). The service can be queried for extracting the WSDL which would be similar to that shown in Figure 8-3.
3. ***Web Service Software Factory:*** The Microsoft Patterns & Practices group has developed prescriptive guidance with a collection of tools, patterns and source code to build web services using proven

```
<?xml version="1.0" encoding="UTF-8"?><definitions
xmlns="http://schemas.xmlsoap.org/wsdl/" xmlns:tns="http://com/"
xmlns:xsd="http://www. w3.org/2001/XMLSchema"
xmlns:soap="http://schemas. xmlsoap.org/wsdl/soap/"
targetNamespace="http://com/" name="LoanServiceWSDL">
<types>
  <xsd:schema>
    <xsd:import namespace="http://com/" schemaLocation="http://hmf-lpt-
376627. corp. tempcomp.ad:8080/LoanApp/LoanServiceWSDL/ _____ container$publishing
$subctx/WEB-INF/wsdl/LoanServiceWSDL_schema1.xsd"
xmlns:wsdl="http://schemas.xmlsoap.org/wsdir
xmlns:soap12="http://schemas.xmlsoap.org/wsdl/soap12/"/>
   </xsd:schema>
 </types>
 <message name="loanRequest">
   <part name="parameters" element="tns:loanRequest"/>
 </message>
 <message name="loanRequestResponse">
   <part name="parameters" element="tns:loanRequestResponse"/>
 </message>
 <message name="loanStatus">
   <part name="parameters" element="tns:loanStatus"/>
 </message>
 <message name="loanStatusResponse">
   <part name="parameters" element="tns:loanStatusResponse"/>
 </message>
 <message name="registerUser">
   <part name="parameters" element="tns:registerUser"/>
 </message>
 <message name="registerl)serResponse">
   <part name="parameters" element="tns:registerUserResponse"/>
 </message>
 <portType name="LoanService">
  <operation name="loanRequest">
   <input message="tns:loanRequest"/>
    <output message="tns:loanRequestResponse"/>
    </operation>
 <operation name="loanStatus">
  <input message="tns:loanStatus"/>
   <output message="tns:loanStatusResponse"/>
  </operation>
 <operation name="registerUser">
   <input message="tns:registerUser"/>
   <output message="tns:registerUserResponse"/>
  </operation>
 </portType>
```

(a)

FIGURE 9-4 *(continued)*

```
<binding name="LoanServicePortBinding" type="tns:LoanService">
<soap:bindingtransport="http://schemas.xmlsoap.org/soap/http" style="document">
<operation name="loanRequest">
<soap:operation soapAction=""/>
<input>
      <soap:body use="literal"/>
        </input>
          <output>
          <soap:body use="literal"/>
        </output>
    </operation>
   <operation name="loanStatus">
   <soap:operation soapAction="/>
   <input>
       <soap:body use="literal"/>
       </input>
         <output>
          <soap:body use="literal"/>
       </output>
    </operation>
   <operation name="registerUser">
     <soap:operation soapAction="/>
     <input>
   <soap:body use="literal"/>
     </input>
      <output>
        <soap:body use="literal"/>
       </output>
     </operation>
   </binding>
      <service name="LoanServiceWSDL">
        <port name="LoanServicePort" binding="tns:LoanServicePortBinding">
          <soap:addresslocation="http://hmf-lpt-
376627.corp.tempcomp.ad:8080/LoanApp/LoanServiceWSDL"
xmlns:wsdl="http://schemas.xmlsoap.org/wsdl/"
xmlns:soap12="http://schemas.xmlsoap.org/wsdl/soap12/">
     </port>
  </service>
```

(b)

FIGURE 9-4 WSDL (a) abstract part; (b) concrete part.

architecture and design patterns. It also addresses several challenges related to building ASP.NET (ASMX) and WCF web services such as exception handling and security (Microsoft, 2006).

Service Enablement of Relational Databases

The extensive adoption of web services has incentivized key database technology providers to develop features that allow web services to be exposed at database level.

```
using System;
using System.Web;
using System.Web.Services;
using System.Web.Services.Protocols;
using DataLayer;
using MessageDefinitions;

[WebService(Namespace = "http://tempuri.org/")]
public class LoanService : System.Web.Services.WebService
{
   public LoanService ()
   {
   }

   [WebMethod]
   public RegistrationResponse RegisterUser(RegistrationRequest Regreq)
   {
       //...
   }
   [WebMethod]
   public LoanResponse LoanRequest(LoanRequest Lnreq)
   {
       //...
   }
   [WebMethod]
   public LoanStatusResponse LoanStatus(LoanStatusRequest Lnstatusreq)
   {
       //...
   }
}
```

FIGURE 9-5 .NET web service.

Service Broker Feature of Microsoft SQL Server: T-SQL stored procedures may be created at database level and exposed as web services by the use of the *service broker* feature of Microsoft SQL Server. The steps involved in exposing stored procedures as web service are as follows (Joshi, 2008):

1. Create a *stored procedure* to expose the functionality as a service.
2. Create an *HTTP endpoint* for the stored procedure. An HTTP endpoint is an interface using which the service consumers can access the web service.
3. Create a *proxy* for the web service (by "Adding Reference" using a tool such as Visual Studio).
4. Invoke the method of the web service.

Web Service Feature for Oracle Database Server: PL/SQL, Java stored procedures, pre-defined SQL queries, DML, and Oracle Advanced Queuing processes in Oracle database may be exposed as web services. The following are the steps to expose web services using the capabilities of Oracle database

(Mensah, 2005). JDeveloper automates these steps with a wizard using the inputs from user:

1. Create a *stored procedure/SQL query/DML/AQ process* to be exposed as a Web Service.
2. Generate a *Java proxy* for the stored procedure or database operations.
3. *Publish* the Java proxy class as standard J2EE Web service in Oracle Application Server runtime (OC4J).
4. On invocation of a method of the web service, the Java proxy invokes the corresponding operation in the database using JDBC. The functionality exposed as a service is then executed in the database and the result set is sent back to the service consumer.

Stored Procedure Web Service Feature for IBM DB2 UDB: Java Stored procedures and SQL queries for IBM database may be exposed as web services. The following are the steps to expose Java stored procedures or SQL queries as web services that IBM RAD (or WSAD tool) automates with a wizard using the inputs from user (Xu, 2006):

1. Create a *Java stored procedure* or *SQL query* to be exposed as a Web Service.
2. Generate a Document Access Definition Extension (*DADX*) group and *DADX file* for the Java Stored Procedure or query.
3. Create a *web service* for the generated DADX file.
4. When the web service is invoked the corresponding Java Stored Procedure or SQL query is executed.

9.2 TECHNOLOGIES FOR SERVICE INTEGRATION

While service consumers can directly invoke services based on the WSDL provided by the service providers; this approach results in several issues in an enterprise context:

1. It becomes necessary for a service consumer to use the same protocol (e.g., web services) as that of a service provider. In many cases, the service consumers and service providers may be designed independently to work on different protocols (such as JMS or .NET Remoting).
2. The message format used by the service consumer for service invocation may be different from the format required by the service provider.
3. A large number of service providers and consumers may result in increased complexity due to several point-to-point connections caused on account of direct invocations between service providers and consumers.

To address the above issues, it becomes necessary for the existence of a *mediator* to not only integrate the service providers and service consumers such that the point-to-point connections are avoided but also to perform transformation, routing and event handling. The architecture pattern that addresses this requirement is the *Enterprise Service Bus (ESB).*

Different vendors have provided their own implementations for ESB. Products that support the concept of ESB are available from:

1. application server providers;
2. middleware vendors;
3. ERP providers;
4. open source.

Table 9-2 lists some of the key vendor-specific tools/products available today for ESB.

Many of the ESB products listed in Table 9-2 come with features and capabilities over and above what is required in an ESB. Visual tools are provided that allow configuration of service providers and service consumers with ESB.

TABLE 9-2 ESB tools/products

Tools/Products → *Vendors* ↓	*Enterprise Service Bus Products*	*Vendor Website Reference*
IBM	WebSphere ESB	http://www-01.ibm.com/common/ssi/rep_ca/0/897/ENUS207-230/ENUS207230.PDF
	Message Broker	http://www-306.ibm.com/software/integration/wbimessagebroker/index.html?S_TACT=105AD02W&S_CMP=campaign
Microsoft	BizTalk (+ ESB Guidance from Microsoft Patterns & Practices)	http://www.microsoft.com/biztalk/solutions/soa/esb.ms
Oracle	Oracle Service Bus	http://www.oracle.com/technologies/soa/service-bus.html
BEA	Aqualogic Service Bus	http://www.bea.com/framework.jsp?CNT=index.htm&FP=/content/products/aqualogic/service_bus/
Apache	Service Mix	http://servicemix.apache.org/home.html

(continued)

TABLE 9-2 *(Continued)*

Tools/Products → Vendors ↓	*Enterprise Service Bus Products*	*Vendor Website Reference*
Cape Clear Software	Cape Clear ESB	http://www.capeclear.com/solutions/it.shtml
Fiorano	Fiorano Business Integration Suite	http://www.fiorano.com
Fuse Source	FUSE ESB (based on ServiceMix)	http://fusesource.com/products/enterprise-servicemix/
Mulesoft	Mule ESB	http://www.mulesoft.org/display/MULE/Home
RedHat	JBoss Enterprise SOA Platform, which includes JBoss ESB	http://www.jboss.org/jbossesb/
Software AG	webMethods	http://www.softwareag.com/Corporate/Images/SAG_wM_ESB_Platform_FS_web_tcm16-34350.pdf
Sonic Software	Progress Sonic ESB	http://www.sonicsoftware.com/products/sonic_esb/index.ssp
Tibco	Active Matrix Service Bus	http://www.tibco.com/software/soa/activematrix_service_bus/default.jsp
Vitria	Business Accelerator ESB	http://www.vitria.com/Business_Accelerator/esb.php
WSO2	WSO2ESB	http://wso2.com

Service Integration with ESB

In order to illustrate the use of ESB, the example of loan approval business process involving process orchestration discussed in Chapter 8 is extended for service integration through BEA AquaLogic ESB.

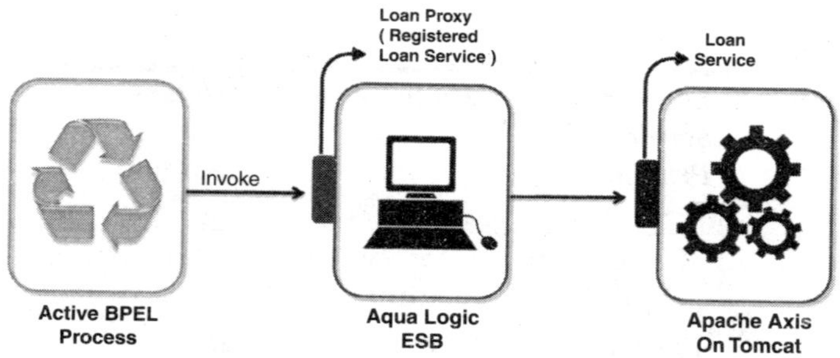

FIGURE 9-6 Service integration with ESB.

Scenario

The *Loan Service* provides web methods invoked during orchestration of loan approval process and is implemented with Apache Axis on Tomcat server. The web methods invoked at various steps of process orchestration are made over the BEA Aqualogic Enterprise Service Bus. Thus, the ESB forms a glue for service integration as shown in Figure 9-6.

Aproxy service (*Loan Proxy*) is registered in AquaLogic for the *Loan Service* developed with Apache Axis and deployed on Tomcat server. The following *invoke* activities (shown in Figure 8-10) of loan approval business orchestrated in ActiveBPEL call *Loan Proxy* service:

1. *InvokeLogLoan* (step 3);
2. *InvokeNotifyLoanOfficer* (step 5);
3. *InvokeNotifyCustomer* (steps 12, 18, 34);
4. *InvokeNotifyManager* (step 24);
5. *InvokeLoanApproval* (steps 16, 22);
6. *InvokeLoanRejection* (steps 10, 29);
7. *InvokeLoanConfirmation* (step 32).

The BEA AquaLogic is configured to route calls to *Loan Proxy* service to the corresponding methods of *Loan Service* on Tomcat server.

Configuration of BEA AquaLogic ESB

AquaLogic configuration involves the following steps:

1. Login into AquaLogic Admin Console.
2. Enter into editing mode by clicking on ***Create*** in the ***Change center panel.***
3. Create a ***WSDL resource*** using the Loan Service WSDL file. This step registers the *Loan Service* WSDL (which is provided by Apache Axis on Tomcat server) as the WSDL resource. The key portions of the Loan Service WSDL are shown in Figure 9-7. Note that all the resources can be created using the ***Create resource*** drop down box available on the right panel.
4. Create a business service using the WSDL resource.

```
<?xml version="1.0" encoding="UTF-8"?>
<wsdl:definitions.......... >
  <!- Message Definitions -->
  <wsdl:message name= ...>
    ...
    ...
  </wsdl:message>

<!-- Interface Definitions -->
 <wsdl:portType name="LoanService">
   <wsdl:operation name="notify" parameterOrder="message loanNo fixedRate duration
interestRate customer currency loanAmount status">
     <wsdl:input message="impl:notifyRequest" name="notifyRequest"/>
       <wsdl:output message="impl:notifyResponse" name="notifyResponse"/>
    </wsdl:operation>

     <wsdl:operation name="logLoan" parameterOrder="loanNo fixedRate duration
interestRate customer currency loanAmount status">
       <wsdl:input message="impl:logLoanRequest" name="logLoanRequest"/>
       <wsdl:output message="impl:logLoanResponse" name="logLoanResponse"/>
      </wsdl:operation>
      <wsdl:operation name="approveLoan" parameterOrder="loanNo fixedRate duration
interestRate customer currency loanAmount status">
      <wsdl:input message="impl:approveLoanRequest" name="approveLoanRequest"/>
      <wsdl:output message="impl:approveLoanResponse" name="approveLoanResponse"/>
      </wsdl:operation>

     <wsdl:operation name="confirmLoan" parameterOrder="loanNo fixedRate duration
interestRate customer currency loanAmount status">
       <wsdl:input message="impl:confirmLoanRequest" name="confirmLoanRequest"/>
        <wsdl:output message="impl:confinnLoanResponse" name="confinnLoanResponse"/>
     </wsdl:operation>

     <wsdl:operation name="rejectl_oan" parameterOrder="loanNo fixedRate duration
interestRate customer currency loanAmount status">
       <wsdl:input message="impl:rejectLoanRequest" name="rejectLoanRequest"/>
       <wsdl:output message="impl:rejectLoanResponse" name="rejectLoanResponse"/
      </wsdl:operation>
   </wsdl:portType>

  <!-- Binding Definitions -->
   <wsdl:binding name= ...>
...
  </wsdl:binding>
  <!-- Service Definition ->
  <wsdl:service name="LoanServiceService">
     <wsdl:port binding="impl:LoanServiceSoapBinding" name="LoanService">
        <wsdlsoap:address location="http://localhost:8080/axis/services/LoanService"/>
      </wsdl:port>
    </wsdl:service>

</wsdl:definitions>
```

FIGURE 9-7 Loan service WSDL.

5. Create a proxy service using the business service align. This will routing to the target business service.
6. Edit the routing in the proxy service message flow and choose the option 'Use inbound operation for outbound'.
7. Activate the changes.

Reference the Proxy Service in Active BPEL

The *Loan Proxy* service is registered in AquaLogic ESB; its WSDL is imported into Active BPEL workspace and used for invocations from the BPEL process. The following BPEL code corresponds to the *Loan Proxy* service WSDL reference in ActiveBPEL:

```
<bpel:import importType="http://schemas.xmlsoap.org/wsdl/"
location="WSDL/LoanProxy.wsdl"
namespace="http://localhost:8080/axis/services/LoanService"/>
```

Invoke Proxy Service

The ***<bpel:import>*** code makes all operations available to the BPEL process. The following BPEL code shows how a BPEL process invokes *approve loan* operation on imported proxy service. Partner Links also need to be created which are shown in complete listing of BPEL in Annexure B.

```
<bpel:invoke inputVariable="approveLoanRequest" name="InvokeLoanApproval"
operation="approveLoan" outputVariable="approveLoanResponse"
partnerLink="LoanServiceLPT" portType="ns2:LoanService">
</bpel:invoke>
```

9.3 TECHNOLOGIES FOR SERVICE ORCHESTRATION

Business processes are externalized and defined as flow of service interactions in Business Process Execution Language (BPEL). A process orchestration engine orchestrates the execution of steps defined for business processes. BPEL is a standard for business process orchestration and has been explained in detail in Chapter 8. Several vendors provide products for the process orchestration engine. The key products for service orchestration are given in Table 9-3.

The implementation of service orchestration using one of the open-source tools, Active BPEL has been described in detail in Chapter 8 and its relationship with service integration has also been discussed in Section 9.2 of this chapter. Active BPEL is an open-source product from Active Endpoints. The Active BPEL engine executes process definitions created for the BPEL standards BPEL4WS 1.1 specification and the WSBPEL 2.0.

TABLE 9-3 Products for service orchestration

Tools/Products → *Vendors ↓*	*Service Orchestration Tools*	*Vendor Website Reference*
IBM	WebSphere Process Server	http://www.ibm.com/software/integration/wps/
Microsoft	Biztalk Server	http://www.microsoft.com/biztalk/default.mspx
Oracle	Oracle BPEL Process Manager	http:// www.oracle.com/technology/bpel
Intalio	Intalio Works BPMs (Community and Enterprise Editions)	http://www.intalioworks.com/product/bpm
Lombardi	Teamworks	http://www.lombardisoftware.com/enterprise-bpm-software.php
Redhat	jBPM	http://www.jboss.com/pdf/jbpm_whitepaper.pdf
Active EndPoints	Active BPEL Community Edition	http://www.activevos.com/community-open-source.php
	Active VOS	http://activevos.com/products-activevos.php

PoCs developed using representative SOA technologies are presented in Annexure A.

9.4 SUMMARY

SOA implementations involve use of several technologies. The technologies for SOA for service enablement, service integration and service orchestration have been presented. Generic technologies that are standards-based and platform-supported have been discussed for service enablement and key vendor-specific tools and products have been provided with references. The loan approval business process example discussed in Chapter 8 has been extended to discuss service integration over ESB. Key vendor-specific tools have also been listed for service integration and service orchestration.

KEY TERMS

Hyper Text Transfer Protocol (HTTP)	A communication protocol developed over TCP/IP that forms the basis of web-based communications.
eXtensible Markup Language (XML)	A canonical text-based markup language without fixed tags (unlike HTML where specific tags are used to specify presentation aspects).
SOAP	SOAP is an XML-based protocol to provide an envelope to data exchanged by web services.
Web Services Definition Language (WSDL)	WSDL is a description language for specifying address, contract and binding related details of web services.
XSD	XSD is an XML language for describing and constraining the content of XML documents.
Java API for XML web services (JAX-WS)	JAX-WS is an API built to make web service development easier than the earlier JAX RPC by providing a library of annotations; a toolkit of Ant tasks and command-line utilities that hide the complexity of the underlying XML message protocol.
Java API for XML binding (JAXB)	JAXB is an API that enables generation of Java classes from XML schemas or vice versa.
Java Messaging Service (JMS)	JMS is a messaging standard that allows application components based on Java EE platform to create, send, receive and read messages.
.NET Remoting	.NET Remoting is a Microsoft API for inter-process communication.

REFERENCES

Fielding, R. (2000) *Architectural Styles and the Design of Network-based Software Architectures*, Dissertation, University of California, Irvine.

Graham, S., Davis, D., Simeonov, S., Daniels, G., Brittenham, P., et al. (2004) *Building Web Services with Java: Making Sense of XML, SOAP, WSDL, and UDDI*, 2nd edn, Sams Publication, Indianapolis.

Joshi, B. (2008) *Creating Native Web Services in SQL Server, developer.com*, internet.com, http://www.developer.com/db/article.php/3767311/Creating-Native-Web-Services-in-SQL-Server.htm

Microsoft (2006) *Web Services Software Factory*, Patterns & Practices Development Center, http://msdn.microsoft.com/en-us/library/aa480534.aspx

McGovern, J., Ambler, S.W., Stevens, M.E., Linn, J., Sharan, V., et al. (2003) *Practical Guide to Enterprise Architecture*, Prentice Hall, New Jersey.

Microsoft (2006) Web Services Software Factory, Patterns and Practices Development Center, http://msdn.microsoft.com/en-us/library/aa480534.asgx

Mensah, K. (2005) *Virtualize Your Oracle Database with Web Services*, Oracle Technology Network.

SDN WSIT (2007) *Web Services Interoperability Technology Features*, http://java.sun.com/webservices/interop/features/index.jsp

Smart, J. (2006) *Web Services Made Easy with JAX-WS 2.0*, java.net, http://java.net/pub/a/today/2006/06/13/web-services-with-jax-ws-2.0.html

Vohra, D. (2004) *Generating an XML Document with JAXB*, ONJava.com, http://www.onjava.com/pub/a/onjava/2004/12/15/jaxb.html

Wikipedia (2010) Representational State Transfer, http://en.wikipedia.org/wiki/Representational_State_Transfer#cite_note-3

Woods, D. and Mattern, T. (2006) *Enterprise SOA: Designing IT for Business Innovation*, O'Reilly, Sebastopol.

W3C (2004) *Web Services Architecture*, W3C Working Group Note 11 February 2004, http://www.w3.org/TR/ws-arch/

Xu, P. (2006) *Create Web Services for DB2 stored procedures using Rational Application Developer V6*, developerWorks, IBM.

Business Case for SOA

CHAPTER 10

CONTENTS

LEARNING OBJECTIVES

After reading this chapter, you would be able to:

- Understand the need to establish a business case for SOA.
- Review the considerations for SOA adoption.
- Study the benefits of SOA.
- Determine cost savings that can result from SOA.
- Learn how to compute ROI for SOA.

SOA has been discussed from architecture and technology perspectives thus far. At an enterprise level, these are related to the *what* and *how* of SOA. However, for an initiative such as SOA to be adopted, a business case must first be established. This constitutes the *why* of SOA in an enterprise context.

Like other IT initiatives, SOA initiatives require investments in hardware and software along with development and deployment efforts to meet the objectives. The results from SOA adoption must justify the investments involved. It is, therefore, important to establish a business case for SOA initiatives to get the necessary sponsorship in terms of funding, support for implementation and buy-in for roll-out. A business case is developed considering the following:

1. stakeholders objectives;
2. benefits of SOA;
3. cost savings;
4. Return on Investment (ROI).

The objective of this chapter is to cover the above considerations that need to be kept in mind when justifying SOA adoption.

10.1 STAKEHOLDER OBJECTIVES

A SOA initiative needs to fulfil the objectives of the stakeholders. Hence, a business case needs to be prepared with the key stakeholders in mind.

Sponsors

SOA initiatives are sponsored by CXOs, Heads of Business or Heads of IT when they result in strategic advantages and financial benefits for the enterprise. The strategic advantages that the sponsors of SOA look for include:

1. alignment of business and IT;
2. reduced time-to-market;

3. agility;
4. vendor independence;
5. competitive edge through leverage of new technologies.

The financial benefits that reinforce a business case for the sponsors are: (a) Financial gains on account of improved competitiveness and (b) cost savings due to the benefits of SOA.

Business

Enterprises have business units that deliver products and services and IT departments that provide hardware and software infrastructure to enable the business through implementation of their business processes.

The success of a SOA initiative depends to a large extent on the value it delivers to the business users in addressing their problems. The buy-in of key stakeholders of business units of an enterprise is usually necessary before an enterprise-wide SOA initiative can be taken up.

One of the issues that stakeholders in business units experience is the difficulty in introducing new products and services or making changes to existing products and services in tune with market trends. While the lack of alignment between goals and objectives of business units and IT departments could be one reason, the lack of flexibility in IT infrastructure to support the business needs (or alternatively the effort and time needed to have the changes effected) could be another reason.

SOA, when properly applied, solves these issues through the dimensions of reuse, agility and integration. The capabilities of SOA solutions, in meeting the objectives of business, need to be brought out appropriately with the key stakeholders of the business in order to establish a business case.

IT

SOA represents the next step in the evolution of programming paradigms as discussed in Chapter 3. The services model presents several opportunities that did not exist earlier. With the availability of IT infrastructure that enables externalizing of business processes and the maturity of packaged application platforms and enterprise platforms to deploy them, IT departments can contribute significantly to strategies that provide competitive edge to the enterprise. IT departments can thus go beyond the usual support role and act as change agents within an enterprise. The leadership role that IT department can play in an enterprise through SOA needs to be underlined to establish the business case for key stakeholders of IT departments.

Also, through the concepts of loose coupling and integration based on ESB, SOA solves many problems that IT departments face from an architecture perspective. In several enterprises, IT infrastructure has evolved over a number of years with a combination of legacy applications and newer technologies without an overarching enterprise-wide holistic view. SOA can be the enabler to create and manage such an enterprise-wide architecture. It can be implemented taking into account current market demands while protecting investments in legacy applications. This aspect can also be emphasized to build the business case for SOA.

10.2 BENEFITS OF SOA

SOA results in several benefits for an enterprise:

1. ***Business agility:*** SOA techniques enable agile system infrastructure by separating business process operations from business applications and moving them into a different layer that manages the orchestration of business processes. By doing this, the complexity and agility of business processes can be managed more easily than if they had been hard-wired using traditional programming languages. The architecture of an enterprise based on SOA would have the business functionality of the applications exposed as a set of services that are orchestrated by a set of business process services. Changes to business functionality of any of the business applications do not impact the rest of the application infrastructure of the enterprise. Likewise, changes to the orchestration element of business process services do not also impact the business applications in a well-architected SOA solution for an enterprise. Thus, SOA brings in the agility that is critical to business transformation in organizations.
2. ***Shorter development cycles:*** As the collection of services in an enterprise becomes rich, the motivation to reuse those services increases and new functionality is more easily built using existing services resulting in incremental business benefit. While the initial learning curve for SOA architects, designers and developers on technologies related to SOA implementation is steep, the development time for enterprise-wide implementations is reduced on the account of reuse, common integration infrastructure and configurable nature of business processes.
3. ***Reduced time-to-market:*** On the account of shorter development cycles for new functionality and ease of change to business processes supported by SOA, IT can respond quickly enough to desired changes in market conditions in order to support business with new products and services for competitive advantage.
4. ***Lower total cost of ownership:*** In an enterprise context, more reuse and common infrastructure implies lesser effort to develop, test and maintain and, therefore, improved productivity resulting in lower total cost of ownership. On a different dimension, SOA implementations when properly architected, designed and implemented are technology- and vendor-neutral and hence many of the problems of vendor lock-in are no longer issues. This gives organizations an advantage in price negotiations with vendors and results in lower hardware and software costs for IT.

5. ***Strategic architecture:*** SOA, when defined at enterprise level, is strategic in nature. It could serve as a blueprint to the enterprise-wide IT implementation and enable governance. Flexibility, scalability and security may be addressed on the basis of the principles of SOA. On the account of the strong endorsement for SOA from most of the IT infrastructure vendors, it is reasonable to assume that most of the products developed over the next 5–10 years will be compatible with SOA and will most likely support a SOA strategy. Therefore, adoption of SOA enables an enterprise to leverage new developments in future that cannot be anticipated today. Use of SOA principles can also bring about other possibilities from an architecture perspective. As organizations go through mergers and acquisitions and also make collaborative arrangements with other enterprises for competitive edge, restructuring of the business would take place that would result in changes to business processes and overall enterprise-wide architecture. An enterprise-wide architecture based on SOA will allow increased degree of agility such business transformations demand by maintaining focus on business processes and their orchestration rather than be limited by technology used for implementing the applications.
6. ***Alignment of IT and business:*** In SOA implementations, business functions are exposed as services and act as "modules" which are implemented by IT applications. IT functions are closely tied to the business functions and therefore to the business objectives. Alignment of business and IT may thus be implemented through externalizing of business processes and their orchestration based on invocation of services exposed by IT applications. As changes occur either in business or IT side of the organization, the alignment may be maintained by suitable configuration rather than custom development. This ability for business and IT to be in tandem with each other can provide significant competitive advantage to the enterprise.
7. ***Interoperability:*** The service-oriented model requires that service providers and service consumers do not make any assumptions of the technology used for their development or for interactions. All communication is based on contracts defined. Also, the data format used is a canonical format (XML). Services, therefore, are designed to be interoperable. Interoperability enables reuse across applications built with different technologies reducing the cost of ownership.
8. ***Effective integration:*** Integration in SOA can happen at two levels – process level or service level. In both the cases, SOA encourages common infrastructure (process orchestration engine or ESB) for applications to implement integration. The need for custom code to integrate applications is reduced and hence the development and maintenance costs are reduced accordingly. Other benefits also result from common infrastructure for integration promoted by SOA. Organizations can build significant competencies on the integration tools that can be leveraged by several initiatives for economies of scale.

9. ***Improved efficiency:*** One of the key benefits of services model is on account of the principle of reuse – "Build once, Use many times." This principle eliminates duplication of functionality in applications resulting in improved productivity, quality and efficiency.

10.3 COST SAVINGS

In order to establish a business case for SOA, it is important to articulate the cost benefit that results from a SOA initiative. Several approaches may be considered for determining cost benefit. One such approach suggested by David Linthicum (Linthicum, 2005) involves computation of cost savings taking into account the reuse of services. Cost-savings computation based on this approach is described as follows.

Cost Savings Computation

The cost savings can be computed as:

$$\text{Development Cost Savings (DCS)} = [(\boldsymbol{N} \times \boldsymbol{R})/100] \times (\boldsymbol{C} \times \boldsymbol{A}) \qquad (10.1)$$

where

$\boldsymbol{N}$ = No. of services that are reusable
$\boldsymbol{R}$ (%) = Degree of reuse (expressed as percentage)
$\boldsymbol{C}$ = Complexity of services (average no. of functions or object points per service)
$\boldsymbol{A}$ = Average cost per function point or object point

Explanation

1. When $\boldsymbol{N}$ services are reusable with a reuse percentage of R then the amount of reuse that represents cost savings is $\boldsymbol{N} \times \boldsymbol{R}/100$.
2. The complexity of services, $\boldsymbol{C}$, represents the measure of average amount of development effort required to develop each of the services. This is dependant on effort (measured in function points or object points) that would be needed to develop the functionality had it not been avoided because of services model.
3. Taking the complexity factor, $\boldsymbol{C}$, into consideration and multiplying it with the average cost for each function point or object point, $\boldsymbol{A}$, results in average cost savings per unit of reuse ($\boldsymbol{C} \times \boldsymbol{A}$).
4. Hence, the total effort saved on development (which otherwise would have been needed) would be the amount of reuse ($\boldsymbol{N} \times \boldsymbol{R}/100$) multiplied by the average cost savings per unit of reuse ($\boldsymbol{C} \times \boldsymbol{A}$).

Illustration

Consider a banking institution that provides loans to customers. For the purpose of illustration of computation of cost savings, assume that the IT department supports the business with a dozen (12) applications and is considering a SOA strategy for the benefits mentioned earlier.

In order to move to SOA, assume that of the 12 applications are modified one per quarter each on an average exposing six services and the reuse percentage reaches a maximum of 18% over 12 quarters, that is over a period of three years. If the complexity, that is, the average number of function points or object points is 400, then, using Eq. (10.1), the cost savings may be computed over a period of three years as follows.

Apply Eq. (10.1) for cost savings for Q2 (Linthicum, 2005) (Note: *In Q1, services are yet to be defined. Hence, reuse and cost savings do not occur):*

No. of services that are reusable $= \boldsymbol{N} = 12$
Degree of reuse (expressed as percentage) $= \boldsymbol{R}\% = 5\%$
Complexity of services (average no. of functions or object points per service) $= \boldsymbol{C} = 400$
Average cost per function point or object point $= \boldsymbol{A} = \$100$

$$\begin{aligned}\text{Cost savings for Q1} &= [(\boldsymbol{N} \times \boldsymbol{R})/100] \times (\boldsymbol{C} \times \boldsymbol{A})\\ &= [(12 \times 5)/100] \times (400 \times 100) = \$24{,}000\end{aligned}$$

The cost savings for each of the quarters can be computed accordingly and is shown in Table 10-1.

TABLE 10-1 Cost-savings computation (illustration)

Cost Savings → *Year/Quarter ↓*		*Services Accessible (N)*	*Degree of Reuse (Rin %)*	*Complexity (C)*	*Average Cost (in $) (A)*	*Cost Savings ($)*
	Q1	6	0	400	100	0
Year 1	Q2	12	5	400	100	24,000
	Q3	18	10	400	100	72,000
	Q4	24	12	400	100	115,200
	Q1	30	12	400	100	144,000
Year 2	Q2	36	12	400	100	172,800
	Q3	42	12	400	100	201,600
	Q4	48	12	400	100	230,400
	Q1	54	15	400	100	324,000
Year 3	Q2	60	15	400	100	360,000
	Q3	66	18	400	100	475,200
	Q4	72	18	400	100	518,400
Development Cost Savings (DCS) for 3 years (in $)						2,637,600

10.4 RETURN ON INVESTMENT (ROI)

Return on Investment (ROI) is one of the most important factors for approval of a business case by decision makers in an enterprise. SOA initiatives provide ROI on all three dimensions, namely reuse, integration and agility. While ROI can be computed on the basis of the estimations on the first two dimensions, it is difficult to quantify the ROI for business agility that SOA offers. Only when market conditions change and IT is able to quickly meet the demands of the business by supporting it with IT solutions, does the value of agility gets established. Hence, ROI computations that follow are based on estimations on reuse and integration dimensions.

ROI may be computed using

$$\text{Return on Investment (ROI)} = (\text{DCS} - \text{EXP})/\text{EXP} \tag{10.2}$$

where

DCS = Development Cost Savings = Cost savings from SOA initiative (due to reuse and integration)

EXP = Expenditure = Expenditure towards hardware, software, network and development effort

Explanation

1. ROI is computed by subtracting expenditure from cost savings and dividing the result by expenditure.
2. Cost savings may be computed using Eq. (10.1).
3. Indicative expenditure is as follows:
   - purchase of hardware (servers, data accelerators, upgrading of network infrastructure, etc.);
   - purchase of software (ESB, process orchestration engine, development tools, etc.);
   - cost of training;
   - cost of effort involved in development of services.

Illustration

Consider the banking institution example used earlier to compute cost savings. The same is extended to compute ROI. For the purpose of illustration, assume that expenditure for the three years is as follows. The ROI computations on a yearly basis are shown in Table 10-2. The assumptions made in this example are as follows:

1. Nine resources are needed to implement SOA at the cost of $60,000 (per resource per year) for a period of three years.

TABLE 10-2 ROI computation (illustration)

ROI → / Year ↓	Cost Savings (DCS in $)	Expenditure (EXP in $)					
		Hardware	*Software*	*Training*	*Development*	*Total*	*ROI*
Year 1	211,200	25,000	100,000	10,000	540,000	675,000	−68.71
Year 2	748,800	75,000	50,000	10,000	540,000	675,000	−28.89
Year 3	1,677,600	100,000	25,000	10,000	540,000	675,000	30.25

2. The expense in the first year is predominantly setting up of software for development purpose, in the second year it is for the server hardware while in the third year it is for the network hardware.
3. Training expense for users and resources has been estimated for all the three years.

It can be noted from Table 10-2 that with time the cost savings and ROI increase on account of reuse and the SOA initiative for the banking institution reaches a break-even and provides 30% rate of return for patterns of cost savings and spend provided in the example.

10.5 BUILD A CASE FOR SOA

Several surveys have been conducted by analyst firms on SOA adoption. One of the surveys conducted by GCR (GCR, 2008) with CXO respondents provides interesting results summarized as follows:

1. The primary drivers for SOA vision are *IT cost savings, customer service improvement* and *faster time-to-market*.
2. The top three areas of impact as a result of SOA deployment have been identified as *customer service improvement, faster time-to-market* and *information visibility*.
3. The four main roadblocks for justifying SOA in organizations are *lack of confidence in a big SOA payoff, securing funding, ROI not strong enough* and *unable to build a business case*.

The survey results provide an important insight: It is important to build a good business case with quantitative data on cost savings and ROI and qualitative difference that SOA can make to an enterprise's business with agility. Only then will there be buy-in from senior management of an enterprise and SOA plans can take off from the drawing board.

10.6 SUMMARY

SOA initiatives involve significant investments that require authorization of senior management in an enterprise. A business case that justifies the investments is essential to convince decision makers of the business value of SOA. The key considerations in establishing a business case for SOA have been discussed in this chapter. The need to understand stakeholder objectives is also presented. The computations involved in arriving at cost savings and ROI have been discussed with an example.

KEY TERMS

CXOs	Chief Executive Officer, Chief Information Officer, Chief Technology Officer, etc. of an organization are collectively referred to as CXOs.
Return on Investment (ROI)	ROI is the percentage of profit on a past, current or future investments on account of an SOA initiative.
Interoperability	Interoperability is the ability of two or more systems built with different technologies to exchange information.

REFERENCES

GCR, (2008) SOA RESEARCH – SOA Justification, ebizQ, http://www.ebizq.net/white_papers/7554.html

Linthicum, D. (2005) *The ROI of Your SOA,* http://www.ebizq.net/topics/soa/features/6092.html?&pp=1

SOA Governance, Security, and Implementation

CHAPTER 11

CONTENTS

LEARNING OBJECTIVES

After reading this chapter, you would be able to:

- Study the approach for enterprise-wide SOA Implementation.
- Learn strategy definition process for an enterprise.
- Understand the steps involved in SOA development.
- Define SOA Governance.
- Determine the process, technologies and people involved in SOA Governance.
- Learn concepts of SOA security.
- Know the technologies for SOA security.

In order to ensure successful SOA implementation in an enterprise, it is necessary to define rules, processes, metrics and organizational constructs for control of SOA implementation to meet the business needs of the enterprise. *Governance* and *security* become important in this context. These key concerns addressed by the *infrastructure layer* for the Strawman architecture for enterprise-wide SOA are discussed in Chapter 4.

This chapter discusses SOA governance and provides an approach to implement SOA in an enterprise.

11.1 SOA GOVERNANCE

SOA Governance is a model of establishing policies, controls, and enforcement mechanisms within the context of the activities and constructs associated with SOA implementation (WebMethods, 2006). It involves *process* that defines policies, *technology* that establishes controls and *people* that enforce mechanisms. SOA implementation involves formulation of strategic architecture and development of services. Hence governance is applicable to both these aspects.

The drivers for SOA Governance are (ebizQ, 2008):

1. implementation of best practices;
2. business and IT alignment;
3. real-time service visibility;
4. reduce risk;
5. measurable ROI;
6. realize service reuse;
7. track and communicate progress of SOA implementation.

Strategic Architecture

As indicated earlier, the principles of enterprise architecture may be applied in arriving at a SOA-based strategic architecture. It follows, therefore, that the principles of enterprise architecture governance are equally applicable to SOA strategic architecture.

Process

The governance for SOA strategic architecture includes:

1. Architecture principles that the strategic architecture would need to comply with. Industry framework such as TOGAF may be customized for SOA initiative of the enterprise.
2. Definition of processes that lead to the formulation of business, application, information and infrastructure architecture.
3. Architectural considerations for SOA infrastructure layer including service security and service governance (design-time and run-time).
4. Decision-making criteria for selection of vendor products and tools.
5. Roadmap for implementation of the strategic architecture.
6. Specification of QoS parameters for services.
7. Recommendation of Service Level Agreement (SLA) requirements (that service providers need to fulfill).

Technologies

1. Establishment of standards for technologies used for development and deployment.
2. Tools (such as IBM Rational System Architect) to specify strategic architecture.
3. Identification of PoCs to validate the strategic architecture.

People

1. Governance team with architects and key stakeholders from across the enterprise with representation from senior management is constituted to ensure that the processes and approval cycles are appropriately followed for changes and deviations.
2. A suitable mix of enterprise, solution and infrastructure architects in the governance team to develop standards, policies, rules and guidelines to implement the strategic architecture and approve changes and deviations.

Development of Services

Services are created, consumed, changed and removed during their lifecycle. The governance of services involves definition of policies and rules for service design (creation), service execution (consumption) and service modification (change and removal).

Governance of Service Design

The process, technologies and people involved in the governance at design-time of services are as follows.

Process

As design of services with the right level of granularity for reuse is critical to success of services and SOA, policies may be defined to validate service definitions and ensure that they conform to relevant industry standards such as WS-Policy and WS-Interoperability. The four types of services, namely, activity services, business process services, client services and data services defined in Chapter 4, and reference models for those types services based on best practices may be made the basis of all service definitions. Procedures may be put in place for review and approval of services.

Technology

The tools used for service design and notation for representing design of services may be standardized at enterprise level. Guidelines for design and development of services ensure that the implementation conforms to established design patterns and other corporate standards.

A service registry plays an important role in policy enforcement by maintaining a catalog of services designed and developed. It does not store the service implementations but stores the technical details that a consumer requires in order to invoke the service (i.e., the address, binding and contract). Permissions for creation, modification or removal of services may be enforced through the features of registry that initiate approval workflows in order to authorize such actions.

A service repository is another important element of governance that holds policies, rules and restrictions. The repository maintains taxonomy for policies defined and has audit and identity management capabilities. In other words, the repository acts as a "centrally managed policy store" (WebMethods, 2006).

It may be noted that service registry and repository elements are often combined in one product as it provides several advantages. At the time of service design, the combined registry/repository provides the dual features of policy definition and enforcement.

People

Governance during service design is mainly the concern of business analysts, architects and developers who build services. The governance team gets involved for approval of policies and for exceptions/deviations.

Governance of Service Execution

The governance that is needed at run-time for services deployed in production is focused on operational aspect of SOA.

Process

During service execution, enforcement of policies to allow only the authorized consumers with appropriate permissions to access the services on the permitted message transports becomes important. Compliance to organization standards is also essential. Service level agreements defined between service providers and consumers may be monitored to ensure that some or all of the following parameters are within specified bounds (Systinet, 2010).

1. throughput (calls/min.);
2. response time(s);
3. availability (%);
4. number of slow calls (>2 s);
5. maximum number of messages/day;
6. service throttling (max concurrent calls);
7. service reuse index (ratio of reusable services across business processes to the number of services exposed);
8. service reuse frequency (average number of times a particular service is reused);
9. service variants index (number of variants/versions for a given service);
10. service failure index (percentage of failed service invocation per unit time);
11. service recovery index (percentage of service recovered over services failed).

Technology

An ESB (with some additional capabilities) has a key role in service execution governance. The policy enforcement can be done by ESB transparent to the service provider and consumer. During service invocations, the ESB mediates the requests, consults the service registry/repository for the policies and applies them as required. Applying a common policy context to such interactions is a unique aspect of governance in SOA.

People

The IT operations team of the enterprise is the primary stakeholder for governance during service execution.

Governance for Service Modification

One of the main aspects of governance is managing changes to services developed on account of changing needs of service consumers. Services once created go through several changes in their capabilities and contracts. The policies applicable to both providers and consumers also go through several changes. Thus, change-time governance is the key to getting the overall SOA governance model right.

Process

Changes to a service may be required on account of change to functionality due to change in business needs or change to the configuration that provides access and consumption of a service. In either case, there is a need to analyze the impact of the required change on the design of the service in addition to managing the changes needed in deployment environment as well as policies and service-level agreements. Accordingly, approvals of the SOA governance team may be required to authorize the changes.

Technology

The technologies required to manage, monitor and control IT systems are relevant to govern the change-time state of service. In addition, tools that support business activity monitoring (BAM) can provide useful information on the run-time model of services. Information from all these sources may be stored in registry/repository and may be used to make decisions on changes proposed to services. Rule engines integrated with service registry/repository can also automate changes that may be needed for IT systems.

People

The SOA governance team is involved to authorize changes. Additionally, the business analysts, architects, designers and developers may also be involved depending on the impact of the change. The best practices identified in SOA implementation and governance are provided in Annexure C.

Technologies for SOA Governance

The technologies for service development, service execution and service modification provide the following capabilities to implement design-time and run-time governance:

1. registry and repository;
2. policy definition and enforcement;
3. service monitoring and management.

Gartner predicts that "By 2013, lack of a systematic investment in composition tools, methodologies and governance will be a leading cause of failure in enterprise SOA initiatives" (Bradley et al., 2009). Hence, it is important to leverage available governance tools and technologies.

Several vendors have comprehensive solutions that provide the required governance capabilities. Organizations can, therefore, take a holistic look at their SOA governance needs and introduce an appropriate solution that not only enables design-time governance through a service registry and repository but also leverages them for service monitoring and management for run-time governance. Table 11-1 lists some of the key vendor-specific tools/products available today for SOA governance.

TABLE 11-1 SOA governance tools

Vendor	*Governance Tool*	*Website Reference*
Amberpoint	AmberPoint Governance System, AmberPoint Management System	http://www.amberpoint.com/products/amberpoint-governance-system.shtml
HP	HP SOA Systinet, HP SOA Policy Enforcer, HP SOA Registry Foundation, HP Business Process Monitor software, HP Business Service Level Management software	http: //www.hp.com/go/soa
IBM	WebSphere Registry and Repository, DataPower, Tivoli Composite Application Manager, Tivoli Security Policy Manager, Rational Asset Manager	http://www-01.ibm.com/software/solutions/soa/gov/
Microsoft	Microsoft Expressions, Microsoft Visual Studio	http://www.microsoft.com
MuleSoft	Galaxy	http://www.mulesoft.org/display/GALAXY/Home
Oracle	Oracle Enterprise Repository, Oracle Web Services Manager, Oracle EM Management Pack Plus for SOA, Oracle Service Registry, Oracle SOA Suite	http://www.oracle.com/us/technologies/soa/soa-governance/index.htm
Progress Software	Actional Enterprise, Actional Application Development	http://web.progress.com/en/Product-Capabilities/soa-governance.html
Sensedia	Sensedia Repository	http://www.sensedia.com/sensedia-repository
Software AG	CentraSite, Mediator, Insight	http://www.softwareag.com/Corporate/Products/wm/soagovernance/default.asp

(continued)

TABLE 11-1 *(Continued)*

Vordel	Vordel Policy Director, Vordel Reporter, Vordel Policy Studio	http://www.vordel.com/products/index.html
WebLayers	WebLayers Center	http://www.weblayers.com

11.2 SOA SECURITY

Security in the context of SOA has three factors. The first is related to securing of interactions between service providers and service consumers. The second is related to securing the deployment environment of applications that expose and consume the services. These are addressed by security solutions for IT infrastructure. Finally, the third factor is related to management of policies for security and their associated infrastructure. The solutions for policy management discussed for SOA governance in earlier section are also relevant for security and may be leveraged to address policy management needed for SOA security.

The focus of this section is on the first factor, that is, in securing interactions between service providers and service consumers.

The key capabilities for securing interactions between service providers and service consumers include (Nagaratnam et al., 2007):

1. authentication;
2. authorization;
3. audit;
4. identity;
5. confidentiality and integrity.

Authentication involves validation of credentials of the requester (service consumer if *unilateral one-pass* and also that of service provider if *mutual two party*) and returning security token. The service consumer then calls the method of the service using the security token.

Authorization provides access to a service based on a set of policies, typically privileges. The authorization information may be centralized or federated. When the service consumer is authenticated, access is permitted based on the policy information specified.

Audit collects data of service invocations, stores and reports it to provide a record of interactions between service providers and service consumers.

TABLE 11-2 SOA security tools

Vendor	*Governance Tool*	*Website Reference*
Layer 7 Technologies	SecureSpan XML Networking Gateway, SecureSpan XML VPN Client, SecureSpan Manager	http://www.layer7tech.com/main/solutions.html
Computer Associates	CA SOA Security Manager	http://www.ca.com/us/products/product.aspx?id=5263
Bloombase	Spitfire SOA	http://www.bloombase.com/products/spitfire/soa/index.html

Identity provides a framework to manage, share, federate and access identity information from identity sources of user and groups.

Confidentiality and *Integrity* protects sensitive information from being disclosed and detects unauthorized modification of data.

The above capabilities need to implemented in the *infrastructure layer* of the enterprise Strawman architecture (discussed in Chapter 4) to address the concern of securing services.

Technologies for SOA Security

Table 11-2 lists some of the key vendor-specific tools/products available today for SOA security.

11.3 APPROACH FOR ENTERPRISE-WIDE SOA IMPLEMENTATION

SOA is successfully adopted in an enterprise when strategic aspects of architecture and technology are suitably envisioned, the key stakeholders are committed to implement the vision and the approach to SOA implementation and governance is properly planned and executed. In the chapters so far, the concepts and techniques to get the right architecture and technology for SOA have been discussed as also the practices that can be employed to get the buy-in of key stakeholders in an enterprise.

This chapter provides an approach to implement SOA in an enterprise and the governance model that needs to be put in place to fully leverage SOA so as to meet the business objectives of the enterprise.

In Chapter 4, a Service Oriented Analysis and Design (SOAD) process with focus on development of services was presented. The implementation of SOA at an enterprise level involves several other activities over and above what are already described in the SOAD process. These activities include: taking an inventory of IT applications, conducting interviews of key stakeholders to gain an understanding of business goals and objectives and determining the scope of IT project(s) to implement SOA. The governance model to manage the initiative needs to also be put in place. All these activities come under the purview of IT strategy and governance.

SOA implementation involves two categories of activities:

1. strategy;
2. development.

Each category of activities may be spun off as a separate project and may be executed by an in-house team or by an external consulting organization. A process may be defined for each category of activities to realize SOA at an enterprise level. In the following sections, each of the categories and the applicable process is discussed.

Strategy

Strategy for SOA in an enterprise is done in the context of business and IT of the enterprise. Hence, all the steps involved in defining an enterprise-wide IT strategy are equally applicable to a SOA initiative. While the push for SOA may come from CXO level or IT side of the organization, it is important that a structured approach be followed for defining the strategy.

Figure 11-1 pictorially depicts a process that could be used for strategy definition. It has three steps:

1. due diligence;
2. AS-IS assessment;
3. TO-BE strategic architecture.

A team that typically includes a technology consultant and a business analyst is put together for strategy formulation.

Due Diligence

A short period of assessment is initially planned to identify the scope of the initiative, take inventory of artifacts available and to ensure that the approach for establishing the strategic architecture is understood and supported by all key stakeholders. This includes Strawman architecture discussed in Chapter 4.

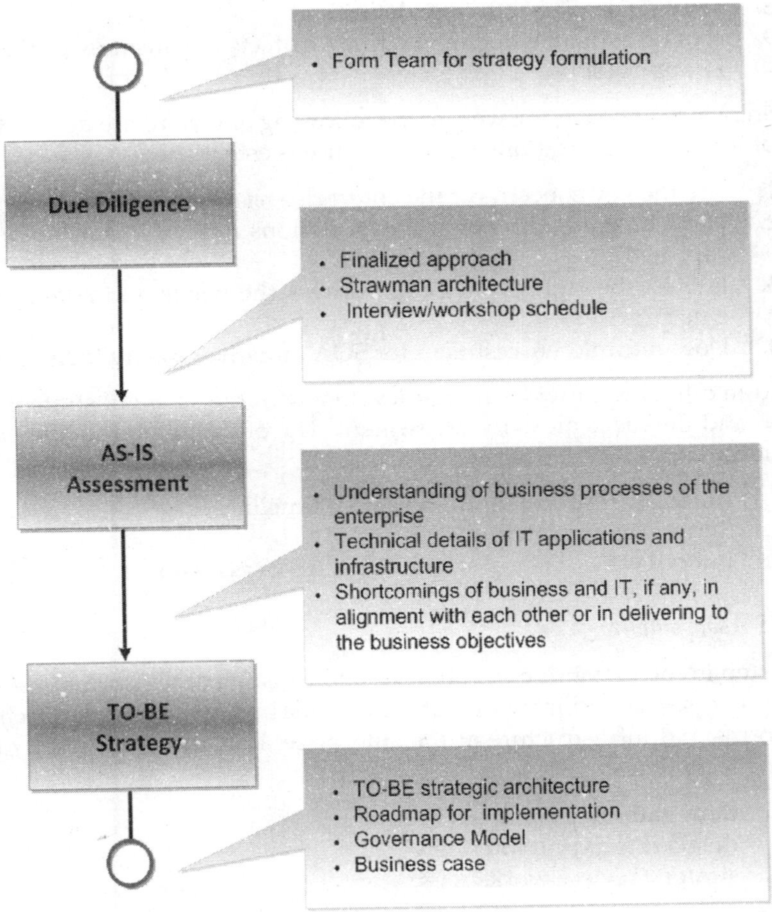

FIGURE 11-1 Process for strategy formulation.

The key activities undertaken as part of due diligence are as follows:

1. review business goals and drivers;
2. understand business growth and competitive landscape;
3. conduct interviews with key stakeholders;
4. assess pain points of business and IT;
5. determine key business processes;
6. take inventory of IT applications, architecture and design artifacts, information/data models and infrastructure (server and network) that host the applications;

7. review enterprise-wide IT architecture;
8. arrive at scope of strategy definition;
9. catalog available documentation/artifacts for business processes and IT applications.

During Due Diligence, answers to the following questions are determined and suitability of SOA as a strategic architecture is established:

1. Are the key concerns of the enterprise *reuse, integration* and *agility*?
2. Have business drivers and expectations from key stakeholders been captured?
3. Is SOA the right strategy to address the needs and concerns of the enterprise?
4. Does return on investment for SOA initiatives justify their cost?

The due diligence provides a high-level view of the scope of strategy formulation and the focus areas for assessment. The outcome of due diligence step includes:

1. finalized approach with indicative timelines;
2. Strawman architecture;
3. interview/workshop schedule for AS-IS assessment.

AS-IS Assessment

This step involves conducting analysis and research of the current set of business processes, IT applications that support the business processes, technology platforms and infrastructure at the enterprise. It is accomplished by the following techniques:

1. data-gathering surveys;
2. detailed technical interviews;
3. strategy review workshops.

The objective of this step is to identify the current portfolio in key areas, giving context to the next stage of TO-BE strategy.

The key activities during this step are as follows:

1. The business analyst in the team (or the consultant with the required business skills) reviews documents or artifacts that represent the activities and workflows of all the key business processes.
2. The technology consultant (or enterprise architect with the required consulting skills) gains an understanding of the key business processes and reviews the documents or artifacts that capture the architecture, data model and infrastructure of IT applications that support the business processes.

3. By mapping business processes to the applications that support their functionality, analysis is conducted to assess the alignment of IT to business strategy.
4. The pain-points of business and IT are reviewed and the strategy needed to eliminate (or atleast mitigate them) are explored.
5. The business goals and drivers are reviewed and the strategic changes needed to architecture to support the business are considered. The need for reuse, agility and integration (the dimensions of SOA) is assessed and a determination made on whether a business case for SOA exists.
6. The readiness of the enterprise in effectively leveraging SOA at enterprise level is determined.

AS-IS assessment gives a picture of the current business and IT in an enterprise. The outcome of AS-IS assessment step is as follows:

1. Understanding of business processes of the enterprise.
2. Technical details of IT applications that support the business.
3. Shortcomings of business and IT, if any, in delivering to business objectives.
4. SOA readiness assessment based on the initiatives taken up by enterprise to:
    - map the business processes of the enterprise;
    - develop an enterprise architecture to align business with IT;
    - leverage the services model;
    - adopt new technologies;
    - govern IT.

TO-BE Strategy

This step involves strategic architecture to support the current and future requirements of the enterprise. Enterprise architecture also has the same objective. Hence, the principles of enterprise architecture may be applied to define the TO-BE strategic architecture. The strategic architecture includes the following:

1. Business architecture that provides a solution at business level (i.e., a model with business elements such as account master, ledger, etc.) needed to implement the current and future requirements based on industry trends.
2. Application architecture that maps the business architecture to applications and provides a solution in terms of applications needed to implement the business architecture. This also involves recommendation of technology solutions in key areas based on technology trends.

3. Information architecture that models the data flows among applications, repositories, OLTP and OLAP data stores, data exchanges with ERP, legacy and external systems, ETL flows, datamarts and datawarehouses.
4. Infrastructure architecture that deals with the technology elements (such as servers, routers, etc.) required to host the applications.

TO-BE strategic architecture provides a solution to current and future business and IT requirements in an enterprise. The key activities performed during this step (typically by a business analyst and technology consultant) are as follows:

1. Identification of business processes for current and future requirements and development of business architecture to address those requirements.
2. Definition of applications that would support the set of business processes to be introduced in future and development of TO-BE application architecture.
3. Mapping of business processes to the existing data models, that is the AS-IS information architecture and creating the TO-BE information architecture taking into the account TO-BE business and application architecture.
4. Recommendation of an infrastructure architecture that would host and integrate applications to deliver the business functionality in a seamless manner. This involves mapping TO-BE business processes and applications, reviewing AS-IS infrastructure and creating TO-BE information architecture.
5. Recommendations of technology stack for development of services and definition of criteria for selection of commercial or open source products. Identification of applications that need to be sunset and applications (not necessarily specific products) that need to be procured.
6. Gap analysis between TO-BE strategic architecture and AS-IS architecture.
7. Formulation of appropriate governance process, including roles, structure and activities, to ensure that the strategic architecture remains relevant and appropriate to the current and future requirements.
8. Roadmap for implementation of TO-BE strategic architecture. A high-level view of the following activities to be undertaken subsequently is provided:
    - plan for transition from AS-IS to TO-BE;
    - process for identification of activity services, business process services, client services and data services;
    - identification of PoCs with representative activity services, business process services, client services and data services in order to validate recommended technologies;

- setup of SOA Governance team for the enterprise with representation of key stakeholders of the enterprise;
- creation of Business Process model.

9. Preparation of a business case for SOA as discussed in Chapter 10.

The outcome of TO-BE strategic architecture step includes:

1. TO-BE strategic architecture;
2. roadmap for implementation of TO-BE strategic architecture;
3. Governance model;
4. business case.

The completion of strategy formulation marks an important milestone in the process of SOA implementation in an enterprise. The blueprint for enterprise-wide SOA is created and the business case prepared for approval by key stakeholders of the enterprise. This calls for a "Go–NoGo" decision and commitment of senior management on funding and adoption of SOA as a strategic initiative for the enterprise. A "Go" decision by the senior management triggers the next set of SOA development activities described in the next sub-section.

SOA Development

On receiving the approval from the senior management of the enterprise, the next category of activities in SOA implementation are initiated. Figure 11-2 pictorially depicts a process that could be used for SOA development. It has five steps:

1. transition planning;
2. validation;
3. business process model creation;
4. service development;
5. service deployment and monitoring.

This category of activities involves significant effort and therefore is executed as one or more projects. One or more teams, depending on the size of the effort, need to be formed with architects, business analysts and developers.

Transition Planning

The process of transitioning the enterprise from its current AS-IS to a future TO-BE strategic architecture is a significant task. It potentially involves defining multiple projects each aligning to a broader transition plan that is prepared taking into account the approved SOA strategy.

The key factors for transition planning are as follows:

1. Gap between TO-BE and AS-IS business architecture: Low impact to business processes of the enterprise would imply that the focus of transition planning would be on IT.
2. Technologies of current applications and changes needed to support the services model.

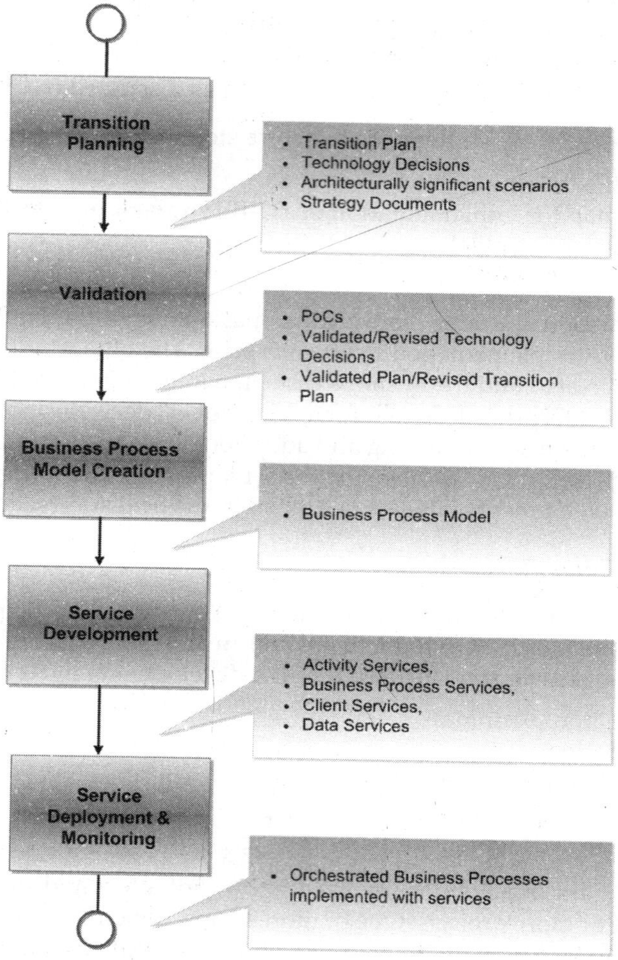

FIGURE 11-2 SOA development process.

3. Scope and complexity of applications that need to be developed for new functionality/business processes not part of the current applications.
4. Extent to which knowledge of domain and technology aspects of current applications is available within the enterprise. In many organizations, legacy applications have evolved (or have been acquired) over number of years with little or no documentation and with the architects, designers and developers of those applications not being available to support the transition. This indicates that significant effort would need to be

planned for extracting the business processes and rules from current applications through reverse engineering and other techniques.

5. Capabilities of project teams involved in transition. Several enterprises leverage outsourcing for such initiatives. The effort required for project teams of outsourced partners to gain an understanding of the business processes and knowledge of the current applications is factored into the transition plan.

Validation

A number of products are available from vendors that can be used for developing SOA solutions. On the basis of the recommendations made as part of strategy formulation, there is a need to:

1. elaborate and validate the technology recommendations through prototypes developed for architecturally significant scenarios;
2. revise the transition plan based on outcome of the activities for development of prototypes.

Proof of Concept (PoC)

Development of PoC is an important step in SOA development. This is because technology recommendations that are included as part of SOA strategy are generally meant for senior management and hence at a high level. Development teams will need to elaborate the recommendations and arrive at detailed specifications required for application development such as a specific version of process orchestration engine or ESB of a given vendor. There is thus a need to validate these decisions made at a lower level of detail through prototypes that implement architecturally significant scenarios and that include creation and consumption of different types of services. The PoCs can also be based on best practices so that they serve as reference implementations during service development step.

The results of PoCs yield useful information on technology issues, the workarounds needed and the effort required to implement the representative scenarios. This data can then be used to fine tune the plans of individual projects as well as the transition plan to ensure that they remain realistic.

Business Process Model

Creation of a business process model is an important step in implementing SOA in an enterprise. One of the key aspects of SOA from an enterprise perspective is orchestration of business processes. This entails modeling of the business processes that are required to implement the TO-BE strategic business architecture.

The agility that SOA brings to an enterprise is enabled by this step. The extent to which business processes in an enterprise can be externalized and made configurable (through process orchestration engine) represents the degree of agility of the enterprise. Hence, business processes need to be defined and modeled to provide the required agility to the enterprise.

Several tools are available to model the business processes such as IBM WebSphere Business Modeler and IDS Aris Business Architect. These tools generate BPEL workflows and UML that can form the basis of design of business process services and activity services.

Service Development

Services may be designed and developed using Service Oriented Analysis and Design (SOAD) Process described in detail in Chapter 4. Using this process (*what*) as basis, different methodologies (*how*) such as iterative, spiral, waterfall can be defined and projects with phases can be planned.

Activity, client and data services can either be developed ground up for new applications or existing functionality may be exposed as services. The prototypes during the validation step, if developed on the basis of the best practices for different types of services, can serve as reference implementations during this step. This step involves significant effort and a number of tools such as IBM Rational Software Architect and Microsoft Visio may be used to model service design. UML 2 profile or SoaML profile for software services may also be considered for this purpose.

Process services are designed and developed for externalized business process and orchestrable workflows. The four types of services are integrated through implementation of ESB. The SOAD process provides new possibilities for multinational, multi-location organizations with distributed IT capability. It is possible to define a TO-BE SOA strategy across such organizations based on enterprise-wide business architecture. Individual business units and IT groups can develop services independently for their application portfolios for reuse across the organization. Enterprises with outsourcing partners may also specify functionality to be developed in terms of services that may be built by leverage of not only multi-location development (onsite–offshore) but also of multi-partner capabilities.

SOA Deployment and Monitoring

SOA deployment involves setting up services on physical infrastructure for consumers to use. It is dependent on the technology platform for which the service is built.

Virtualization technologies can play an important role in deployment. The service-level workloads can be monitored and spread across servers and storage by provisioning new resources when required. Another factor in service deployment in enterprises is their management through service registries and repositories. Multiple versions of deployed services can co-exist and be made available to service consumers as per defined policies. Deployed services may be monitored at run-time for service levels defined and accordingly policies enforced at run-time. Effective service deployment and monitor requires a broader context of SOA governance.

11.4 SUMMARY

This chapter deals with implementing SOA (including SOA infrastructure layer that address the SOA governance and security needs) in an enterprise. SOA implementation at enterprise level involves SOA strategy formulation and SOA development. The steps involved in SOA strategy formulation, namely, due diligence, AS-IS assessment and TO-BE strategy are presented. This is followed by description of steps required for SOA development – transition planning, validation, business process model, service development and service deployment and monitoring. There is a need to govern SOA during and after implementation. These are covered with focus on governance for service design, service execution and service modification keeping in mind process, technology and people factors. The concepts of securing services are explained and technologies to implement SOA security are discussed.

KEY TERMS

Due Diligence A short period of assessment is planned during strategy definition phase for a SOA initiative to identify the scope of the SOA initiative.

AS-IS Assessment AS-IS Assessment involves conducting analysis and research of the current set of business processes, IT applications that support the business processes, technology platforms and infrastructure at the enterprise.

TO-BE Strategic Architecture TO-BE Strategic Architecture is a step in strategy definition for an SOA initiative that involves formulation of strategic architecture to support the current and future requirements of the enterprise.

Virtualization Virtualization is a technique for abstraction of computer resources. Single resource through virtualization may be setup as multiple logical resources. Alternatively, multiple physical resources may be setup as single logical resource.

Governance SOA Governance is a model of establishing policies, controls, and enforcement mechanisms within the context of the activities and constructs associated with SOA implementation.

Repository	A service repository is an tool for development-time governance of services. The repository maintains taxonomy for policies defined and has audit and identity management capabilities.
Business Activity Monitoring (BAM)	BAM is automatic monitoring of events associated with activities in an executing business process.

REFERENCES

Bradley, A. Sholler, D., Natis, Y., Schulman, J. and Blechar. M. (2009) *Predicts 2010: Addressing Key Advancements in Application Architecture*, Gartner Document ID: G00173052.

ebizQ (2008) *How Much Business Value is Your SOA Delivering?*, SOA Governance, an ebizQ publication.

Gartner (2009) *Magic Quadrant for Integrated SOA Governance Technology Sets*, Gartner ID Number: G00166481 Survey Report.

Systinet (2010) *HP SOA Systinet*, www.hp.com

WebMethods (2006) SOA Governance, http://www1.webmethods.com/PDF/whitepapers/SOA_Governance.pdf

Trends in SOA

CHAPTER 12

CONTENTS

LEARNING OBJECTIVES

After reading this chapter, you would be able to:

- Look at trends in SOA.
- Review technologies in relation to SOA.
- Know how convergence of SOA and BPM is taking place.
- Understand how Web 2.0 is presenting a lightweight option to SOA.
- Review the Open Source options for SOA development.
- Examine SOA Appliances.
- Look at the advances in SOA.
- Event-Driven Architecture and Complex Event Processing.
- Study the concepts of Software as a Service (SaaS) and a Reference model for SaaS platform.
- Understand a major trend in SOA – Cloud Computing.

Chapters 2–11 have covered in detail the architecture, design, implementation and governance of SOA for enterprise applications. In this concluding chapter, the trends in SOA are presented. Trends in SOA may be viewed under three categories:

1. SOA adoption;
2. technologies in relation to SOA;
3. advances in SOA.

12.1 SOA ADOPTION

In the past couple of years, SOA has gained signed significant adoption in the enterprise. According to Forrester, "Sixty-eight percent of enterprises say they are using SOA or will be using it by the end of 2010. Fifty-six percent are using SOA now, and that number jumps to 74% when considering only Global 2000 organizations". Further, the majority of enterprises adopting SOA have been satisfied enough to expand their use of SOA (Heffner, 2009).

According to ebizQ's survey on SOA governance, *agility, enterprise integration, business process optimization* and *IT asset reuse* were the top four reasons for adopting SOA (ebizQ, 2008). The survey results reinforce the dimensions of SOA outlined in Chapter 2 of the book.

With regard to SOA adoption in different geographies, Gartner indicates that "Although there are still some minor differences, many companies throughout

Asia exhibit an SOA adoption profile much like companies elsewhere in developed markets (such as North America and Europe)" (Lheureux, 2008).

IDC research shows that SOA adoption depends on the following critical success factors (Rogers, 2008):

1. business alignment;
2. organizational change management;
3. communications;
4. trust;
5. architecture;
6. scale and sustainability;
7. governance.

12.2 TECHNOLOGIES IN RELATION TO SOA

Several technologies that have evolved independent of SOA are being increasingly adopted for SOA implementations.

SOA and BPM Products

Business Process Management (BPM) is a discipline that automates and optimizes business processes and their performance in an enterprise. BPM products provide tools for modeling processes, development of process orchestration solutions, modules for deployment of business processes and management of their key performance indicators to meet operational targets. BPM implementations help enterprises preserve investments, identify threats, reduce risks, better structure processes and transform businesses. The BPM suite from Pegasystems is an example of BPM products.

BPM products are of two types (Lawson, 2007):

1. human-centric suites that evolved from imaging technology;
2. integration-centric suites that grew out of enterprise application integration tools.

On account of process orchestration being a key aspect of SOA, BPM is being seen as a key technology for SOA. This is resulting in BPM products being enhanced to better support needs of SOA in organizations leading the way for BPM products becoming part of SOA implementation of enterprises. Traditionally, BPM was business-driven while SOA was IT-driven. However, with increased focus in enterprises on business-IT alignment and enterprise-wide IT strategies, there is convergence of objectives leading to convergence of SOA and BPM. Gartner predicts that business process management will become the driver for SOA implementations and may eventually lead to their convergence (Sinur and Hill, 2006).

SOA and Web 2.0

Web 2.0, a term first coined at the first O'Reilly Media Web 2.0 conference in 2004, enables services such as social networking, aggregation services, tracking and filtering content and collaboration (Anderson, 2007). It represents a range of technologies that include:

1. Asynchronous JavaScript and XML (AJAX);
2. Representational State Transfer (REST);
3. JavaScript Object Notation (JSON);
4. Really Simple Syndication (RSS);
5. Mashup;
6. Weblog (or Blog);
7. Wiki.

One of the trends noticed is the use of Web 2.0 technologies acting as front-ends to SOA back-end environments (Taft, 2007). Of particular value is the use of web 2.0 technologies for developing *client services* discussed in Chapter 7 that could be used to implement *enterprise presentation layer* systems such as Portal or other mobile applications with improved reliability, scalability and governance. AJAX and Mashups are two important technologies of Web 2.0 that several products such as JackBe Presto provide and complement the capabilities of SOA.

Web 2.0 also offers an option in *lightweight* SOA through what Gartner refers to Web-Oriented Architecture (Hinchcliffe, 2005). Services may be exposed and consumed by any technology and not necessarily web services. When web service is used as the technology for exposing and consuming services in service-oriented applications, the SOAP envelope constitutes an overhead and both the service provider and consumer need to support it. An alternative to this is the use of Web 2.0 technologies especially Representational State Transfer (REST) that provides a simple communications interface using XML and HTTP discussed in Chapter 9. Every resource is identified by a URI and HTTP is used through GET, POST, PUT and DELETE command requests (Hinchcliffe, 2006). Gartner predicts that "By 2014, WOA (REST)-style services will be in use in 80% of organizations pursuing SOA" (Bradley et al., 2009).

Really Simple Syndication (RSS) is an XML-based web feed format for syndication, that is for publishing frequently changing web content such as news. RSS content can be subscribed by access of the link that supports it and by regular checks to get the updates. Mail systems such as Microsoft Outlook can also be enabled for receiving RSS feeds. When used in conjunction with REST, RSS can play an important part in lightweight SOA of being the glue to data from different sources.

JSON is a lightweight data interchange format written to be an alternative to XML. It provides a simple object serialization approach for remote calls and thus is an option when architecting lightweight SOA solution based on AJAX, REST and RSS as it is fast, compact and easy to consume in a browser.

A new trend, referred to as Enterprise 2.0, is seen in enterprises for communication using Web 2.0 technologies such as blogs, wikis and group messaging software for capture of tacit knowledge that includes best practices and relevant experiences from across an enterprise in order to make it available to users (McAfee, 2006). The back-end knowledge management systems for such enterprises may be based on SOA (Kambhampaty, 2007).

SOA and Open Source

SOA products for service development, process orchestration and ESB sourced from commercial vendors come with several advanced features but can be expensive. Open source products, on the other hand, are more rudimentary in their features but can meet specific requirements for web service development, integration and process orchestration. Cost and simplicity, therefore, have been the main reasons for a variety of open source products being available for implementation. The trend is towards increased open source SOA solutions. Table 12-1 lists the key open source products currently available for SOA development.

Commercial vendors are also supporting open-source SOA by providing certified releases of stack of open-source products for SOA development. For example, Progress Software provides open-source SOA stack called FUSE with certified releases of Apache SOA projects.

TABLE 12-1 Key open source products for SOA

Requirement	*Open Source Solution*	*Source*
Web service development	Axis 2	Apache Software Foundation
	CXF	Apache Software Foundation
ESB	WSO2 ESB	WSO2
	FUSE ESB	Fuse Open Source Community
	MULE ESB	Mulesoft
Process Orchestration	ActiveBPEL Community Edition	Active Endpoints
	Intalio Works BPMS Community Edition	Intalio
	jBPM Community Edition	jBoss Community

SOA Appliances

While most of SOA infrastructure has been software specific, hardware products are being introduced to manage SOA functions that operate between the network layer and the application layer (Kelly, 2006). These hardware devices called *SOA Appliances* are XML devices that handle specific tasks related to messaging layer efficiently. The messaging layer is important because it allows any service consumer to invoke any service provider over common integration infrastructure and hence the communication is no longer point-to-point. Thus, security cannot be addressed at network level by the use of SSL and HTTPS. It needs to be addressed at message level by the use of standards such as WS-Security.

SOA Appliances provide an option to parse SOAP and XML at message level in hardware and perform specialized processing for security. Such processing is CPU-intensive and can be done efficiently in hardware. IBM Data Power and Layer 7 Secure Span XML Networking Gateway are examples of SOA appliance devices currently available.

12.3 ADVANCES IN SOA

With the prediction of increased adoption of SOA by analyst organizations, research organizations, product vendors and various industry segments are looking at ways to leverage the services model. Several innovations are also possible to the basic model of exposing and consuming services. This section presents the trends observed in this regard.

Event-Driven Architecture (EDA)

In SOA, a request (service call) from the service consumer results in a synchronous response from the service provider. However, when asynchronous capabilities are needed for interactions between service providers and service consumers a system of events is needed.

Gartner introduced a design paradigm based on events called event-driven architecture (EDA) in which events are published by event producers which are received by event consumers. In EDA, event producers are not aware of who consume the event and therefore are decoupled from service consumers. Event consumers *subscribe* to the events that providers *publish*. When events occur, the event consumers are notified to perform the necessary processing. Thus, EDA provides asynchronous capabilities between decoupled components based on the publish/subscribe model.

EDA can bring the asynchronous capabilities to SOA. It can also bridge decoupled service boundaries as the services that produce or consume do not depend on the availability of a published service for the interactions. Thus EDA complements the capabilities of SOA and is sometimes referred to as *event-driven SOA*. Tibco's Ajax Message Bus is an example of a product that enables *event-driven SOA* to stream data and events to clients.

EDA in conjunction with SOA may be used for (Hoof, 2007):

1. asynchronous communication between services;
2. communication between workflows in business processes;
3. Processes where request/response-based communication may not be suitable, for example, processes that cross organization boundaries.

The combination of asynchronous event-driven processing with synchronous request/response processing in service-oriented applications makes them more scalable, flexible and dynamic as the components that process the events are mostly uncoupled from each other. Gartner predicts that "By 2012, 50% of large, new application systems will include event-driven functions to improve business responsiveness" (Bradley et al., 2009).

Messaging infrastructure is needed for publish/subscribe model to work. As most ESBs provide support for messaging infrastructure in addition to transformation and routing of services, they are well-suited to meet the combined requirements of SOA and EDA. With such an ESB infrastructure in place, events may cause invocation of services. Services may also trigger an event (Michelson, 2006).

Complex Event Processing (CEP)

The next step to invoking components in an asynchronous manner to events produced in EDA is to detect patterns in the events generated to bring intelligence to business applications in real-time. Such processing is referred to as *complex event processing* (CEP) or *event stream processing*.

An example of CEP is to detect fraud from the events corresponding to usage of a credit card. Another example is stock trading based on patterns detected in events that represent market conditions.

In order to be able to detect patterns in the events generated, CEP applications use rule engines to filter and aggregate events. While in traditional business intelligence systems data is static and processing (queries) on the data is dynamic, in CEP, processing in terms of rules is static while data in terms of events is dynamic.

As CEP may be seen as next step to EDA, SOA applications and infrastructure can play the part of being the source of events as in the case of EDA.

Software as a Service (SaaS)

The basic concept of SOA is to encapsulate coarse-grained functionality and expose it as a service. With the increased adoption of SOA, the principles of service orientation have been leveraged not only from an IT perspective but also to define a business model in which the service consumer only pays for the services consumed. This "pay-as-you-go" model is attractive for small and medium businesses which cannot afford large IT investments in development of functionality that is standard and even commodity-like (e.g., payroll or tax) that is non-core to their business. Such a model is similar to "renting" software rather than "buying or building" it and is referred to as *Software as a Service*. Since this is essentially services model and SOA is an approach for services model, it follows that SOA is fundamental to SaaS.

From a business perspective, when the type of service is standard and the volume of services consumed is low, there is cost savings for the service consumer of SaaS in hardware, software and development effort required to have the functionality built in-house. SaaS service providers also provide free and automatic upgrades to services offered to consumers with better end-user experience.

From a technical perspective, SaaS may be seen as a judicious mix of SOA technologies, Web 2.0 technologies and implementation of SaaS patterns. The functionality that is provided based on "pay-as-you-go" is exposed as services. The service consumers in SaaS are not applications but users – either individual users or users who represent an organization. These service consumers are called *tenants*. The characteristics of the tenants are that they need no "special" infrastructure – a browser should be all that they would need in most cases, no maintenance and they "pay as they go".

In a SaaS application, there is a distinction between a *tenant* and an *end-user*. The *tenant* is an organization with data store logically separated from other tenants. *End-users* are provided accounts and granted access by *tenant* organization to some portion of the tenant's data (deVadoss, 2007).

The service provider deals with service instances, that is run-time representation of a service offered by the service provider, the code bases from which the instances are built, the databases that hold the data for the tenants and security required in providing services. It is possible to define one instance for one tenant or one instance for many tenants or many instances for many tenants.

In SaaS, a single code base serves multiple tenants (unlike in Application Service Provider model). SaaS vendors typically use a *multi-tenant* architecture, which means multiple users of tenant organizations are consuming the same services, but with virtually separate data. The data of multiple tenants may physically be in one database or different databases. The generic requirements of a platform to support SaaS are as follows:

1. hosted platform;
2. multi-tenant;
3. subscription-based business model;
4. secure and performing;
5. services-based integration model;

6. parameterized (customization-based on metadata);
7. multiple delivery channels;
8. SLA based service.

Platform for SaaS that is based on SOA envisioned to address the above generic requirements would include:

1. ***Tenant presentation layer:*** provides customized UI and functionality for multiple tenants based on SLA.
2. ***Service bus:*** loosely couples Business Services provided by instance layer.
3. ***Instance layer:*** provides scalable framework for Business Services to support single/multiple instances as well as supports service security, scalability, metering and management.
4. ***Hosted application layer:*** exposes functionality in hosted applications as services.
5. ***Infrastructure layer:*** provides hardware and software to deploy the hosted applications.

A reference model to address the generic requirements of SaaS platform is shown in Figure 12-1. The reference model may be implemented with the use of technologies for SOA and Web 2.0.

Explanation

The *tenant presentation layer* provides UI for single or multiple tenants. The service bus loosely couples the tenant presentation layer with *Business Services*. *Instance layer* provides a scalable framework for Business Services to support single/multiple instances. Service security, scalability, metering and management are addressed by the instance layer. *Hosted application layer* offers functionality as services based on SaaS model. They are registered with instance layer and managed by it. The hosted application layer may host products or applications from one source or multiple sources.

Products based on Web 2.0 technologies (such as those from JackBe and Tibco) may be considered for implementing the *tenant presentation layer* and the *service bus*. A service delivery platform (such as Microsoft Connected Services Framework) may be considered for implementing the *instance layer* and providing business services to the tenants. *Hosted applications layer* and *infrastructure layer* are typically implemented in data centers and expose services that are delivered to tenants based on SaaS model.

Cloud Computing

The hosted "pay as you go" model of SaaS discussed in the earlier sub-section may be *extended* and *generalized* to not only provide and consume *software as a service* but also *infrastructure* and *platform as service*. In order for this to be

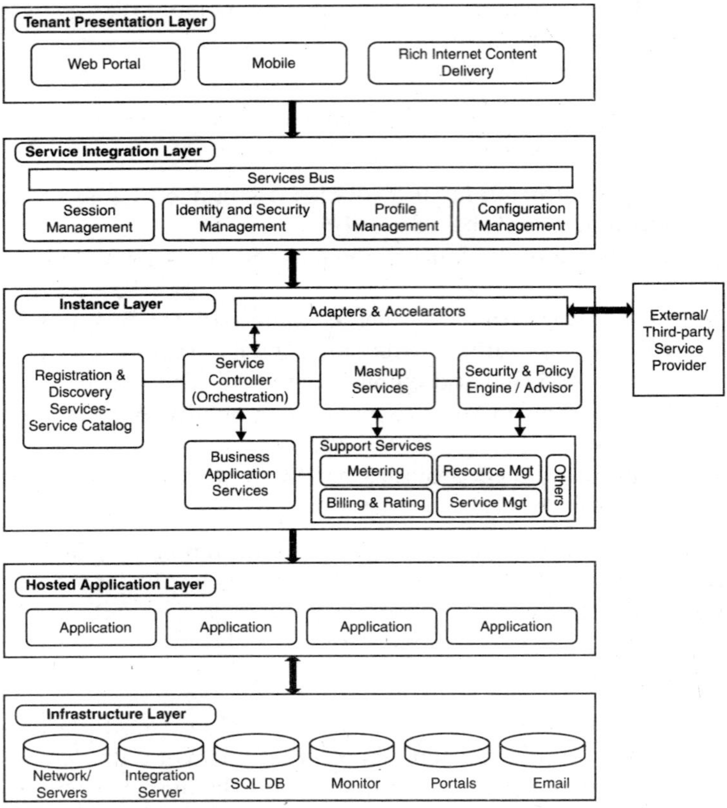

FIGURE 12-1 Reference model for SaaS platform.

technically feasible and economically viable, a ubiquitous computing/communication infrastructure is essential. The "Internet," being that all-pervading infrastructure, provided the foundation for such a computing paradigm that is referred to as *cloud computing*.

Cloud computing is the evolution of leveraging the services model from within an enterprise to beyond the enterprise. A set of computing resources on the internet may expose functionality as a service or computing resource as a service or even a computing platform as a service. The capabilities of cloud for providing infrastructure, platform or software as a service will be referred to as *cloud capabilities*.

With the emergence of the cloud computing paradigm, the adoption of the services model is bound to increase. Gartner predicts that "By 2014, more than 65% of programmatic enterprise access to cloud services will be through SOA-style methods and technologies" (Bradley et al., 2009).

Several possibilities exist for business solutions to leverage SOA and cloud in many innovative ways. The next chapter introduces cloud computing and the subsequent two chapters discuss cloud computing platforms and SOA with cloud services to provide insights into leveraging SOA both in the enterprise and beyond.

12.4 SUMMARY

This chapter presents trends in SOA. Trends have been observed in technologies that have developed independent of SOA but have seen increased adoption for SOA implementation. SOA-BPM convergence is a possibility and the background to this is presented. Web 2.0 technologies have helped define a lightweight model for SOA and a trend towards use of Web 2.0 technologies as front-ends in organizations has also been observed. Open Source is providing a rich set of products and their usage is expected to grow over the next few years. Some of the key open-source products have been listed for ready reference. The trend towards use of hardware in SOA for processing of SOAP and XML in message layer is discussed. Advances in SOA have also been described. The complementary nature of event-driven architecture to provide event-based asynchronous capabilities to services is explained. The business model of providing Software as a Service (SaaS) and a platform to support such applications are discussed in the chapter. The major trend in SOA–cloud computing is introduced and a context set for a detailed discussion in subsequent.

KEY TERMS

Business Process Management (BPM) — BPM is a discipline that automates and optimizes business processes and their performance in an enterprise.

Web 2.0 — Web 2.0 is a set of web technologies that enable services such as social networking, aggregation, tracking and filtering content and collaboration.

Asynchronous JavaScript and XML (AJAX) — AJAX is a set of web development techniques to create highly responsive and interactive web applications. The key aspect of the techniques is asynchronous data transfer with the use of XMLHttpRequest object.

Representational State Transfer (REST) — REST is an alternative technology to SOAP and web services that provides a simple communications interface using XML and HTTP. Every resource in REST is identified by a URI and HTTP is used through GET, POST, PUT and DELETE command requests

Really Simple Syndication (RSS)	RSS is an XML-based web feed format for syndication, that is for publishing frequently changing web content such as news. RSS content can be subscribed by access of the link that supports it and by regular checks to get the updates.
JavaScript Object Notation (JSON)	JSON is a lightweight data interchange format written to be an alternative to XML.
Event-driven architecture (EDA)	EDA is an advanced SOA architecture that includes events. EDA provides asynchronous capabilities between decoupled components based on the publish/subscribe model.
Software as a Service (SaaS)	SaaS is a software application delivery model where a service provider develops a software application and hosts and operates the application for use by its customers.

REFERENCES

Anderson, P. (2007) *What is Web 2.0? Ideas, Technologies and Implications for Education,* JISC Technology and Standards Watch, UK.

Bradley, A., Sholler, D., Natis, Y., Schulman J., and Blechar, M. (2009) *Predicts 2010: Addressing Key Advancements in Application Architecture,* Gartner Document ID: G00173052.

deVadoss, (2007) Securing Data in Hosted Applications, Microsoft, http://www.microsoft.com/technet/community/columns/secmgmt/sm0807.mspx

ebizQ (2008) *How Much Business Value is Your SOA Delivering?*, SOA Governance, an ebizQ publication.

Heffner, R. (2009) *Topic Overview: Insights for CIOs — SOA And Beyond,* Forrester, December 15, 2009.

Hinchcliffe, D. (2005) *Dion Hinchcliffe's SOA Blog: RSS Is the Web 2.0 "Pipe",* http://www.web2journal.com/read/152507.htm

— (2006) *The SOA with Reach: Web-Oriented Architecture,* http://blogs.zdnet.com/Hinchcliffe/?p=27

Hoof, J. (2007) *SOA and EDA: Using Events to Bridge Decoupled Service Boundaries,* http://searchsoa.techtarget.com/tip/0,289483,sid26_gci1246430,00.html

Kambhampaty S. (2007) Architecting Knowledge Management Systems, *Strategic Knowledge Management in Multinational Organizations,* Information Science Reference,Hershey, PA.

Kelly, D. (2006) *The Rise of SOA Appliances*, ebizQ, http://www.ebizq.net/topics/soa/features/7051.html?page=2

Lheureux, B. (2008) *Hot Questions about SOA from Asia*, Gartner Research Document ID Number: G00163150.

Lawson, L. (2007) *What's the Deal with BPM and SOA*, http://www.itbusinessedge.com/blogs/mia/?p=131

McAfee, A. (2006) *Enterprise 2.0: The Dawn of Emergent Collaboration*, MIT Sloan Management Review, Volume 47, Number 3, MIT Sloan School of Management, MA.

Michelson, B. (2006) *Event-Driven Architecture Overview*, Elemental links, http://elementallinks.typepad.com/bmichelson/2006/02/eventdriven_arc.html

Rogers, S. (2008) *A Study in Critical Success Factors for SOA*, IDC Research.

Taft, D. (2007) *The Merging of SOA and Web 2.0*, eWeek.com, http://www.eweek.com/article2/0,1759,2158558,00.asp

Schulte, R., Sholler, D., Bradley, A. (2008) *Key Issues for SOA, EDA and WOA*, Gartner Research Document ID: ID Number: G00158197.

Sinur, J. and Hill, J. (2006) *Predicts 2007: Align BPM and SOA Initiatives Now to Increase Chances of Becoming a Leader by 2010*, Gartner, ID No.: G00144274.

Cloud Computing Concepts

13

CHAPTER

CONTENTS

LEARNING OBJECTIVES

After reading this chapter, you would be able to:

- Understand the cloud computing paradigm.
- Distinguish between different types of cloud and cloud services.
- Gain insights into technologies that enable cloud computing.
- Know the opportunities in cloud computing.

The increased adoption of SOA has resulted in extensive development of technologies for service enablement, integration and orchestration and has also provided enterprises with an alternative business model in offering "Software as a Service" (SaaS). Many enterprises are in the process of migration of their legacy infrastructure to new technologies to build service-oriented applications or expose the functionality of their existing applications as services in order to leverage service-oriented architecture (SOA).

The services model based on SOA has enabled an eco-system of service providers, service hosters and service consumers globally. IT organizations have the option of not only developing full-scale applications through composition of services that are developed in-house but also utilizing services developed by external service providers that may be available in the "cloud" (Boss et al., 2007).

13.1 CLOUD COMPUTING PARADIGM

"Cloud computing is a computing paradigm in which tasks are assigned to a combination of connections, software and services accessed over a network. This network of servers and connections is collectively known as the cloud" (Search-SOA, 2009). The emergence of this paradigm may be seen as a progression from *cluster computing* to *grid computing* to *cloud computing* to address the need of scalable computing on demand. In this paradigm, users do not need to have knowledge, expertise and control over technology infrastructure. The cloud computing technologies enable cloud service providers to abstract the infrastructure details from the users and provide computing capabilities on a *pay as-you-go* basis.

An analogy from civil engineering may be useful here to understand the cloud computing paradigm. A *"home"* is analogous to a certain infrastructure capability. When the residents of the home need additional infrastructure on a short-term basis to accommodate greater number of residents, then a *"hotel"* can represent such a scalable infrastructure where the infrastructure is maintained and managed transparently to the user. The user is charged by the hotel on a *pay as-you-go* basis.

Cloud computing is a style of computing in which scalable IT capabilities are provided as a service using Internet technologies often to multiple external service consumers. In the traditional hosting model of applications, fixed resources are allocated to the software application. While some innovations were made in the traditional model to bring additional processing power on demand, cloud computing involves concepts and technologies to enable truly *"elastic"* resource allocation according to the demand. Infrastructure of IT systems has often been one of the limiting factors for businesses in reaching out to new geographies, handle increased traffic and perform live upgrade for new features (Smith, 2008). Cloud computing can effectively address these challenges.

The elastic nature of a cloud results in several characteristics for cloud computing solutions (Malcom, 2009):

1. First of all, cloud allows for computing capacity to be brought in and removed on demand.
2. Through the use of technologies that enable this dynamic computing infrastructure, the implementation details of the cloud are made transparent to the users (or user systems) of the cloud and thus interactions with the cloud are essentially "service-centric."
3. Usage of cloud capabilities is typically through self-service. The user requests the cloud service provider for resources (computing, storage, software, process, etc.). Cloud services are provisioned accordingly on request and automatically de-provisioned after use.
4. A cloud platform is a minimally managed or self-managed platform, Software automation for provisioning (and de-provisioning services), scheduling and reserving resource capacity, configuring and reporting, controlling access to resources and enforcing policies enable self-management capabilities.
5. "Pay as you go" is also a characteristic of cloud computing. Cloud consumers pay only for the resources they use and hence cloud computing platforms provide mechanisms to capture usage information.

The nature and characteristics of cloud computing present several advantages and disadvantages to solution providers and users. These are listed in Table 13-1.

13.2 TYPES OF CLOUD

On the basis of deployment of cloud infrastructure, the following types of cloud may be defined:

1. ***Public cloud:*** Public cloud, as the name implies, is referred to deployment of cloud infrastructure outside a user's organizational context and is accessed over internet using web technologies.

TABLE 13-1 Pros and cons of cloud computing

Pros	*Cons*
Provides solution for high scalability requirements especially for short duration, high computing demand scenarios (spikes).	Effort for migration to a cloud platform may be significant for existing applications as cloud is a new paradigm.
Infrastructure needed by cloud service consumers limited to what is needed to leverage the cloud; no other software licensing costs.	Risks in adherence to Service Level Agreement (SLA) have to be managed when cloud infrastructure is outside the organization.
On demand Infrastructure provisioning through dynamic capacity management.	Issues related to security, data confidentiality and reliability have to be resolved.
Higher resource utilization efficiency.	Enforcement of compliance and regulation policies present several challenges.
Consumption based billing.	Cloud computing platforms are yet to mature and hence early adopters of cloud computing platforms may need to address vendor lock-in related issues.

2. ***Private cloud:*** When the cloud infrastructure is deployed within the organizational context of the user essentially to leverage the scalability benefits (than those related to management of infrastructure), it is referred to as private cloud.
3. ***Hybrid cloud:*** A hybrid cloud combines some resources offered in a cloud externally with others in an organization. Cloud resources are used as an extension of existing infrastructure with an enterprise. This approach to leveraging the cloud is more practical and is likely to gain wider adoption and hence is the focus of the next chapter.

The capabilities of the above three types of clouds may be grouped under three categories (William, 2008):

1. ***Infrastructure as a Service (IaaS):*** When computing infrastructure, in terms of CPU, memory, operating system, etc., is virtualized and provided as a service to users, the cloud computing capability is referred to as *Infrastructure as a Service (IaaS)*. Such a type of cloud is also referred to *instance cloud*. Thus, a user can request an IaaS service provider to provide a *"compute unit"* with a certain processing *power, memory* and *storage* that may be accessed over Internet through a set of web services.

The compute unit represents a *machine image* whose configuration is set up as per user requirements. An example of IaaS is Amazon Elastic Compute Cloud (Amazon EC2). Amazon EC2 is discussed in detail in the next chapter. The *hotel* analogy from civil engineering described earlier is relevant for this type of cloud service.

2. ***Platform as a Service (PaaS):*** In addition to computing infrastructure, if additional services needed to run and deploy applications developed with certain technologies are made available by cloud service provider then the cloud computing capability is referred to as Platform as a Service (PaaS). Examples of PaaS are Microsoft Azure and IBM CloudBurst. Further, when the architecture of a cloud platform is based on fabric architecture, it is referred to as *fabric cloud*.

   An *exhibition facility* may be seen as an analogy from civil engineering for PaaS. An exhibition facility not only provides the infrastructure but rather a platform for service providers to meet users with a certain interest to showcase their capabilities.
3. ***Software as a Service (SaaS):*** When application functionality that addresses specific business requirements is offered as a service then such a cloud computing capability is referred to as Software as a Service (SaaS). Example of SaaS is CRM capability provided by Salesforce.com with Force.com cloud computing services.

13.3 TECHNOLOGIES THAT ENABLE CLOUD COMPUTING

The cloud computing technologies may be represented in several layers (Johnston, 2009). Figure 13-1 depicts the generic stack of layers for cloud computing.

Description of layers in cloud computing:

1. At the lowest level is the *hardware* that contains servers with CPU, memory, storage and network.
2. The infrastructure layer also has *operating system, hypervisor, virtualization software* and *fabric controller*.
3. A *hypervisor* is a software component that allows multiple operating systems or multiple instances of a single operating system to run on server hardware. Examples of hypervisors include Microsoft Azure Hypervisor, VMware ESX and ESXi and Xen (IBM, 2009).
4. *Virtualization software* allows *virtual machines* (VMs) to be created from a set of servers that execute as though they are real machines with certain compute capability, operating system, storage and network. The virtualization software manages the *creation, configuration, lifetime management* and *IO management* of virtual machines (Neil, 2006).

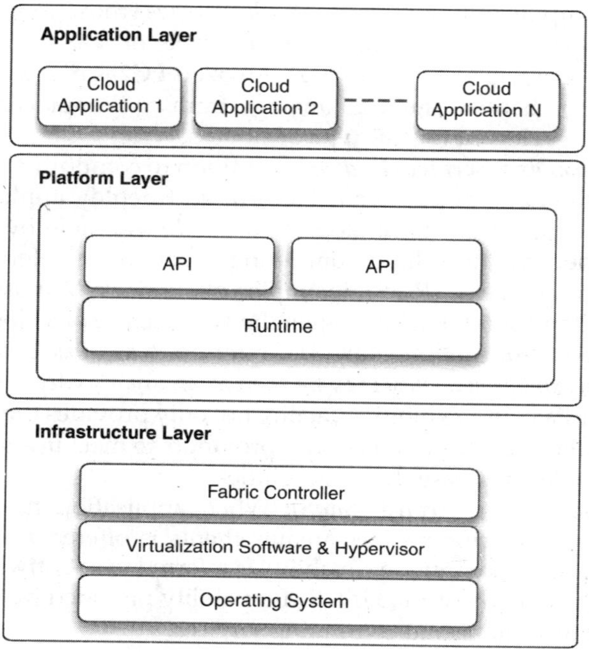

FIGURE 13-1 Cloud computing layers.

5. The *fabric* consists of nodes, which may be physical machines, VMs, or (eventually) partial VMs. *Fabric controller* maps service specifications to available resources, manages service life cycle, monitors system status, recovers from failures and maintains SLA. Essentially, the cloud services are run by the fabric controller.
6. The *platform layer* provides application programming interface (API) for specific technologies such as Microsoft .NET services for Azure or IBM Websphere for CloudBurst that applications developed for cloud can leverage.
7. The application layer consists of applications developed using the capabilities of platform layer to provide cloud services to consumers.

13.4 OPPORTUNITIES IN CLOUD COMPUTING

Industry analysts have projected significant growth in cloud computing market. Gartner projects the world-wide cloud computing market to reach $150.1 billion by 2013.

According to IDC, by 2012, customer spending on IT cloud services will grow almost threefold, to $42 billion, accounting for 9% of customer spending.

With significant possibilities projected by industry analysts, there is a clear business case for all the major participants in the cloud computing marketplace, namely, *cloud platform providers*, *cloud service providers* and *cloud end users*.

Cloud Platform Providers

Technology providers can extend their offerings to leverage the elastic and dynamic nature of cloud and target small and medium business customers through high volume and low cost *pay-as-you-go* model. Thus, while technology providers can continue to sell licenses of software products to enterprises, a cloud option may also be provided to customers who either cannot afford the licenses or who are looking for a competitive offering.

Cloud Service Providers

Service providers, on the other hand, can provide innovative solutions for consumers world-wide through the public cloud. These service providers can focus on the business solution and have the cloud infrastructure address the problems of scalability. Cloud service providers can also provide services to develop, maintain and host cloud platform and applications.

End Users

End user organizations quite often want to focus on their core business and reduce the continuous need to manage the IT infrastructure for non-core activities. As the offerings from cloud platform providers and cloud service providers mature, there is a possibility of moving at least the non-core IT functions to the cloud.

13.5 SUMMARY

The objective of this chapter is to present the concepts of cloud computing. The cloud computing paradigm is explained. Recent trends indicate that cloud computing is likely to grow at a significant rate in view of its elastic and dynamic nature. The different types of cloud and cloud services are described. Insights are provided into technologies that enable cloud computing. The opportunities for cloud platform providers, service providers and end users are discussed.

KEY TERMS

Cloud Computing — Cloud computing is a computing paradigm in which tasks are assigned to a combination of connections, software and services accessed over a network. This network of servers and connections is collectively known as the cloud.

Public cloud	Public cloud refers to deployment of cloud infrastructure outside a user's organizational context and is accessed over internet using web technologies.
Private cloud	When the cloud infrastructure is deployed within the organizational context of the user essentially to leverage the virtualization and scalability benefits, it is referred to as private cloud.
Hybrid Cloud	A hybrid cloud combines the services offered by public cloud with services developed within an organization.
IaaS	When computing infrastructure, in terms of CPU, memory, operating system, etc., is virtualized and provided as a service to users, the cloud computing capability is referred to as Infrastructure as a Service (IaaS).
PaaS	A cloud computing platform with capabilities needed to deploy and cloud applications or services is referred to as Platform as a Service (PaaS).
SaaS	When application functionality that addresses specific business requirements is offered as a service then such a cloud computing capability is referred to as Software as a Service (SaaS).

REFERENCES

Boss, G., Malladi, P., Quan, D., Legregni L. and Hall H., (2007) *Cloud computing*, IBM Whitepaper, http://download.boulder.ibm.com/ibmdl/pub/software/dw/wes/hipods/Cloud_computing_wp_final_8Oct.pdf

Brodkin, J. (2008) *Seven Cloud-Computing Security Risks*, NETWORKWORLD, http://www.networkworld.com/news/2008/070208-cloud.html

Chaganti, P. (2008) *Cloud Computing with Amazon Web Services*, Part 1, developerWorks, IBM.

IBM Education Assistant (2009) *CloudBurst – Hypervisor Integration*. CloudBurst_Hypervisor_Integration.pdf

Johnston, S (2009) *Cloud Computing Stack Showing Infrastructure, Platform and Application Layers as well as Clients and Servers*, http://en.wikipedia.org/wiki/File:Cloud_Computing_Stack.svg

Malcom, D. (2009) *The Five Defining Characteristics of Cloud Computing*. Tech News on ZDNet.

Neil (2006) *Hypervisor, Virtualization Stack, and Device Virtualization Architectures*. Microsoft WinHEC.

SearchSOA. (2009) *Cloud Computing*, http://searchsoa.techtarget.com/sDefinition/0,,sid26_gci1287881,00.html

Smith, E. (2008) Under the Hood: Inside The Cloud Computing Hosting Environment, Microsoft PDC 2008.

William Blair and Company (2008) *The Next Stage of Computing, Technology: Software & Services*. Industry Report (08-063).

Cloud Computing Platforms

14

CHAPTER

CONTENTS

LEARNING OBJECTIVES

After reading this chapter, you would be able to:

- Distinguish between different cloud computing platforms.
- Know the salient features of the key cloud computing platforms.
- Gain an understanding of the cloud offerings from the major cloud platform providers.

Several technology providers have developed offerings for the cloud. These offerings may be grouped under two categories:

1. *Cloud computing platforms* that provide capabilities for cloud service providers to develop services for the cloud.
2. *Cloud services* that provide capabilities to end users and end user applications. This category is discussed in detail in the next chapter.

Leveraging the cloud to develop services requires an understanding of the capabilities of available cloud computing platforms. An overview of the five cloud computing platforms is presented in the following sections:

1. Amazon EC2;
2. Google App Engine;
3. IBM CloudBurst;
4. Microsoft Azure;
5. Salesforce Force.com.

Each of the sections presents the features of a cloud computing platform. In order to provide consistency, the description of each of the platform summarizes the salient features. The cloud offerings are presented based on the layers shown in Figure 14-1.

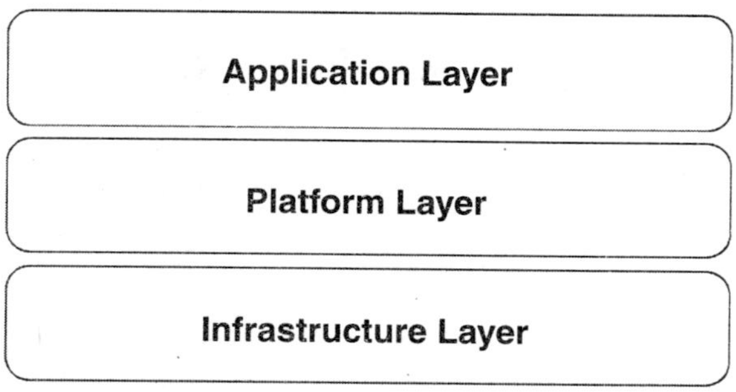

FIGURE 14-1 Cloud platform layers.

14.1 AMAZON EC2

Amazon is a pioneer in public cloud computing and a leader in Infrastructure as a Service (IaaS) with its offering *Amazon Elastic Compute Cloud (EC2)*. EC2 provides instances with a variety of operating systems running on virtual machines that may be accessed through a web service interface. Each of the instances is called Amazon Machine Image (AMI) with full root/Administrator access (Amazon, 2009).

The salient features of Amazon EC2 are summarized in Table 14-1.

Amazon EC2 uses XEN based virtualization for its infrastructure layer (Perilli, 2006). While developers can use the instances to build applications and deploy them, EC2 does not provide platform level support for development of applications. It does, however, provide the following support services that can be leveraged by cloud applications:

1. *Amazon SimpleDB* that provides core database functions of data indexing and querying in the cloud.
2. *Amazon CloudFront* for content delivery to distribute content to end users with low latency, high data transfer speeds.
3. *Amazon Simple Storage S3* to store and retrieve large amounts of data on Internet.

TABLE 14-1 Amazon EC2 features

Cloud offering	Amazon EC2
Description	Collection of web services offered over the Internet
Cloud capability	IaaS (bBased on XEN Hypervisor)
Target users	Individual users, enterprise customers
Target applications	Not applicable
Scalability and failover	User to implement scalability and failover
Development support	Amazon provides instances (machine images) with several operating systems. Developers may use any development tools that run in the instances.
Languages supported	Not applicable
Storage support	Simple Storage Service, SimpleDB, Relational Database Service

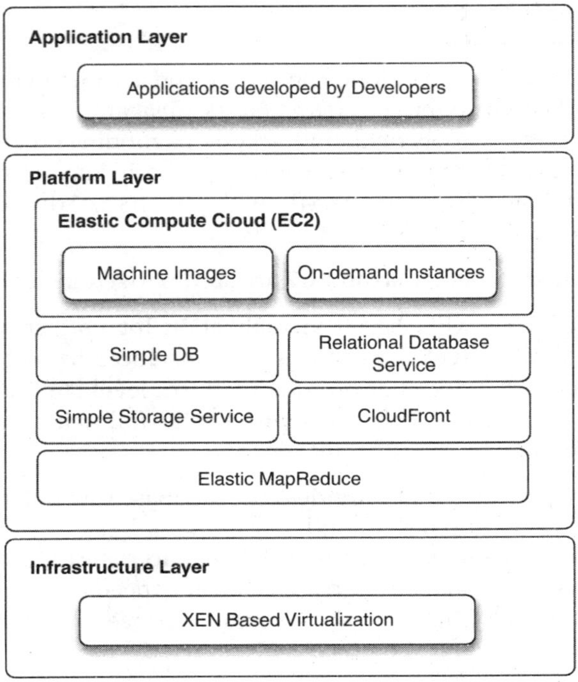

FIGURE 14-2 Cloud offering from Amazon.

4. *Amazon Elastic MapReduce* to provision capacity to perform data-intensive tasks for applications such as web indexing and data mining.
5. *Amazon Relational Database Service (Amazon RDS)* to setup, operate and scale MySQL in the cloud.

Amazon also provides a *virtual private cloud* capability to secure and provide a seamless bridge between an organization's existing IT infrastructure and the public cloud services. The cloud offering from Amazon may be depicted pictorially as shown in Figure 14-2.

14.2 GOOGLE APP ENGINE

Google offers *Google App Engine* as the platform for building web-based applications and deploying them on the cloud. Google App Engine supports both Java and Python runtime environments and so applications can be developed with Java or Python languages and deployed on Google cloud infrastructure.

Applications developed for Google App Engine run in a separate secure environment (sandbox) with limited access to operating system including no access to file system. Also, application code runs only in response to a request or a task (scheduled or queued) and accesses other computers on the Internet through URL fetch and email services. The Google App Engine SDK provides application programming interface (API) for Java and Python using which applications can be developed (AppEngine, 2009).

The salient features of Google App Engine are summarized in Table 14-2.

Google App Engine uses proprietory virtualization technology for its cloud platform. It provides several services to perform common operations when managing applications such as URL Fetch to access resources on the web, mail, memcache for high-performance in memory caching, image manipulation and for task management (AppEngine, 2009).

Google App Engine also provides access to the following services for use in applications:

1. *Datastore* is a distributed data storage service provided by App Engine that has a query engine and support transactions. The datastore is unlike a traditional database and has entities that are "schemaless" on which the application code imposes a structure.
2. Google Accounts is user authentication capability with which App Engine integrates. Users already with a Google Account created for a different application (such as Google Mail) may be authenticated with the same account rather than have a separate account created.

TABLE 14-2 Google App Engine features

Cloud offering	Google App Engine
Description	Platform for developing and hosting web applications in Google-managed data centers
Cloud capability	PaaS
Target users	Mostly individual users
Target applications	Only web applications
Scalability and failover	Supports auto scaling/provisioning
Development support	Provides support for basic editing, local simulation, and deployment tools with plug-ins for Eclipse IDE. Java and Python SDK and runtime environments.
Languages supported	Java/Python
Storage support	BigTable, Datastore APIs

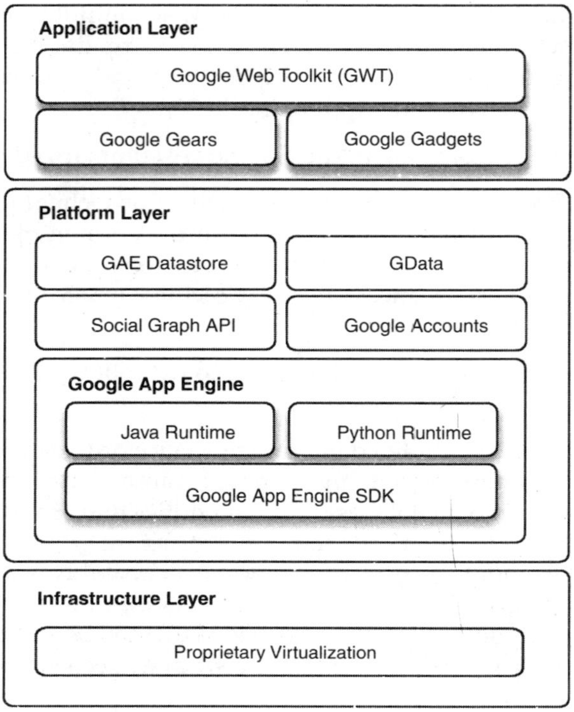

FIGURE 14-3 Cloud offering from Google.

Developers not only can use the Google App Engine SDK that provides APIs for Java and Python to develop programs to deploy to the cloud infrastructure but can also leverage any of the following application development capabilities that Google provides:

1. *Google Web Toolkit (GWT)* for front-end application development in Java (Niccolai, 2008).
2. Gears to enhance the capabilities of the browser (Niccolai, 2008).
3. *Google Gadets* to add dynamic content to any page.
4. *Social Graph API* to access public connections in social networking.
5. *GData* to use a protocol to read and write data on the web.

The cloud offering from Google may be depicted pictorially as shown in Figure 14-3.

14.3 IBM CLOUDBURST

CloudBurst is a private cloud offering from IBM. It is a pre-packaged integrated system of hardware storage, networking, virtualization and also service management software to create a private cloud. CloudBurst provides Platform as a Service (PaaS) which can be further enhanced with IBM CloudBurst WebSphere Appliance to manage WebSphere images in the cloud. In short, IBM CloudBurst delivers a cloud computing infrastructure into an enterprise and WebSphere CloudBurst Appliance delivers the WebSphere-based application environment into the IBM CloudBurst cloud (Gaur, 2009).

The salient features of IBM CloudBurst are summarized in Table 14-3.

CloudBurst uses VMWARE hypervisor for virtualization at infrastructure layer (IBM Education, 2009). A monitoring service based on Tivoli monitoring manages operating system, database and middleware servers.

The hardware for CloudBurst consists of different configurations of IBM BladeCenter servers. The private cloud also comes with automation software and pre-packaged automation templates. The automation software is *Tivoli's provisioning manager* which provides automation workflows and script enabled service component. It automatically provisions required server, storage and software when needed by developers without human intervention. It also automatically de-provisions unused capacity, making it available for other users and increasing efficiency of data center assets (IBM, 2009).

A Service Catalog is provided that lists pre-engineered services that developers can choose from. A self-service portal is also provided that allows developers to access IT infrastructure.

TABLE 14-3 IBM CloudBurst features

Cloud offering	IBM CloudBurst
Description	Pre-packaged Integrated Cloud Computing Platform (with hardware, server, storage, virtualization and service management software)
Cloud capability	PaaS (based on VMWARE Hypervisor)
Target users	Enterprise users
Target applications	Enterprise applications
Scalability and failover	Supports scaling/provisioning. Additionally, allows scaling and provisioning of WebSphere images with IBM WebSphere CloudBurst Appliance
Development support	Any development environment supported by the operating system run by the hypervisor
Languages supported	Any language supported by the development environment
Storage support	Any storage supported by operating system

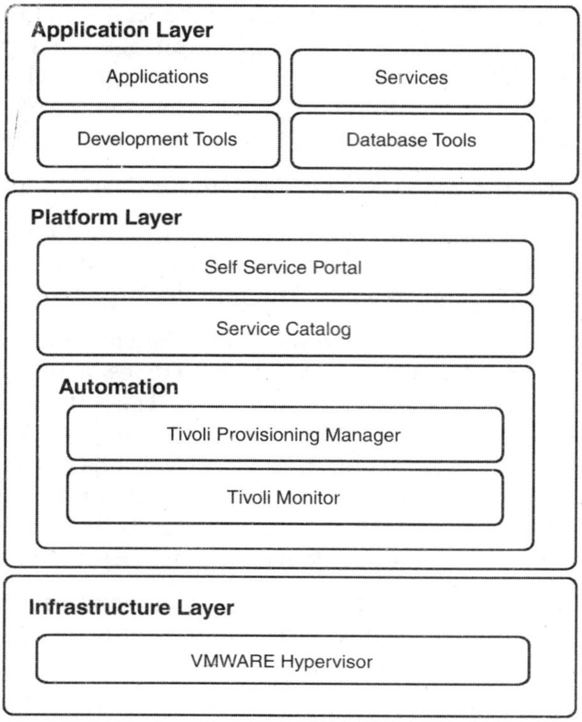

FIGURE 14-4 Cloud offering from IBM.

The CloudBurst offering from IBM may be depicted pictorially as shown in Figure 14-4.

14.4 MICROSOFT AZURE

The PaaS offering from Microsoft is Azure. Windows Azure has three main components (Chappell, July 2009):

1. Compute service that runs applications.
2. Storage service that stores data.
3. Fabric that supports the compute and storage services.

Azure enables both public and hybrid models for cloud. Applications may be developed *on-premise* of enterprises for Microsoft Windows (using .NET, C#, etc.) and deployed on the cloud to benefit from the *compute service* available in cloud that runs in the Microsoft data center. Organizations may choose to leverage only the *storage service* of Azure to store both unstructured and relational data (using *SQL Azure services*). Alternatively, enterprises may also deploy some

TABLE 14-4 Microsoft Azure features

Cloud offering	Microsoft Azure
Description	Cloud Computing Platform that supports both public and hybrid models
Cloud capability	PaaS (based on Windows Azure Hypervisor)
Target users	Enterprise and individual users
Target applications	Windows applications built to leverage SQL Azure Services and Azure AppFabric
Scalability and failover	Supports scaling/provisioning through Fabric architecture and fault tolerance through replication
Development support	Visual Studio
Languages supported	C#, C++
Storage support	Storage Service available

of the applications on the cloud while the rest of them run in their data centers all interconnected using Windows Azure *AppFabric*. Formerly called ".NET Services," *AppFabric* provides a service bus for workflow services and connectivity across network and organizational boundaries (Azure Platform, 2009).

The salient features of Microsoft Azure are summarized in Table 14-4.

Windows Azure creates and manages virtual machines (VMs) that run instances of Windows 2008 using Windows Azure Hypervisor (based on Hyper–V). The *fabric* consists of nodes, which may be physical machines, VMs, or (eventually) partial VMs. Fabric controller maps service specifications to available resources, manages service life cycle, monitors system status, recovers from failures and maintains service level agreement (SLA). Essentially, the cloud services are run by the fabric controller.

The cloud offerings from Microsoft may be depicted pictorially as shown in Figure 14-5.

The compute service runs applications based on two instance types (Chappell, March 2009):

1. Web role that takes incoming web requests (HTTP/HTTPS) and runs code in a VM with IIS.
2. Worker role that are "self-directed" and run tasks like a batch program.

The storage service stores data in blobs, tables or queues and for fault tolerance replicates data three times.

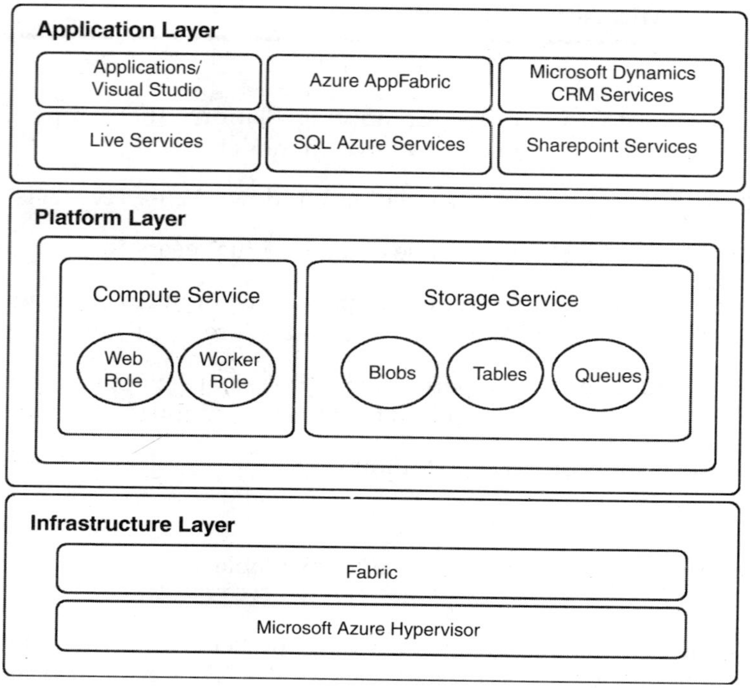

FIGURE 14-5 Cloud offering from Microsoft.

In order to deploy an application in the cloud, a user logs into the Azure Portal with Windows Live ID and creates a *hosting* account in order to run applications and a *storage account* to store data. The user then deploys the application specifying the number of instances it needs.

Live Services uses an open-standards programming interface and resource model that spans devices and reach a community of millions of Windows Live ID users.

SQL Services extends the Microsoft SQL Server into the cloud and enables relational queries, search, and also data synchronization with mobile users and remote offices.

14.5 SALESFORCE FORCE.COM

Salesforce.com is a leader in *customer relationship management* (CRM) solution based on the SaaS model. Force.com is a Platform as a Service (PaaS) offering for the cloud for application development and deployment.

Force.com is based on *multitenant architecture* in which all users and apps share a single, common infrastructure and code base. It supports a metadata-driven development model in which data models, objects, forms and workflows are defined by metadata in a declarative manner (developerforce, Winter '10).

Force.com provides a set of API that defines web service calls to access all data stored in the platform. It also provides a framework called *Visualforce* for creating user interfaces for applications in the cloud.

A cloud computing programming language called *Apex* has been designed by Force.com for building business applications to manage data and processes for the Force.com platform which is based on Java. Applications developed for Force.com platform may be shared using a facility called *AppExchange*.

The salient features of Force.com are summarized in Table 14-5.

The cloud offerings from Salesforce.com may be depicted pictorially as shown in Figure 14-6 (salesforce.com, 2008).

Force.com is based on the multi-tenant architecture. In order that a statically compiled executable application can meet the unique challenge of multi-tenancy of being dynamic in nature, a runtime engine exists that generates application components from metadata. In Force.com, there is a clear separation of the compiled runtime engine (kernel), application data, the metadata that describes the base functionality of an application, and the metadata that corresponds to each tenant's data and customizations. This clear separation makes it possible

TABLE 14-5 Force.com features

Cloud offering	Force.com
Description	Force.com is an integrated set of tools and application services to build applications and run on the same infrastructure that delivers the current Salesforce CRM applications
Cloud capability	PaaS (based on multi-tenant architecture)
Target users	Enterprise customers
Target applications	Business applications (e.g., Sales, CRM applications)
Scalability and failover	Web, CRM
Development support	Provides a component-based user interface framework called Visualforce
Languages supported	Apex
Storage support	Proprietary metadata-based data support

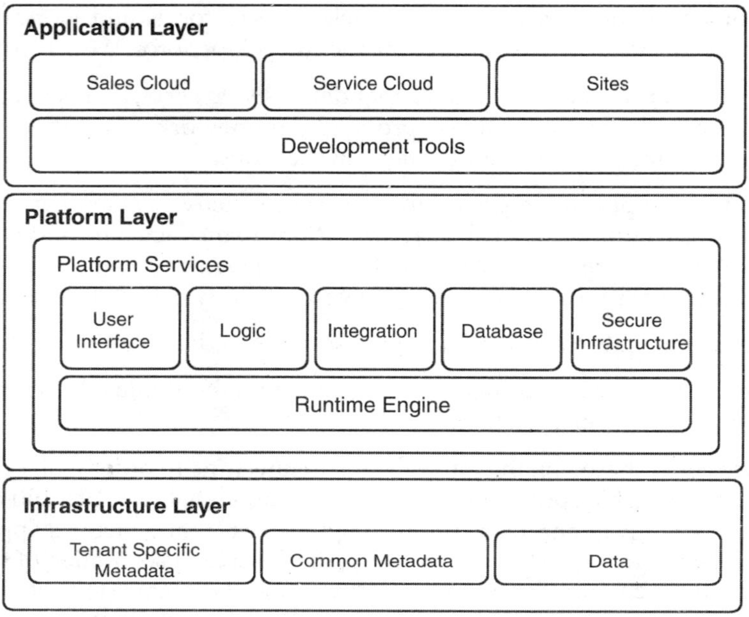

FIGURE 14-6 Cloud offering from Salesforce.com.

to independently update the system kernel, modify the core application, or customize tenant-specific components at no risk of one affecting the others.

In order to build user interfaces, Force.com *Sites* enables creation of public web applications and web sites that run natively on Force.com. User interfaces may also be developed using Force.com's *Builder*, a tool which provides a facility to change the layout and the order of data fields on pages, create complex reports and create different views of the data for different users (Chinnam, 2009).

Force.com incorporates workflow engine capabilities in order to provide common, reusable process components such as task creation, record assignment, time-based actions and even event-based system integration. These components can be made a part of application logic. Apex programs may also be written to extend applications to include business logic and functionality.

Integration capabilities are provided to applications using Force.com's Web Services API. This API may be used to integrate with applications built with .NET, Java and PHP, middleware products such as those available from Tibco and Microsoft's BizTalk, ETL tools such as Informatica and ERPs such as SAP R/3 (through pre-packaged connectors).

Proprietary metadata-based support is provided to describe database objects such as tables and fields. Data operations can accordingly be performed on the database objects.

In order to support development of business applications better, Salesforce.com provides *Sales Cloud* and *Service Cloud* which may be leveraged in conjunction with capabilities provided by Force.com (onCloudComputing, 2009)

14.6 SUMMARY

The objective of this chapter is to present various cloud computing platforms presently available. In order to leverage the key cloud computing platforms it is necessary to know the salient features of the key cloud computing platforms. It is also necessary to gain a clear understanding of the offerings for the cloud from the major cloud platform providers.

KEY TERMS

Cloud Computing Cloud computing is a computing paradigm in which tasks are assigned to a combination of connections, software and services accessed over a network. This network of servers and connections is collectively known as the cloud.

Public Cloud Public cloud refers to deployment of cloud infrastructure outside a user's organizational context and is accessed over internet using web technologies.

Private Cloud When the cloud infrastructure is deployed within the organizational context of the user essentially to leverage the virtualization and scalability benefits, it is referred to as private cloud.

Hybrid Cloud A hybrid cloud combines the services offered by public cloud with services developed within an organization.

IaaS When computing infrastructure, in terms of CPU, memory, operating system, etc., is virtualized and provided as a service to users, the cloud computing capability is referred to as Infrastructure as a Service (IaaS).

PaaS A cloud computing platform with capabilities needed to deploy and cloud applications or services is referred to as Platform as a Service (PaaS).

SaaS When application functionality that addresses specific business requirements is offered as a service then such a cloud computing capability is referred to as Software as a Service (SaaS).

REFERENCES

Amazon (2009) *Amazon Elastic Compute Cloud* (Amazon EC2). http://aws.amazon.com/ec2/

AppEngine (2009) *What Is Google App Engine?* Google. http://code.google.com/appengine/docs/whatisgoogleappengine.html

Chinnam, C. (2009), *Architecture of Force.com Platform*. SalesForce.com Deep Dive.

developerforce (Winter '10) *Force.com Platform Fundamentals*. http://www.salesforce.com/us/developer/docs/fundamentals/index.htm

Chappell, D. (March 2009) *Introducing Windows AZURE*. Sponsored by Microsoft Corporation.

Chappell, D. (July 2009) *Windows AZURE and ISVS – A Guide for Decision Makers*, Sponsored by Microsoft Corporation.

Gaur, N. (2009) *IBM CloudBurst and WebSphere CloudBurst Appliance Compared*. SYS-CON Media Inc.

IBM Education Assistant (2009) *CloudBurst – Hypervisor Integration*. CloudBurst_Hypervisor_Integration.pdf

IBM (2009) *A Breakthrough in Service Delivery for Data CenterWorkloads – IBM CloudBurst, IBM.*

Malcom, D. (2009) *The five defining characteristics of cloud computing*. Tech News on ZDNet.

Neil, M. (2006) *Hypervisor, Virtualization Stack, And Device Virtualization Architectures*. Microsoft WinHEC.

Niccolai, M. (2008) *Google App Engine New York Hack-a-thon*. Google App Engine Blog.

onCloudComputing (2009) *With Salesforce CRM the Sant Corporation Runs its Entire Business in the Cloud*. Cloud Computing News and Resources. Aug 12, 2009.

Perilli, A. (2006) Amazon launches Xen-powered virtual datacenter on demand. virtualization.info

salesforce.com (2008) *The Force.com Multitenant Architecture Understanding the Design of Salesforce.com's Internet Application Development Platform*. WHITE PAPER.

Azure Platform (2009) *Microsoft Windows Azure Platform* AppFabric. MSDN. http://msdn.microsoft.com/en-us/azure/netservices.aspx

SOA with Cloud Services

15 CHAPTER

CONTENTS

LEARNING OBJECTIVES

After reading this chapter, you would be able to:

- Understand the possibilities with cloud services.
- Know the considerations for cloud services.
- Gain insights into SOA with enterprise and cloud services.
- Understand the implementation aspects of SOA with enterprise and cloud services.

In Chapters 3–12, the application of the principles of SOA in an enterprise context was discussed. In the last two chapters, the concepts of cloud computing and the platforms that enable cloud computing have been elaborated.

Cloud computing brings about several interesting possibilities for service-oriented architecture (SOA) and vice versa. In order to support the "pay as you go" model, greater rigor will be needed on service design which would lead to increased maturity in SOA practices. Cloud infrastructure also provides a scalable environment for services. The emphasis on architecture in SOA solutions and the focus on governance will help build better cloud solutions (Linthicum, 2010). All the cloud platform may be leveraged keeping the services model in mind. This is because the course-grained nature of a service and the principle of loose coupling enable masking of the implementation detail which is essential to a cloud platform. Also, the maturity of the technologies enabling the services model and global adoption across industry verticals has resulted in new possibilities.

Cloud service providers can expose business functionality as services on the cloud that may be consumed based on "pay as you go" model. These are referred to as *cloud services.* Enterprises can focus on building applications and services that are core to their business and leverage the cloud and cloud services to fulfill all the other needs. The efficiency of the business adopting the approach of "building what they must" and "buying what they can" at a service level (rather than at an application level) is likely to be higher as an increasing number of rich services will be available on the cloud at competitive prices in the "cloud marketplace." With the issues of deployment and management of applications and their associated infrastructure being the concern of the cloud service provider, enterprises can focus on synergy and reuse among applications developed across different regions, thereby increasing the overall efficiency and return on investment (ROI) to their applications.

This approach of combining of cloud services and enterprise services to address the business needs of an organization is discussed in this chapter.

15.1 CLOUD SERVICES

Three kinds of cloud services may be defined (Chappell, 2008):

1. *SaaS user services* that are exposed by a SaaS application deployed in the cloud.
2. *Attached services* that are exposed by cloud applications to provide extra functionality to support on-premise enterprise applications.
3. *Cloud platform services* that provide cloud services for creating applications.

Attached services provide functionality in the cloud to support SOA (Katzan, 2009). This kind of cloud services is the focus of rest of the chapter.

In order to explore the possibilities with cloud services, the following scenarios may be considered:

Scenario 1

Consider an online store that offers several products to users for purchase over the Internet. Such an Internet application would include several business processes, namely:

1. User Registration process;
2. Shopping Cart process;
3. Payment process;
4. Fulfillment process.

Each step of the business processes mentioned above may be implemented as an *activity service* (discussed in Chapter 4). For instance, the User Registration process may involve the following three steps:

1. submission of profile by user;
2. approval of user by store;
3. mailing of User ID/Password to user.

Further, the data of the products and registered users may be exposed as data services. Also, the content required by store dashboard (e.g., number of orders received on a given day, amount of revenue generated, etc.) may be made available by client services.

Now in the online store illustration provided in earlier section, consider that the store decides on introducing a fraud detection step in its payment process. Fraud detection is a specialized function that would typically not fall under the core competence of the online store. There is also a significant cost in developing and maintaining such functionality. Instead, such services may easily be utilized from the "cloud" (e.g., Credit Card Fraud detection service available from StrikeIron).

This illustration may be taken forward much further. Since the core business of the Online store is conducting business – receiving orders and payments online and fulfilling the same, and not managing the IT infrastructure, migrating the shopping cart application to a cloud platform such as Google App Engine of Microsoft Azure is a possibility depending on the technology of the shopping cart application. Further, any storage and compute capability needed for migration may also be "procured" from Amazon EC2 or Microsoft Azure cloud. Should the Online store see the need, it can take the cloud possibility to the point of even leveraging the *sales cloud* and *service cloud* capabilities with salesforce.com to have CRM functionality, all from the cloud.

Scenario 2

Consider a large enterprise with several hundred servers and large number of applications dealing with data that cannot be moved out of the enterprise's data center due to security reasons. Managing hundreds of users in data centers and optimally utilizing them to address peak loads is considerable effort and cost. A private cloud platform such as IBM's CloudBurst deployed in the organizations data center can provide the required benefits.

15.2 CONSIDERATIONS FOR CLOUD SERVICES

While several interesting possibilities exist in combining cloud services and enterprise services, it is necessary to keep in mind several considerations in doing so. The following are the key considerations when leveraging services from the cloud (Chaganti, 2008):

1. **Security:** Security needs to be ensured for interactions with services in the cloud.
2. **Availability:** A service outside the enterprise context may not be available all the time due to various reasons. Strategies to leverage alternative services or cache content provided by cloud services need to be considered.
3. **Metering:** The service consumption may need to be logged and metered to ensure reconciliation of payments to providers of cloud services.
4. **Data formats:** The formats in which data is provided by cloud services may be different from the standards within an enterprise. Data may need to be transformed to the required format to address the needs of the enterprise.
5. **Legal:** The terms of use of cloud services and statutory obligations on transfer of data beyond the enterprise boundary need to be considered as well.

15.3 ENABLEMENT SERVICES

The considerations for leveraging the cloud services will require enhancements to the Strawman architecture for SOA (discussed in Chapter 4) that is based on services only within an enterprise. While the Activity services (A), Business Process services (B), Client services (C), and Data services (D) continue to be

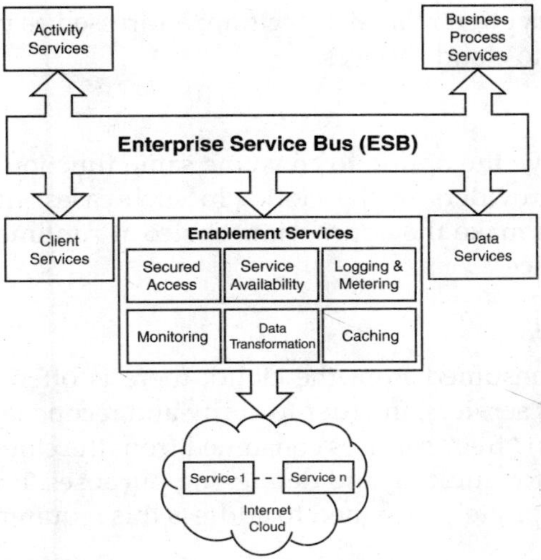

FIGURE 15-1 Strawman architecture for SOA with enterprise and cloud services.

relevant, a new type of services, termed as Enablement services (E), deserves to be included as depicted in Figure 15-1.

Enablement services encapsulate access to the cloud services. Taking into account the needs of the business processes in the enterprise, those enablement services will have to be identified that interact with the services in the cloud.

One of the key principles employed in architecting enterprise-level solutions is to localize interactions with external systems to specific sub-system(s) in an enterprise sometimes referred to as gateway. The enablement services and the associated infrastructure constitute a gateway to cloud services to ensure that changes in the cloud have minimal impact on the applications within the enterprise. In fact, the enablement services abstract cloud services such that services and applications in the enterprise are not even aware that the services are being offered by providers in the cloud. The advantage with this approach to leveraging the cloud is that existing services that are not core to the business of the enterprise may be replaced by cloud services and vice versa.

The key functions supported by enablement services are:

1. secured access;
2. service availability;
3. logging and metering;
4. monitoring;
5. data transformation;
6. caching.

The enablement services ensure that the necessary security checks are done for any access made outside the firewall of the enterprise. Authentication, authorization and encryption related aspects are addressed as part of the providing secured access to cloud services.

Service Availability

An enterprise may have the option to consume same functionality provided by multiple service providers in the cloud. In such cases, the enablement services defined could make the appropriate choice at runtime based on the availability of the service.

Logging and Metering

For "paid" services consumed from the cloud, there is often a need to log and meter the usage of services, in order to verify and reconcile invoices from service providers. Even "free" services consumed from the cloud may require some level of logging for auditing and debugging purposes. Enablement services have to be appropriately designed to address this requirement.

Monitoring

The invocations to cloud services have to be monitored on a regular basis to fine-tune and address issues related to service quality. The infrastructure for enablement services should be such that monitoring of interactions with cloud services is possible.

Data Transformation

It is quite likely that data provided by the services from the cloud is not in the format required by the business processes in the enterprise. Also, data from multiple service invocations may need to be combined suitably. This would usually require enablement services to apply data transformation techniques on data received from cloud services.

Caching

Services, such as those related to "News," may provide content that changes at a relatively slow rate. Data received from such services is cached by enablement services to optimize service invocations.

Depending on the nature and extent to which services in the cloud are used, the enablement services designed and deployed may vary from simple to significantly complex.

One of the key requirements in the design of enablement services is the ability to change the services consumed from the cloud. This is because service providers will continuously offer enhanced services. Also, new service providers will provide alternatives and competitive pricing. Service composition based on Mashup techniques (with the use of tools such as JackBe Presto) can provide the flexibility required.

The enablement services may be implemented on different types of infrastructure based on the complexity of cloud services and the extent of functionality required. For simple scenarios requiring very little of functionality discussed, an application server (or even a proxy server) may serve the purpose of encapsulating access to cloud services. To address more sophisticated requirements, enterprise service bus (ESB) or hybrid cloud infrastructure (e.g., Microsoft Azure) may be required to implement the enablement services. Also, the Strawman architecture presents a logical perspective based on the architecture principle of separation of concerns. The actual implementation may utilize the existing ESB and other infrastructure for optimization and efficient utilization of resources.

15.4 IMPLEMENTATION OF SOA WITH ENTERPRISE AND CLOUD SERVICES

The Strawman architecture shown in Figure 15-1 is a starting point to define the SOA architecture for an enterprise based on enterprise and cloud services.

The following are some of the key activities that need to be undertaken to arrive at the SOA architecture:

1. Understanding of the business processes of the enterprise.
2. Gathering of technical details of IT applications and infrastructure that implement the business processes.
3. Insights into shortcomings/drawbacks of the current business processes or IT applications/infrastructure.
4. Determination of future business goals and drivers.
5. Identification of types of services that would be leveraged from the cloud.
6. Development of Proof-of-Concept (PoC) applications in order to make technology decisions.
7. Definition of SOA architecture for the enterprise.
8. Formulation of SOA Governance Model.

When the SOA architecture for the enterprise is determined, the key steps for implementation include the following:

1. Service Oriented Analysis and Design Process (SOAD) for identification of activity, business process, client, data and enablement services.
2. Service development.
3. Service deployment.
4. Monitoring of enterprise and cloud services.
5. Governance.

15.5 SUMMARY

The objective of this chapter is to present an approach of combining cloud services and enterprise services in order to address the business needs of an organization. The scenarios for leveraging cloud services are discussed. The considerations for cloud services are detailed. The Strawman architecture for SOA with enterprise and cloud services, including a new type of service known as enablement service, is discussed.

KEY TERMS

Strawman architecture	Strawman architecture is the initial architecture that serves as a starting point for developing the target architecture. It is refined over number of iterations and results in the development of the target architecture.
Activity services	The activity services or business services encapsulate functionality exposed as services in various business applications. These services are reusable business level services that can be orchestrated as part of a configured business process.
Business Process Services	Business process services handle orchestration of business processes implemented as a set of services. These services control the flow and interaction of the different services.
Client Services	Client services deliver content to the business users that require an aggregated enterprise view. They provide presentation content to the "frontend" applications of the enterprise.
Data Services	Data services encapsulate access to data in various sources such as relational databases, spreadsheets, data warehouses or a system external to the organizational context.
Enablement services	A new type of services, referred to as enablement services, have been defined that encapsulate access to cloud services.

REFERENCE

Chaganti, P. (2008) *Cloud Computing with Amazon Web Services, Part 1*, developerWorks, IBM.

Chappell, D. (2008) *A Short Introduction to Cloud Platforms*, Chappell & Associates.

Katzan, H. (2009) *Cloud Software Service: Concepts, Technology, Economics, Service Science*, **1**(4), 256–269.

Linthicum, D. (2010) *Cloud Computing and SOA Convergence in your Enterprise*, Addison-Wesley.

ANNEXURE A

SOA Technologies – PoC

The technologies for SOA were presented in Chapter 9. In order to provide greater insight into their capabilities, this annexure presents several proof-of-concept (PoC) implementations developed with representative technologies for service enablement, integration and orchestration.

A.1 LOAN MANAGEMENT SYSTEM – PoC REQUIREMENTS

The scenario is that of a bank that issues loans to customers. The PoC implements the following functionality (also explained in Chapter 8) of a Loan Management System (LMS).

1. A bank customer initiates the loan approval process by requesting a loan. This results in a notification being sent to a loan officer who makes a decision to approve or reject the loan.
2. If the loan officer rejects the loan request, a notification is sent to the bank customer about the same.
3. Alternatively, if the loan officer approves the loan then system checks if the loan amount is more than 10,000 (in any currency say dollars).
4. In case the loan amount is less than 10,000 (say in dollars) then a notification is sent to the bank customer about the approval of the loan.
5. If the loan amount is more than 10,000 (say in dollars) then a confirmation is required from a manager and he/she is notified. Manager makes the final decision on loan approval and notifications are sent accordingly.

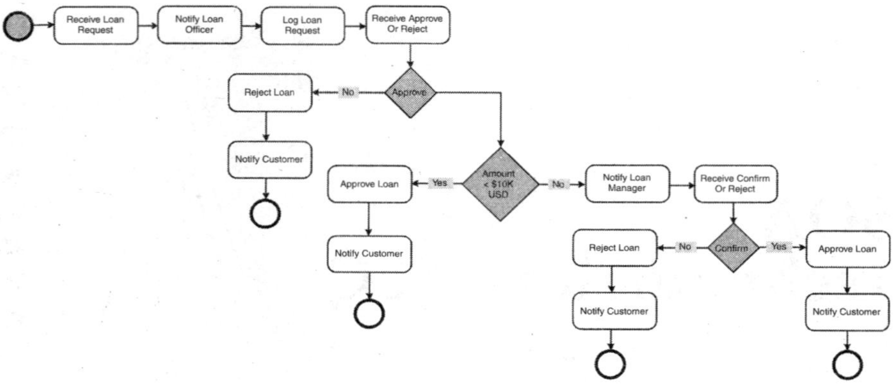

FIGURE A.1 Business process LMS.

The business process model for the functionality of an LMS is depicted in Figure A.1.

Three types of actors interact with LMS – Customer, Loan Officer and Loan Manager.

The key use cases of LMS are as follows:

Use Case 1: Request Loan
Actor: Customer
The customer provides details of the loan that he/she wishes to avail.

Use Case 2: Approve Loan
Actor: Loan Officer
The loan officer examines each of the loan requests and approves/rejects the loan.

Use Case 3: Confirm Loan
Actor: Loan Manager
When the loan amount exceeds a certain limit as defined by the policy (in this case $10,000), an additional approval is needed by the loan manager. The loan manager reviews the approved loan requests and confirms the loan.

A.2 ARCHITECTURE OF AN LMS

The solution for the Loan Management System consists of service-consumer application and service-provider application integrated by an ESB. The loan approval business process of LMS is externalized and exposed as a process service (*Loan Process Service*) by the BPEL orchestration engine. As a part of the

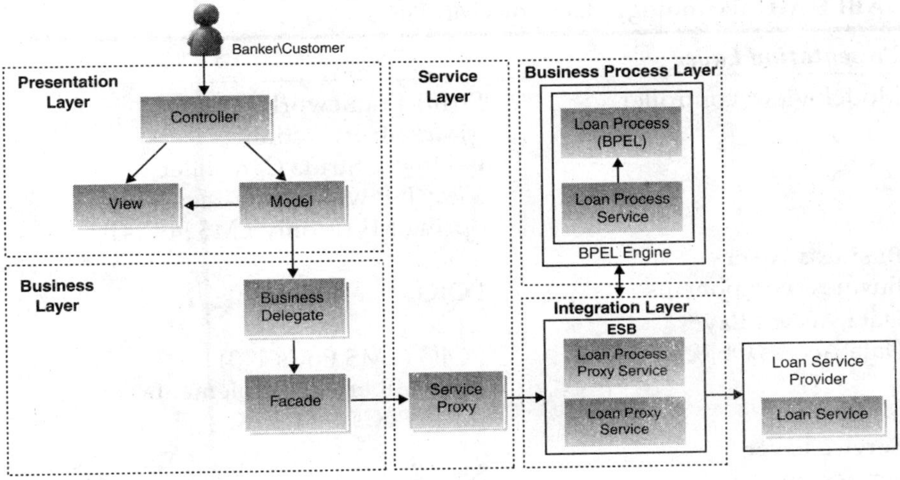

FIGURE A.2 Architecture of LMS.

orchestration of process service, the BPEL engine invokes the activity service (*Loan Service*) exposed by the service provider application.

The architecture of an LMS is depicted in Figure A.2. It may be noted that the purpose of PoC is to illustrate the technologies used for service enablement, integration and orchestration rather than build a complete application. Hence, only the layers and patterns required for the PoC have been shown in the architecture and implemented in the system.

The architecture of an LMS has the following layers:

1. ***Presentation layer:*** mode-view-controller components.
2. ***Business layer:*** business delegate components and façade components.
3. ***Service layer:*** service proxy for loan service.
4. ***Integration layer:*** ESB and process orchestration engine.

The presentation layer implements the *MVC pattern* to provide the user interface for users. The business layer is encapsulated by *business delegate* pattern. It also implements the *façade pattern* to interact with the service layer. The service layer implements the *service proxy pattern* to provide the business layer with an interface to the service. The integration layer implements the *Loan Process Service* which is a process service exposed by the BPEL orchestration engine. The integration layer also implements the ESB to integrate the service provider and service consumer. The service provider application exposes an activity service (*loan service*) that is invoked by the orchestration engine as part of the orchestration of process service.

TABLE A.1 Technology stack for LMS PoCs

Presentation Layer	
Model–view–controller	Struts Framework *Model:* Struts Action *Controller:* Struts Controller *View:* JSP with Struts Tags Spring MVC (only LMS PoC 4)
Business Layer	
Business components	POJO
Data Access Layer	
Data Access Objects	POJO (LMS PoCs 1–3) JPA – Hibernate Implementation (LMS PoCs 4–5)
Service Layer	
Service proxy	POJO
Business Process Layer	
BPEL engine	ActiveBPEL deployed in Tomcat (LMS PoCs 1–3) Intalio BPMS deployed in Tomcat (LMS PoCs 4–5)
Integration Layer	
ESB	BEA AquaLogic Service Bus (LMS PoC 1) OR WSO2 ESB (LMS PoC 2, LMS PoC 4, LMS PoC 5) OR IBM WebSphere ESB (LMS PoC 3)
Server for service provider	Tomcat Server with Apache Axis for web service run-time
Server for service consumer	Tomcat Server

Note: The objective of including the PoCs is to illustrate the use of the principles of SOA (and not to showcase best practices).

Technology Stack

The technologies used to implement the LMS PoCs provided on the companion CD-ROM are given in Table A.1.

A.3 IMPLEMENTATION OF LMS PoCs 1–3

The MVC pattern for presentation layer is developed using the Apache Struts framework. Patterns of business layer and service layer are implemented as Java objects. The process service is orchestrated in ActiveBPEL while AquaLogic ESB is used for integration. The process orchestration engine and ESB are deployed in Tomcat Server.

This section presents sample code used in various layers.

Presentation Layer (of Service Consumer)

The screens that provided the UI for user interactions for the three key use cases are developed as JSP pages.

Screen shot of the UI used by customer

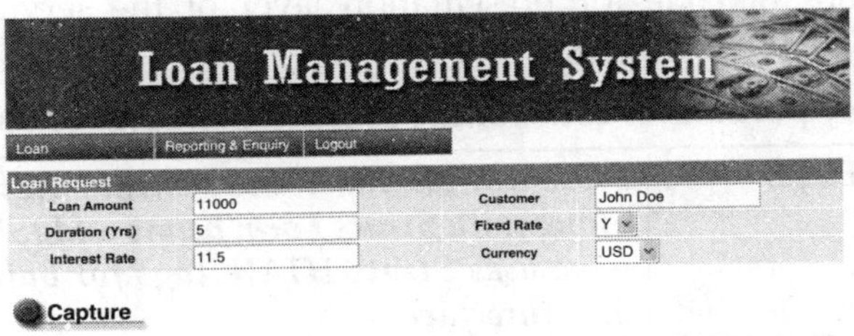

FIGURE A.3 Request Loan screen.

Screen shots of UI used by loan officer

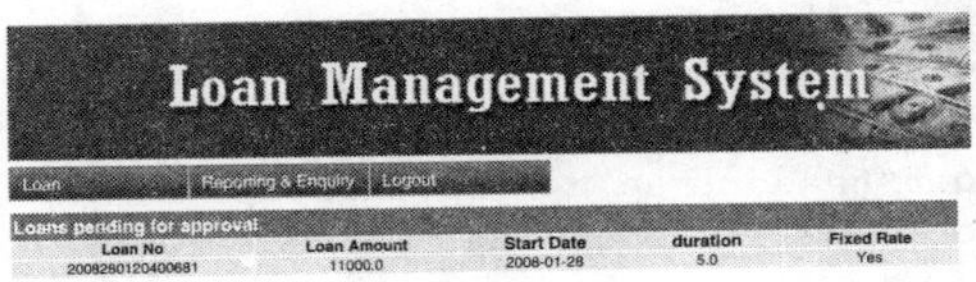

FIGURE A.4 Pending Approvals screen.

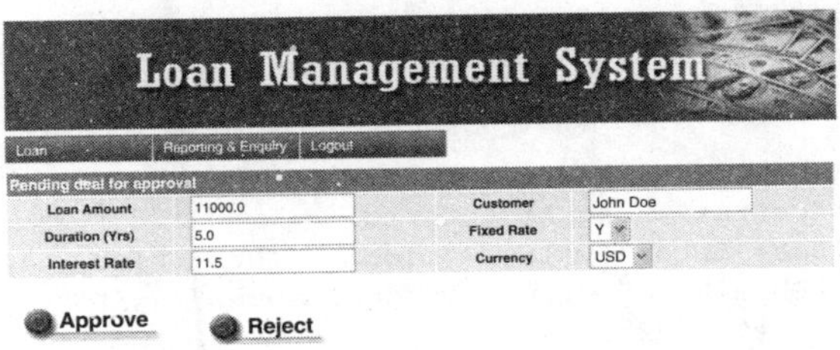

FIGURE A.5 Approve Loan request screen.

Screen shots of UI used by loan manager

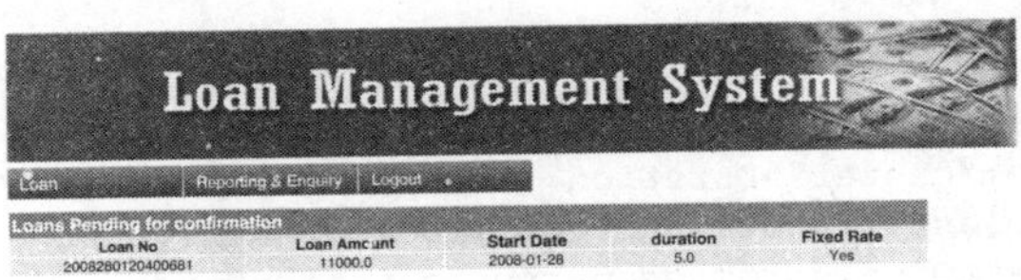

FIGURE A.6 Pending confirmations screen.

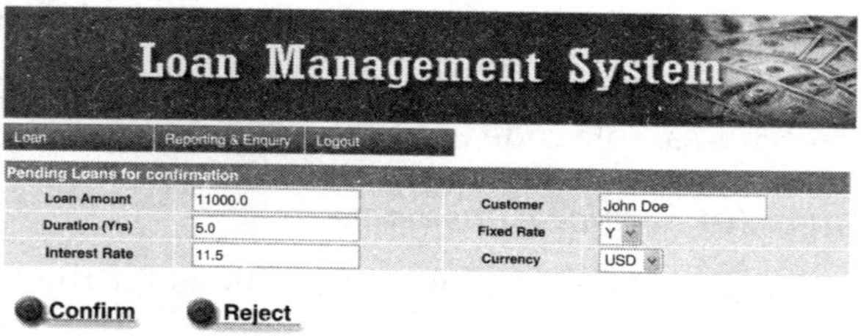

FIGURE A.7 Confirm Loan screen.

The key portions of code for presentation layer of the service consumer application are given in Table A.2.

TABLE A.2 Key portions of code for the presentation layer of LMS PoCs 1–3

Presentation Layer	*Presentation layer uses Struts Action classes along with Struts Form beans and JSP pages. JSP page uses Struts HTML tags for building of the user interface.*
JSP Page	

```
<%@ taglib uri="/WEB-INF/struts-html.tld" prefix="html"%>
<%@ taglib uri="/WEB-INF/struts-bean.tld" prefix="bean"%>
<html:html>
<HEAD>
<TITLE>Deal Input - Capture Deal</TITLE>
</HEAD>
<BODY>
<jsp:include page="header.jsp"></jsp:include>
<html:form action="/deal_capture.do" method="POST">
<br>
<table cellpadding="0" cellspacing="1" width="75%" border="0">
<tr>
        <td class="header1" valign="middle"
        colspan=4>Loan Request</td>
</tr>
<tr>
        <td class="intd2bold" valign="middle"
        align="center">Loan Amount</td>
        <td class="intd2" valign="middle"><html:text
        name="LDDealForm" property="dealAmount"/></td>
        <td class="intd2bold"
        valign="middle" align="center">Customer</td>
        <td class="intd2" valign="middle"><html:text
        name="LDDealForm" property="customer"/>
        </td>
</tr>
<tr>
        <td class="intd2bold" valign="middle"
        align="center">Duration (Yrs)</td>
        <td class="intd2" valign="middle"><html:text
        name="LDDealForm" property="duration" value="5"/></td>
        <td class="intd2bold" valign="middle"
```

(continued)

TABLE A.2 *(Continued)*

```
        align="center">Fixed Rate</td>
        <td class="intd2" valign="middle"><html:select
        name="LDDealForm" property="fixedRate">
        <html:optionsCollection name="LDDealForm"
        property="myFixedRate"/></html:select></td>
</tr>
<tr>
        <td class="intd2bold" valign="middle" align="center">Interest
        Rate</td>
             <td class="intd2" valign="middle"><html:text
        name="LDDealForm" property="interestRate"
        value="4.5"/></td>
        <td class="intd2bold"
        valign="middle" align="center">Currency</td>
        <td class="intd2" valign="middle"><html:select
        name="LDDealForm" property="currency">
        <html:optionsCollection name="LDDealForm"
        property="myCurrency"/></html:select></td>
</tr>
</table>
<br>
<html:hidden name="LDDealForm" property="status" value="NEW"/>
<a href="javascript:document.LDDealForm.submit()"><html:img
src="images/capture.jpg" hspace="4" border="0"/></a>
</html:form>
</BODY>
</html:html>
```

Struts Form Action	**When a user submits a JSP page, form bean populates the required data which is used in action class. *Action* classes use *business delegate* to access the functionality of business layer.**

```
package com.lms.action;

import javax.servlet.http.HttpServletRequest;
import javax.servlet.http.HttpServletResponse;

import org.apache.struts.action.ActionError;
import org.apache.struts.action.ActionErrors;
import org.apache.struts.action.ActionForm;
import org.apache.struts.action.ActionForward;
import org.apache.struts.action.ActionMapping;

import com.lms.bd.LDDealCaptureBD;
import com.lms.bo.Deal;
import com.lms.exceptions.LDException;
import com.lms.formbeans.LDDealForm;

public class LDDealCaptureAction extends LDBaseAction {

    public ActionForward executeAction(ActionMapping mapping,
    ActionForm form,
                            HttpServletRequest request, HttpServletResponse
        response) {
```

(continued)

TABLE A.2 (*Continued*)

```
        ActionErrors errors = new ActionErrors();
        ActionForward forward = new ActionForward();
        LDDealForm lDDealForm = (LDDealForm) form;
        Deal deal = lDDealForm.populateDeal(); try {
                if(!isValidUser()) {
                    throw new LDException("User is not logged in");
                }
        } catch (LDException e) {
                errors.add(e.getMessage(),
        new ActionError(e.getMessage()));
                lDDealForm.setMessage(e.getMessage());
                e.printStackTrace();
        }
        try {
                LDDealCaptureBD businessDelegate =
        new LDDealCaptureBD();
                businessDelegate.logLoanRequest(deal);
        } catch (LDException e) {
                errors.add(e.getMessage(), new ActionError(
                        e.getMessage()));
                lDDealForm.setMessage(e.getMessage());
        }
        if (!errors.isEmpty()) {
                saveErrors(request, errors);
                forward = mapping.findForward("ERROR");
        } else {
                lDDealForm.setMessage("Deal captured successfully.
        Your deal reference number is " + deal.getDealNo());
                forward = mapping.findForward("SUCCESS");
        }
        return (forward);
      }
}
```

Business Layer (of Service Consumer)

The business layer implements the *business delegate* and *façade* patterns. The key portions of code for business layer of the service consumer application are given in Table A.3.

TABLE A.3 Key portions of code for the business layer of LMS PoCs 1–3

Business Layer	***Business layer implements business components and façade components. Business delegate components delegate the request to appropriate façade component. For each business delegate component, there is one façade component.***
Business Delegate Component	

```
package com.lms.bd;

import java.text.SimpleDateFormat;
```

(continued)

TABLE A.3 (*Continued*)

```
import java.util.Date;
import java.util.List;
import com.lms.bo.Deal;
import com.lms.exceptions.LDException;
import com.lms.facade.LDDealCaptureFacade;

public class LDDealCaptureBD {
    public void logLoanRequest(Deal deal) throws LDException {
    LDDealCaptureFacade facade = new LDDealCaptureFacade();
    deal.setDealNo(generateDealNumber());
    facade.logLoanRequest(deal);
}
    private String generateDealNumber() {
    String dealNumber = dateFormat.format(new Date());
    return dealNumber + Math.round(Math.random()*100);
}
```

Facade Component	**Facade component interacts with service proxy component to communicate with integration layer.**

```
package com.lms.facade;

import com.lms.bo.Deal;
import com.lms.exceptions.LDException;
import com.lms.proxy.ServiceProxy;

public class LDDealCaptureFacade {
    public void logLoanRequest(Deal deal) throws LDException {
    ServiceProxy proxy = new ServiceProxy();
        proxy.log(deal.getDealNo(), deal.getFixedRate(),
        deal.getDuration(), deal.getInterestRate(),
    deal.getCustomer(), deal.getCurrency(), deal.getDealAmount(),
    deal.getStatus());
    }
}
```

Service Layer (of Service Consumer)

The service layer implements the *service proxy* pattern. The key portions of code for service layer of the service consumer application are given in Table A.4.

TABLE A.4 Key portions of code for the service layer of LMS PoCs 1–3

Service Layer	*Service Proxy is a proxy class which manages the remote communication with service provider.*
Service Proxy	

```
package com.lms.proxy;

import java.net.MalformedURLException;
import java.net.URL;
import java.rmi.RemoteException;

import javax.xml.namespace.QName;
```

(*continued*)

TABLE A.4 (*Continued*)

```
import javax.xml.rpc.Service;
import javax.xml.rpc.ServiceException;
import javax.xml.rpc.ServiceFactory;
import com.lms.exceptions.LDException;
public class ServiceProxy {
   private static String url =
   "http://localhost:7001/LoanProcessProxy?wsdl";
   private static String nameSpaceUri =
   "http://localhost:8080/aqualoans/services/LoanProcess";
   private static String serviceName = "LoanProcessService";
   private static String portName = "LoanProcessServicePort";
private LoanProcess proxy;
         public ServiceProxy() throws LDException {
    try {
              URL urlWsdl = new URL(url);
     ServiceFactory serviceFactory = ServiceFactory.newInstance();
     Service service = serviceFactory.createService(urlWsdl, new
         QName(nameSpaceUri, serviceName));
              proxy = (LoanProcess) service.getPort(new QName
(nameSpaceUri, portName), LoanProcess.class);
         } catch (ServiceException e) {
              e.printStackTrace();
              throw new LDException(e.toString());
         } catch (MalformedURLException e) {
              e.printStackTrace();
              throw new LDException(e.toString());
         }
    }
public void log(java.lang.String loanNo, java.lang.String fixedRate,
double duration, double interestRate, java.lang.String customer, java.
lang.String currency, double loanAmount, java.lang.String
status) throws LDException {
    try {
          proxy.log(loanNo, fixedRate, duration, interestRate,
 customer, currency, loanAmount, status);
         } catch (RemoteException e) {
                    e.printStackTrace();
                    throw new LDException(e.toString());
         }
}
public  void  approveOrReject(java.lang.String  loanNo,  java.lang.
String fixedRate, double duration, double interestRate, java.lang.
String customer, java.lang.String currency, double loanAmount, java.
lang.String status) throws LDException {
    try {
                    proxy.approveOrReject(loanNo, fixedRate,
duration, interestRate, customer, currency, loanAmount, status);
         } catch (RemoteException e) {
                    e.printStackTrace();
```

(*continued*)

TABLE A.4 (*Continued*)

```
                    throw new LDException(e.toString());
            }
    }
    public void confirmOrReject(java.lang.String loanNo, java.lang.
String fixedRate, double duration, double interestRate, java.lang.
String customer, java.lang.String currency, double loanAmount, java.
lang.String status) throws LDException {
    try {
                    proxy.confirmOrReject(loanNo, fixedRate,
duration, interestRate, customer, currency, loanAmount, status);
            } catch (RemoteException e) {
                    e.printStackTrace();
                    throw new LDException(e.toString());
            }
    }
}
```

Integration Layer

The integration layer implements the *ESB* pattern. It also implements the process orchestration engine that orchestrates the business process exposed by *Loan Process Service*. The diagram and BPEL code for orchestrated business process are given in Annexure B.

As indicated in Chapter 9, several technology options are available for implementing the ESB. In order to provide insights into the process involved in implementing the ESB, PoCs have been developed with the following key technology options and described in this section:

1. BEA AquaLogic Service Bus (LMS PoC 1);
2. WSO2 ESB (LMS PoC 2);
3. IBM WebSphere-ESB (LMS PoC 3).

The code for the PoCs is provided on the CD for ready reference.

Integration with BEA AquaLogic Service Bus

The *Loan Service* provides web methods invoked during orchestration of a loan approval process and is implemented with Apache Axis on Tomcat server. The web method invocations at various steps of process orchestration are made over the BEA AquaLogic Enterprise Service Bus. Thus, the ESB forms a "glue" for service integration as shown in Figure A.8.

A proxy service (*Loan Proxy*) is registered in BEA AquaLogic for the *Loan Service* developed with Apache Axis and deployed on Tomcat server. The BEA AquaLogic is configured to route calls to the *Loan Proxy* service to the corresponding methods of *Loan Service* on Tomcat server. The steps involved in creating a proxy service using BEA AquaLogic Service Bus are discussed in Chapter 9.

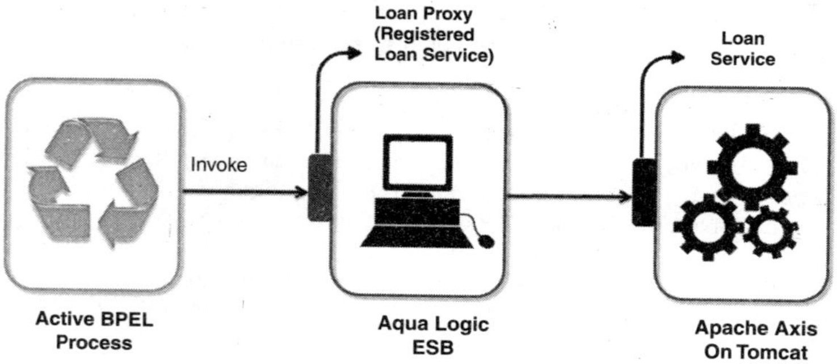

FIGURE A.8 Process service integration with AquaLogic ESB.

When the customer requests for a loan, a long-running process is triggered and the process logs the loan request, sends a notification to the loan officer and the process waits for the loan officer's intervention for approval or rejection. The state may be viewed using Active BPEL monitor.

Figure A.9 shows the state of the long-running process after a customer requests for a loan. It is found to be waiting for the approval of the loan officer.

Integration with WSO2 ESB

This section describes the integration of services using WSO2 ESB product. Figure A.10 depicts the integration scenario where *Loan Service* is accessed via WSO2 ESB for the same Loan Management solution.

Configuration of WSO2 ESB

Creation of proxy service in WSO2 ESB involves the following two steps:

1. Log into WSO2 administration page at the URL http://localhost:9443/esb on the server where WSO2 ESB is installed.
2. Choose *Proxy Services → Add* function from the left menu. Provide as input the name of the proxy service as shown in Figure A.11.
3. Specify target endpoint by selecting the option *Specify as Anonymous → Address Endpoint* from the pull-down menu to the right of the *Target Endpoint* label shown in Figure A.12. Provide as input the location of the service and click *Save.*
4. Specify outgoing sequence by selecting the option *Specify as Anonymous → Add Mediator → Core → Send* from the pull-down menu to the right of the Outgoing message label shown in Figure A.13. Click *Save* option on this screen.
5. Click on *Advanced* (button shown in Figure A.11) to specify more configuration options on the main proxy service screen.

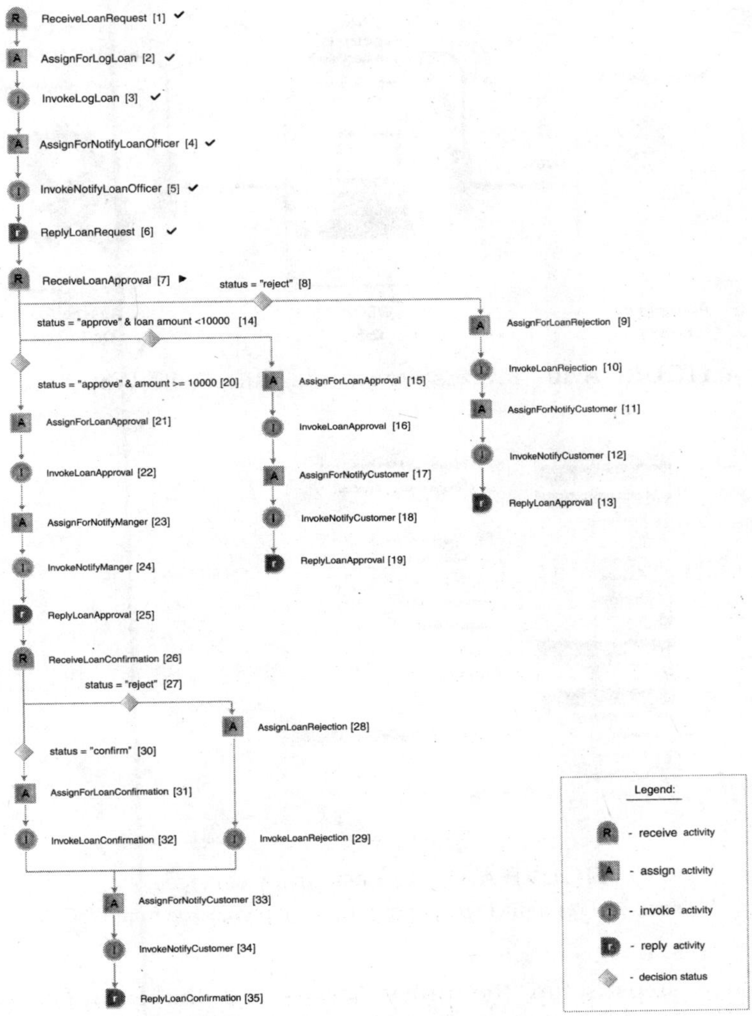

FIGURE A.9 State of business process (after receiving request for loan from customer).

6. Retain the default transport configuration and click on the *Next* button.
7. Retain the default QOS Configuration and click on the *Next* button.
8. Select *Publish WSDL → Specify Source URL* option. Provide as input the location of the WSDL file as shown in Figure A.14. Click on the *Finish* button.
9. Save the configuration with *Configuration → Save* button on the menu as shown in Figure A.15.

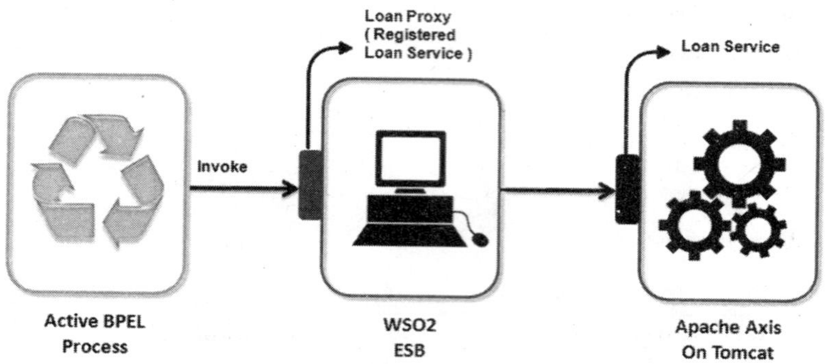

FIGURE A.10 Process service integration with WSO2 ESB.

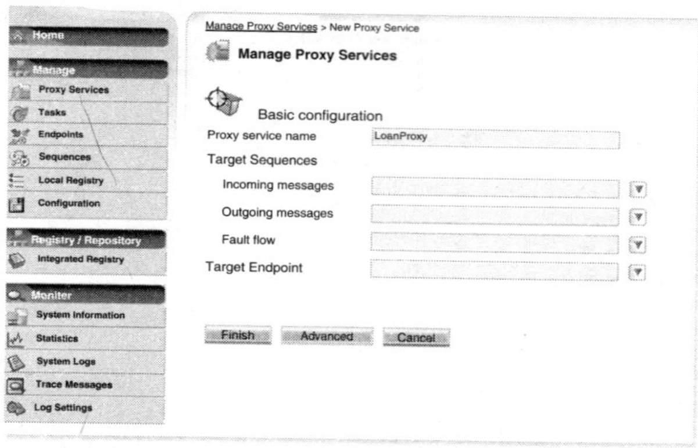

FIGURE A.11 Choose proxy services.
Source: WSO2 product offering (printed with permission from WSO2).

The above steps setup the proxy service for the *Loan Service* web service. During the process orchestration, ActiveBPEL based business process uses the proxy service to access the *Loan Service* via the WSO2 ESB.

Integration with IBM WebSphere ESB

This section describes the integration of services using IBM WebSphere ESB Version 6.1 product. This section describes the integration scenario where *Loan Service* is accessed via IBM WebSphere ESB for the same Loan Management solution.

Integration with IBM WebSphere ESB is accomplished by the use of mediation components. All components in IBM WebSphere ESB are SCA components and can be wired with other components. External components are accessed

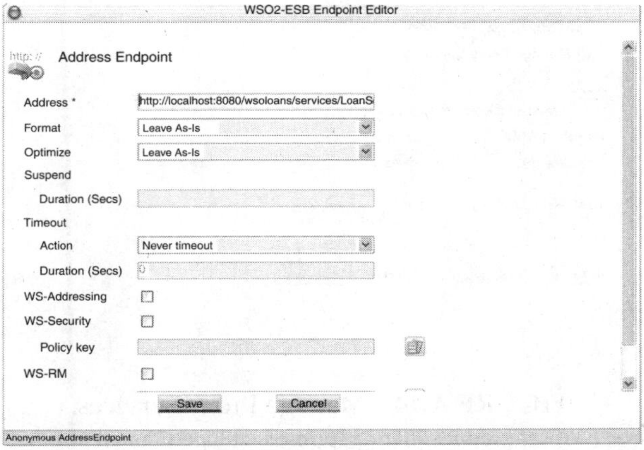

FIGURE A.12 Specify address endpoint.
Source: WSO2 product offering (printed with permission from WSO2).

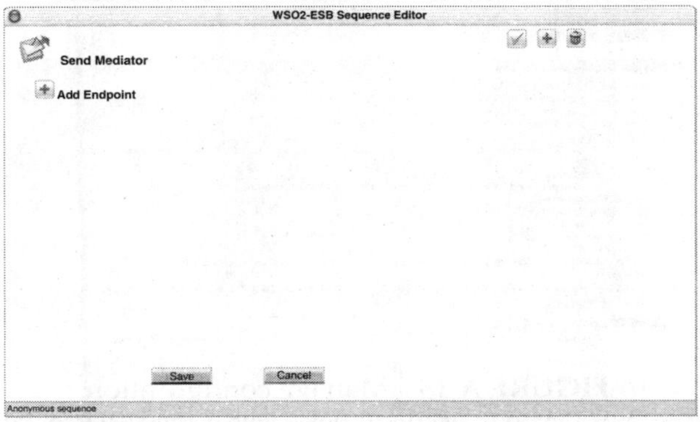

FIGURE A.13 Specify outgoing sequence.
Source: WSO2 product offering (printed with permission from WSO2).

through *imports* defined and mediation components are exposed to external systems via *export* bindings (e.g. Web service binding).

The IBM WebSphere ESB is configured to route calls to *Loan Service* through a mediation flow.

Configuration of IBM WebSphere ESB

The creation of mediation flow in IBM WebSphere ESB (i.e. WID) involves the following steps:

1. Open IBM WebSphere Integration Developer. This is a development tool for developing SOA applications.

FIGURE A.14 Manage Proxy Services.
Source: WSO2 product offering (printed with permission from WSO2).

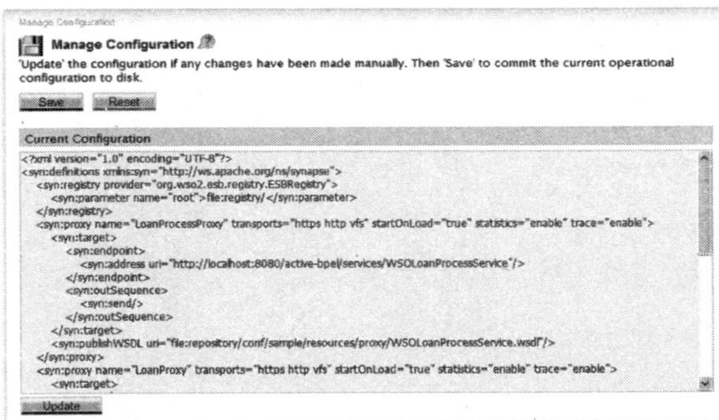

FIGURE A.15 Manage configuration.
Source: WSO2 product offering (printed with permission from WSO2).

2. Create a mediation module using *File* → *New* → *Mediation module*. Uncheck *Create Mediation component* checkbox in the dialog box as shown in Figure A.16.
3. A new project is created for configuring mediation flow.
4. Import *LoanService.wsdl* into the project. Use *File* →*Import* →*File System* option.
5. This creates an interface (*Loan Service*), web service (*Loan Service)* port and import component (*LoanServiceImport1*) in the project.
6. Open the assembly diagram.
7. Drag the web service (*Loan Service*) port onto the assembly diagram. A prompt appears for component creation as shown in Figure A.17. Select **Import with Web Service Binding** option.

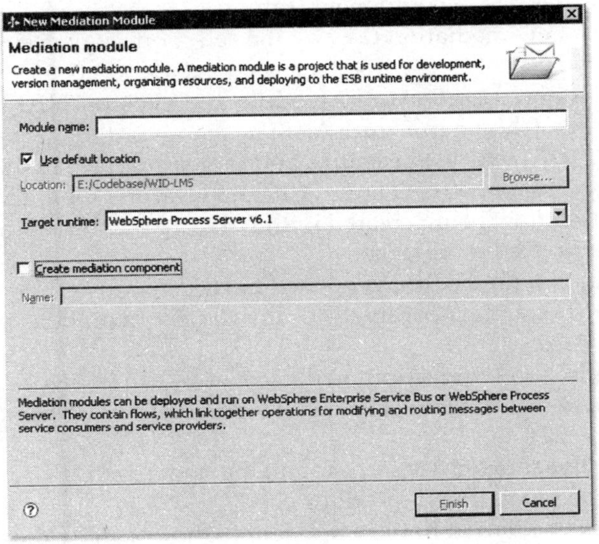

FIGURE A.16 Create a Mediation module.
Source: IBM WebSphere product offering (printed with permission from IBM).

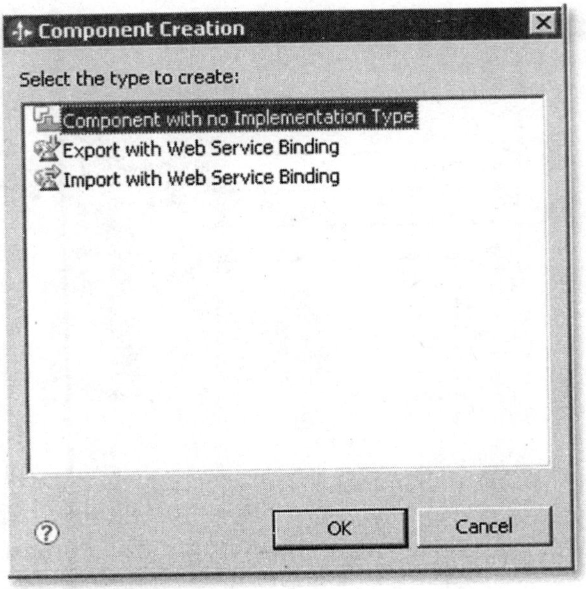

FIGURE A.17 Component creation.
Source: IBM WebSphere product offering (printed with permission from IBM).

8. This creates a SCA component (Import).
9. Create a new mediation flow by the selection sequence *File → New → Mediation flow*.
10. Create a new *LoanProxyApp* module and click on *Next* button in the dialog box (shown in Figure A.18).
11. Select *LoanService* as the source and target interface in the subsequent dialog box as shown in Figure A.19 and click on *Finish*. This results in a mediation flow being created with *LoanService* interface as source and *LoanServicePartner* as target.
12. A mediation flow editor is opened next.
13. Wire the source operation to the target operation as shown in Figure A.20.
14. Then wire the source input to *Callout* as shown in Figure A.21.
15. Now wire the *Callout* response to the input response as shown in Figure A.22.
16. Repeat the above three steps for all the operations.
17. Close the mediation flow editor.
18. Drag the mediation flow component to the assembly diagram.
19. Wire the mediation flow component with *LoanService* import component. An Assembly Diagram window should appear as shown in Figure A.23.

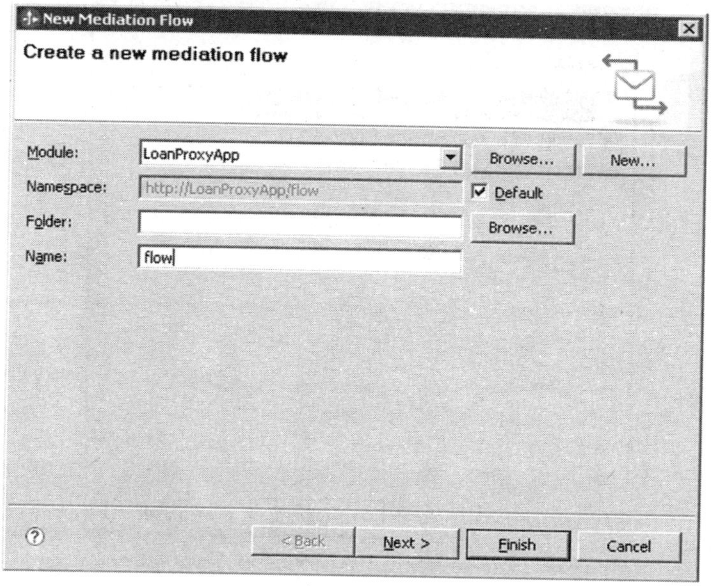

FIGURE A.18 Create a new mediation flow.
Source: IBM WebSphere product offering (printed with permission from IBM).

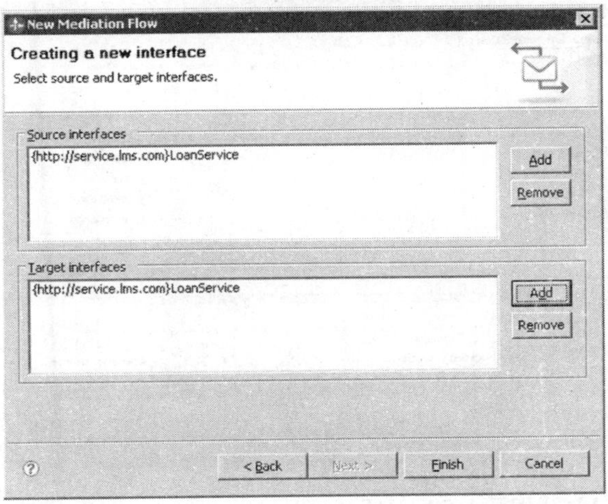

FIGURE A.19 Create a new interface.

Source: IBM WebSphere product offering (printed with permission from IBM).

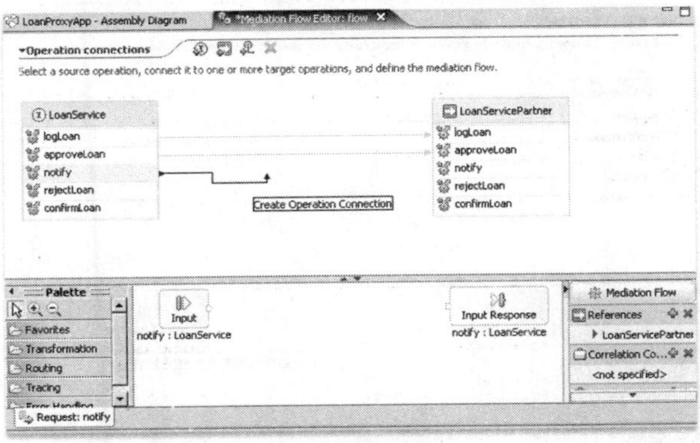

FIGURE A.20 Wire source operation to target operation.

Source: IBM WebSphere product offering (printed with permission from IBM).

20. Right click on the mediation flow component and select *Generate Export → Web Service Binding* as shown in Figure A.24.
21. A transport selection dialog box prompts for selection of the transport. Select *soap/http*.
22. This creates an export component on the assembly diagram which is wired to the mediation component.
23. Select export component and configure property *Preferred Interaction Style* as *Synchronous* as shown in Figure A.25. Repeat the same for mediation flow component and *Loan Service* import component.

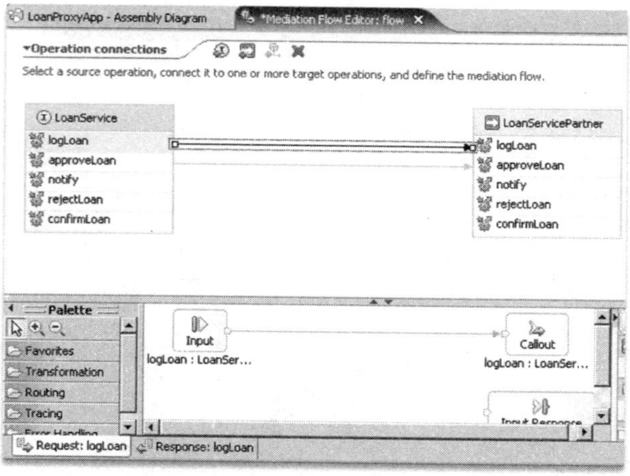

FIGURE A.21 Wire source input to *Callout*.
Source: IBM WebSphere product offering (printed with permission from IBM).

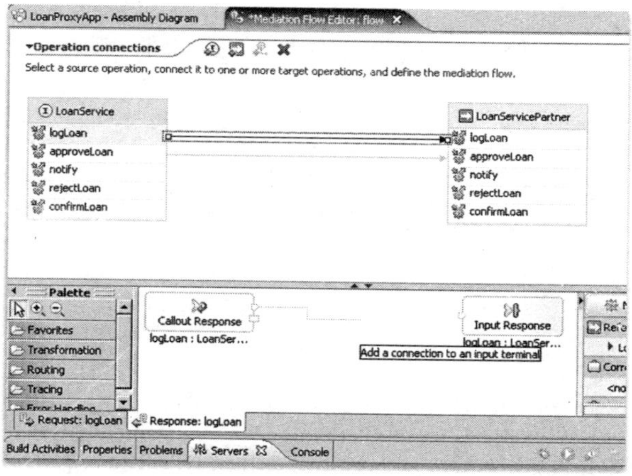

FIGURE A.22 Wire *Callout* to the input response.
Source: IBM WebSphere product offering (printed with permission from IBM).

24. The completed assembly diagram should look like that shown in Figure A.26.
25. Add the project to the server as shown in Figure A.27.
26. Restart the server.

The above steps create the mediation flow that is necessary for routing calls to *Loan Service*. This also makes the mediation flow available to external systems through a web service.

FIGURE A.23 Wire the mediation flow component with import component.
Source: IBM WebSphere product offering (printed with permission from IBM).

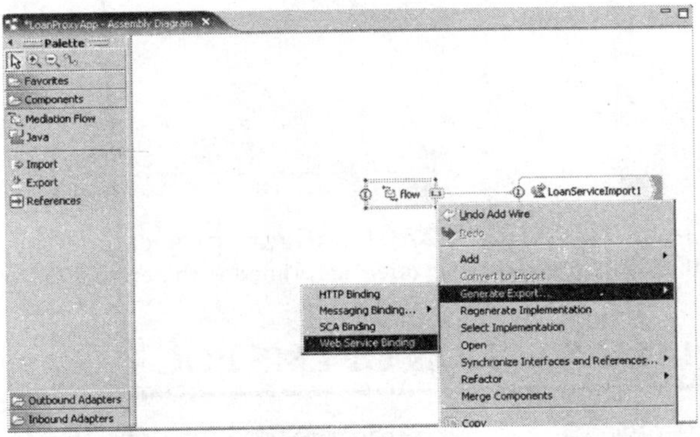

FIGURE A.24 Generate web service binding.
Source: IBM WebSphere product offering (printed with permission from IBM).

FIGURE A.25 Specify preferred interaction style.
Source: IBM WebSphere product offering (printed with permission from IBM).

FIGURE A.26 Completed assembly diagram.
Source: IBM WebSphere product offering (printed with permission from IBM).

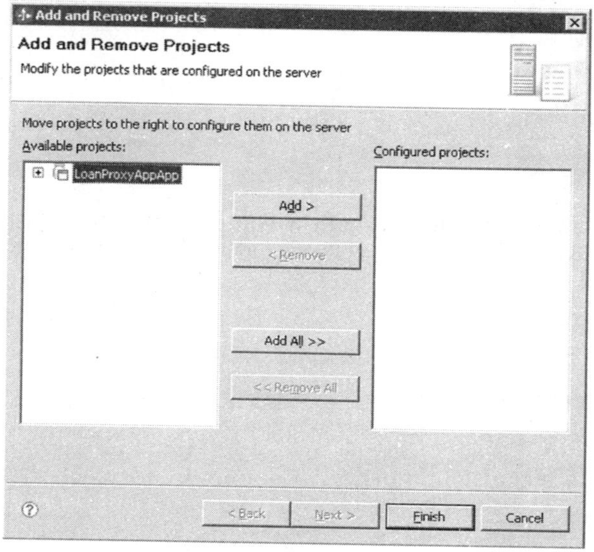

FIGURE A.27 Configure project.
Source: IBM WebSphere product offering (printed with permission from IBM).

A.4 IMPLEMENTATION OF LMS POC 4

With Spring framework gaining widespread adoption, increasing number of applications are being developed with Spring framework leveraging the dependency injection principle supported by it. LMS PoC4 has been developed to illustrate how the principles of service orientation may be employed when developing applications with Spring framework.

The architecture of LMS PoC4 is same as the other PoCs as shown in Figure A.28. Service consumer component has a *presentation layer, business layer* and *service layer*. User interacts with application using service consumer application only. Presentation layer is implemented using MVC pattern and the model delegates the request to *façade* object in business layer which calls the *service proxy* object. Service proxy calls the *loan process proxy* service which is deployed in a BPEL engine (Intalio BPMS) implemented in Business Process layer.

The presentation layer of the service consumer component is built using Spring Web MVC, business layer with POJOs and the service proxy is developed using JAX-WS web service client.

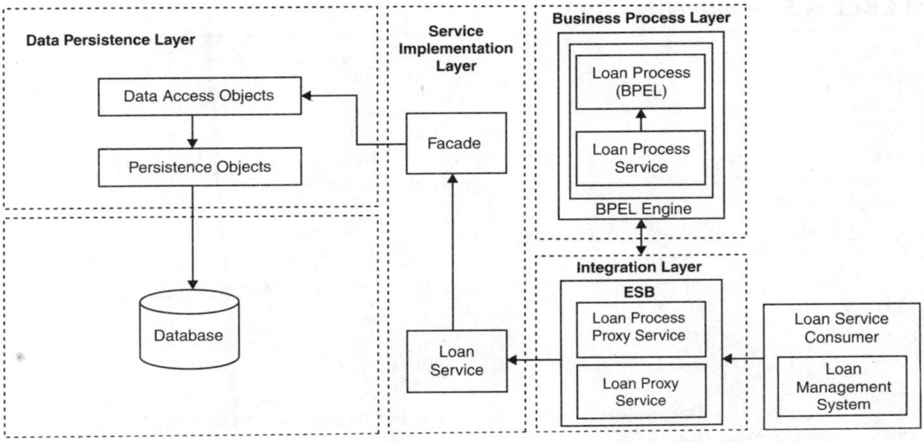

FIGURE A.28 Architecture of LMS PoC 4 (Spring based PoC).

The service provider component implements the services exposed by it. These services (exposed by service provider component) constitute the *services layer* referred to in Chapter 4. Each service has a *service implementation layer* and a *data persistence layer*. The service implementation layer is implemented using Spring Web Services and POJOs and data persistence layer is implemented using Java Persistence API (hibernate implementation).

The *Loan Service* exposed by service provider component is accessed through proxy service (deployed on WSO2 ESB) as part of orchestration of *Loan Process* deployed in an Intalio BPEL engine. The service requests from service consumer application cause orchestration of *Loan Process* service resulting in invocation of *Loan Service*. The *Loan Service* calls a façade object which then calls a data access object (DAO) in data persistence layer. The DAO makes use of the persistence object to insert or modify the loan data into the database as required by the service functionality.

Presentation Layer (of Service Consumer)

The key portions of code for presentation layer of the service consumer application are given in Table A.5.

TABLE A.5 Key portions of code for presentation layer of LMS PoC 4

Presentation Layer	*Presentation layer uses Spring MVC along with Service beans.*
JSP Page	

```
<%@ include file="jsp/include.jsp"%>
<html>
```

(continued)

TABLE A.5 (*Continued*)

```
<HEAD>
<TITLE>Deal Input - Capture Deal</TITLE>
</HEAD>
<BODY>
<jsp:include page="header.jsp"></jsp:include>
<form action="/deal_capture.htm" method="POST">
<br>
<table cellpadding="0" cellspacing="1" width="75%" border="0">
<tr>
      <td class="header1" valign="middle" colspan=4>Loan Request</td>
</tr>
<tr>
      <td   class="intd2bold"   valign="middle"   align="center">Loan
Amount</td>
      <td   class="intd2"   valign="middle"><input   type"text"   name=
"dealAmount"/></td>
      <td class="intd2bold" valign="middle" align="center">Customer
</td>
      <td   class="intd2"   valign="middle"><input   type="text"   name=
"customer"/>
      </td>
</tr>
<tr>
      <td class="intd2bold" valign="middle" align="center">Duration
(Yrs)</td>
      <td   class="intd2"   valign="middle"><input   type="text"   name=
"duration" value="5"/></td>
      <td   class="intd2bold"   valign="middle"   align="center">Fixed
Rate</td>
      <td class="intd2" valign="middle">
      <select name="fixedRate">
            <c:forEach var="rate" items="${fixedRates}">
                  <option value="<spring:transform value="${rate.
                  rateValue}"/>">
                  <c:out value="${rate.rateText}"/>
                  </option>
            </c:forEach>
      </select></td>
</tr>
<tr>
      <td class="intd2bold" valign="middle" align="center">Interest
Rate</td>
            <td  class="intd2"  valign="middle"><input  type="text"
name="interestRate" value="4.5"/></td>
      <td class="intd2bold" valign="middle" align="center">Currency
</td>
      <td class="intd2" valign="middle">
      <select name="currency">
            <c:forEach var="currency" items="${currencies}">
```

(*continued*)

TABLE A.5 (*Continued*)

```
                        <option value="<spring:transform value="$
{currency}"/>">
                        <c:out value="${currency}"/>
                        </option>
                </c:forEach>
        </select></td>
</tr>
</table>
<br>
<input type="hidden" name="status" value="NEW"/>
<a href="javascript:document.LDDealForm.submit()">
<html:img src="images/capture.jpg" hspace="4" border="0"/></a>
</html:form>
</BODY>
</html>
```

Business Layer (of Service Consumer)

The key portions of code for business layer of the service consumer are given in Table A.6.

TABLE A.6 Key portions of code for business layer of LMS PoC 4

Business Layer	***Business layer implements business components and façade components. Façade components interact with service proxy component to communicate with integration layer.***
Façade Component (DealFacade.java)	

```
package com.lms.ld.facade;

import org.springframework.beans.factory.annotation.Autowired;

import com.lms.loanprocess.loanprocess.LoanServiceProxyIfc;
import com.lms.loanprocessservice.Loan;

public class DealFacade {

        @Autowired
        LoanServiceProxyIfc loanProxy;

        public void capture(Loan loan) {
                loanProxy.receiveLogLoan(loan);
        }

}
```

Service Layer (of Service Consumer)

The key portions of code for service layer of service consumer are given in Table A.7.

TABLE A.7 Key portions of code for service layer of LMS PoC 4

Service Layer	*Service Proxy is a proxy that manages the remote communication with service provider.*
Service Proxy (CanonicServiceForclient.java)	

```
package com.lms.loanprocess.loanprocess;

import java.net.MalformedURLException;
import java.net.URL;
import javax.xml.namespace.QName;
import javax.xml.ws.Service;
import javax.xml.ws.WebEndpoint;
import javax.xml.ws.WebServiceClient;
import javax.xml.ws.WebServiceException;
import javax.xml.ws.WebServiceFeature;

@WebServiceClient(name = "CanonicServiceForclient", targetNamespace =
"http://lms.com/LoanProcess/LoanProcess", wsdlLocation = "file:/C:/
Documents%20and%20Settings/shankar/Desktop/wsdl/LoanProcess-LoanPro-
cess.wsdl")
public class CanonicServiceForclient
    extends Service
{

    private final static URL CANONICSERVICEFORCLIENT_WSDL_LOCATION;
    private final static WebServiceException CANONICSERVICEFORCLI-
    ENT_EXCEPTION;
    private final static QName CANONICSERVICEFORCLIENT_QNAME = new
    QName("http://lms.com/LoanProcess/LoanProcess",
"LoanManagementSystem-PoC/LoanProcess/LoanProcess/client");

    static {
        URL url = null;
        WebServiceException e = null;
        try {
            //url = new URL("file:/C:/Documents%20and%20Settings/
srinivas.konduru/Desktop/wsdl/LoanProcess-LoanProcess.wsdl");
            //url = new URL("file:/META-INF/wsdl/LoanProcess-Loan-
Process.wsdl");
          url = new URL("http://localhost:8080/ode/processes/Loan-
ManagementSystem-PoC/LoanProcess/LoanProcess/client?wsdl");
        } catch (MalformedURLException ex) {
            e = new WebServiceException(ex);
        }
        CANONICSERVICEFORCLIENT_WSDL_LOCATION = url;
        CANONICSERVICEFORCLIENT_EXCEPTION = e;
    }

    public CanonicServiceForclient() {
        super(__getWsdlLocation(), CANONICSERVICEFORCLIENT_QNAME);
    }

    public CanonicServiceForclient(WebServiceFeature... features) {
        super(__getWsdlLocation(), CANONICSERVICEFORCLIENT_QNAME,
features);
    }
```

(continued)

TABLE A.7 (*Continued*)

```
    public CanonicServiceForclient(URL wsdlLocation) {
        super(wsdlLocation, CANONICSERVICEFORCLIENT_QNAME);
    }
    public CanonicServiceForclient(URL wsdlLocation, WebService
Feature... features) {
        super(wsdlLocation, CANONICSERVICEFORCLIENT_QNAME, features);
    }
    public CanonicServiceForclient(URL wsdlLocation, QName service-
Name) {
        super(wsdlLocation, serviceName);
    }
    public CanonicServiceForclient(URL wsdlLocation, QName service-
Name, WebServiceFeature... features) {
        super(wsdlLocation, serviceName, features);
    }
    /**
     *
     * @return
     *  returns Forclient
     */
    @WebEndpoint(name = "canonicPort")
    public LoanServiceProxyIfc getCanonicPort() {
        //return super.getPort(new QName("http://lms.com/LoanPro-
cess/LoanProcess", "canonicPort"), Forclient.class);
        return super.getPort(new QName("http://lms.com/LoanProcess/
LoanProcess", "LoanManagementSystem-PoC/LoanProcess/LoanProcess/
clientSOAP11port_http"), LoanServiceProxyIfc.class);
    }
    /**
     *
     * @param features
     * A list of {@link javax.xml.ws.WebServiceFeature} to configure
on the proxy.  Supported features not in the <code>features</code>
parameter will have their default values.
     * @return
     *  returns Forclient
     */
    @WebEndpoint(name = "canonicPort")
    public LoanServiceProxyIfc getCanonicPort(WebServiceFeature...
features) {
        return super.getPort(new QName("http://lms.com/LoanProcess/
LoanProcess", "canonicPort"), LoanServiceProxyIfc.class, features);
    }
    private static URL __getWsdlLocation() {
        if (CANONICSERVICEFORCLIENT_EXCEPTION!= null) {
            throw CANONICSERVICEFORCLIENT_EXCEPTION;
        }
        return CANONICSERVICEFORCLIENT_WSDL_LOCATION;
    }
}
```

(continued)

Service Provider

The key portions of code for service provider are given in Tables A.8 and A.9.

TABLE A.8 Key portions of code for service implementation of LMS PoC 4

Service Provider	*Service Provider exposes services that are consumed by the service consumer. Code for service implementation (of Loan Service) is shown below.*
Service Implementation Layer or Services Layer (LoanServiceEndPoint.java)	

```
package org.lms.service;

import java.text.MessageFormat;

import org.lms.ApproveLoanRequest;
import org.lms.ConfirmLoanRequest;
import org.lms.Loan;
import org.lms.LoanResponse;
import org.lms.LogLoanRequest;
import org.lms.NotifyRequest;
import org.lms.RejectLoanRequest;
import org.lms.dao.LoanDAO;
import org.springframework.ws.server.endpoint.annotation.Endpoint;
import org.springframework.ws.server.endpoint.annotation.Payload-
Root;

@Endpoint
public class LoanServiceEndPoint implements LoanService {

      private static String SUCCESS_MESSAGE = "Request is success-
fully completed";
      private static String ERROR_MESSAGE = "There was problem in
the request execution. ERROR: {0}";

      private LoanDAO loanDAO;

      @PayloadRoot(localPart=LOG_LOAN_REQUEST, namespace=NAMESPACE)
    public LoanResponse logLoan(LogLoanRequest request) {

            System.out.println("LOG LOAN - Loan No: " + request.
getLoan().getLoanNo());
            LoanResponse response = new LoanResponse();
            try {
                  loanDAO.createLoan(copy(request.getLoan()));
                  response.setMessage(SUCCESS_MESSAGE);
            } catch (Throwable e) {
                  e.printStackTrace();
                  response.setMessage(MessageFormat.format(ERROR_
MESSAGE, new Object[]{e.getMessage()}));
            }
        return response;
    }

    @PayloadRoot(localPart=APPROVE_LOAN_REQUEST,
namespace=NAMESPACE)
```

(continued)

TABLE A.8 (*Continued*)

```
     public LoanResponse approveLoan(ApproveLoanRequest request) {
             System.out.println("APPROVE LOAN - Loan No: " +
request.getLoan().getLoanNo());
             LoanResponse response = new LoanResponse();
             try {
                     loanDAO.modifyLoan(copy(request.getLoan()));
                     response.setMessage(SUCCESS_MESSAGE);
             } catch (Throwable e) {

                     e.printStackTrace();
                     response.setMessage(MessageFormat.format(ERROR_
MESSAGE, new Object[]{e.getMessage()}));
             }
      return response;
         }
    @PayloadRoot(localPart=REJECT_LOAN_REQUEST, namespace=NAMESPACE)
      public LoanResponse rejectLoan(RejectLoanRequest request) {
             System.out.println("REJECT LOAN - Loan No: " +
request.getLoan().getLoanNo());
             LoanResponse response = new LoanResponse();
      try {
             loanDAO.modifyLoan(copy(request.getLoan()));
             response.setMessage(SUCCESS_MESSAGE);
      } catch (Throwable e) {
             e.printStackTrace();
             response.setMessage(MessageFormat.format(ERROR_MESSAGE,
new Object[]{e.getMessage()}));
      }
        return response;
      }
    @PayloadRoot(localPart=CONFIRM_LOAN_REQUEST,
namespace=NAMESPACE)
      public LoanResponse confirmLoan(ConfirmLoanRequest request) {
             System.out.println("CONFIRM LOAN - Loan No: " +
request.getLoan().getLoanNo());
             LoanResponse response = new LoanResponse();
             try {
                     loanDAO.modifyLoan(copy(request.getLoan()));
                     response.setMessage(SUCCESS_MESSAGE);
             } catch (Throwable e) {
                     e.printStackTrace();
                     response.setMessage(MessageFormat.format(ERROR_
MESSAGE, new Object[]{e.getMessage()}));
             }
    return response;
      }
    @PayloadRoot(localPart=NOTIFY_REQUEST, namespace=NAMESPACE)
      public LoanResponse notify(NotifyRequest request) {
             System.out.println("Notify - Loan No: " + request.get-
Loan().getLoanNo());
```

(continued)

TABLE A.8 *(Continued)*

```
            LoanResponse response = new LoanResponse();
    return response;
      }
private static org.lms.bo.Loan copy(Loan loan){
            org.lms.bo.Loan loanBO = new org.lms.bo.Loan();
            loanBO.setLoanNo(loan.getLoanNo());
            loanBO.setCurrency(loan.getCurrency());
            loanBO.setCustomer(loan.getCustomer());
            loanBO.setDuration(loan.getDuration());
            loanBO.setFixedRate(loan.getFixedRate());
            loanBO.setInterestRate(loan.getInterestRate());
            loanBO.setLoanAmount(loan.getLoanAmount());
            loanBO.setStatus(loan.getStatus());
            return loanBO;
    }
    public LoanDAO getLoanDAO() {
            return loanDAO;
      }
      public void setLoanDAO(LoanDAO loanDAO) {
            this.loanDAO = loanDAO;
      }
}
```

TABLE A.9 Key portions of code for data persistence of LMS PoC 4

Service Provider	*Service Provider exposes services that are consumed by the service consumer. Code for accessing data persistence of service is shown below.*
Data Persistence Layer	

```
package org.lms.dao;
import java.util.List;
import javax.persistence.EntityManager;
import javax.persistence.PersistenceContext;
import org.lms.bo.Loan;
import org.lms.bo.User;
import org.springframework.stereotype.Repository;
import org.springframework.transaction.annotation.Transactional;
@Repository
public class LoanDAOImpl implements LoanDAO {
      @PersistenceContext
      private EntityManager _entityManager;
      @Transactional
      public void createLoan(Loan loan) {
             _entityManager.persist(loan);
      }
```

(continued)

TABLE A.9 (*Continued*)

```
      @Transactional
      public void modifyLoan(Loan loan) {
            _entityManager.merge(loan);
      }
      @SuppressWarnings("unchecked")
      public List<Loan> fetchLoans() {
            return _entityManager.createNamedQuery("LOAN_ALL").
getResultList();
      }
      @SuppressWarnings("unchecked")
      public List<Loan> fetchLoans(String loanStatus) {
            return _entityManager.createNamedQuery("LOAN_BY_STA-
TUS").setParameter("loanStatus", loanStatus).getResultList();
      }
      public User fetchUser(String username) {
            return _entityManager.find(User.class, username);
      }
}
```

A.5 IMPLEMENTATION OF LMS POC 5

With the release of EJB 3.0 specification, several enterprises have adopted the specification for enterprise applications developed for the Java platform. The purpose of LMS PoC 5 is to provide insights on development of service-oriented Java applications that are based on EJB 3.0 specification. The architecture of LMS PoC 5 is same as the other PoCs and is shown in Figure A.29.

The service consumer component has a *presentation layer*, a *business layer* and a *service layer*. The user interacts with application using service consumer application only. The presentation layer is implemented using MVC pattern and the model delegates the request to façade object in business layer which

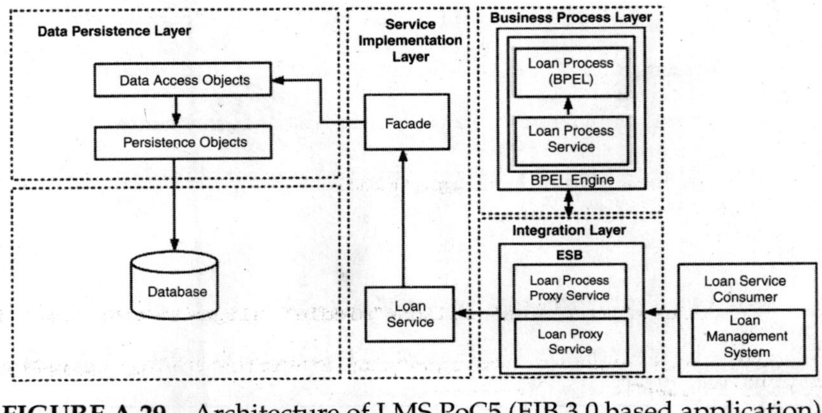

FIGURE A.29 Architecture of LMS PoC5 (EJB 3.0 based application).

calls the *service proxy* object. Service proxy calls the *loan process proxy* service which is deployed in a BPEL engine.

The presentation layer is developed using Struts 2 MVC framework, the business layer is built of POJOs and the service proxy using JAX-WS web service client.

The service provider component implements the services exposed by it. These services constitute the *services layer* referred to in Chapter 4. Each service has a *service implementation layer* and a *data persistence layer*. The service implementation layer is implemented using JBOSS JAX-WS Web Services and POJOs and the data persistence layer is implemented using Java Persistence API (hibernate implementation).

The proxy service is deployed in WSO2 ESB and loan process is deployed in BPEL engine (Intalio BPMS) implemented in Business Process layer.

Presentation Layer (of Service Consumer)

The key portions of code for presentation layer of service consumer are given in Table A.10.

TABLE A.10 Key portions of code for presentation layer of LMS PoC 5

Presentation Layer	***Presentation layer uses Struts Action classes along with Struts Form beans and JSP pages. JSP page uses Struts HTML tags for building of the user interface.***
JSP Page (Display_deal_capture.jsp)	

```
<%@taglib prefix="s" uri="/struts-tags"%>
<s:form method="POST" namespace="/loans">
<br>
<table cellpadding="0" cellspacing="1" width="75%" border="0">
<tr>
      <td class="header1" valign="middle" colspan=4 >Loan Request</td>
</tr>
<tr>
      <td class="intd2bold" valign="middle" align="center">Loan
Amount</td>
      <td class="intd2" valign="middle"><s:textfield name="loan.
dealAmount"/></td>
      <td class="intd2bold" valign="middle" align="center">Customer
</td>
      <td class="intd2" valign="middle"><s:textfield name="loan.
customer"/>
      </td>
</tr>
<tr>
      <td class="intd2bold" valign="middle" align="center">Duration
(Yrs)</td>
      <td class="intd2" valign="middle"><s:textfield name="loan.
duration" value="5"/></td>
```

(continued)

TABLE A.10 (*Continued*)

```
      <td  class="intd2bold"  valign="middle"  align="center">Fixed
Rate</td>
      <td class="intd2" valign="middle">
      <s:select name="loan.fixedRate" list="rates" listKey="rateValue"
listValue="rateText"/>
      </td>
</tr>
<tr>
      <td class="intd2bold" valign="middle" align="center">Interest
Rate</td>
              <td class="intd2" valign="middle">
              <s:textfield name="loan.interestRate" value="4.5"/>
      </td>
      <td class="intd2bold" valign="middle"align="center">Currency</
td>
      <td class="intd2" valign="middle">
      <s:select name="loan.currency" list="currencies"/>
      </td>
</tr>
</table>
<s:hideen name="status" value="NEW"/>
<s:a action="/deal_capture.htm">
      <html:img src="images/capture.jpg" hspace="4" border="0"/>
</s:a>
</s:form>
```

Struts Form Action (*DealAction.java*)	**When a user submits a JSP page, form bean populates the required data which is used in *action class.***

```
package com.lms.ld.action;

import com.lms.ld.facade.DealFacade;
import com.lms.loanprocessservice.Loan;

public class DealAction {
          private Loan loan;

          public String capture() {
                    DealFacade dealfacade = new DealFacade();
                              dealfacade.capture(loan);
     return "success";
   }

          public Loan getLoan() {
                    return loan;
          }
          public void setLoan(Loan loan) {
                    this.loan = loan;
          }
}
```

Business Layer (of Service Consumer)

The key portions of code for business layer of service consumer are given in Table A.11.

TABLE A.11 Key portions of code for business layer of LMS PoC 5

Business Layer	***Business layer implements business components and façade components. Façade components interact with service proxy component to communicate with integration layer.***
Façade Component (DealFacade.java)	

```
package com.lms.ld.facade;

import com.lms.loanprocess.loanprocess.LoanServiceProxyIfc;
import com.lms.loanprocessservice.Loan;

public class DealFacade {

      LoanServiceProxyIfc loanProxy;

      public void capture(Loan loan) {

              loanProxy = new CanonicServiceForclient();
              loanProxy.receiveLogLoan(loan);
      }

}
```

Service Provider

The key portions of code for service provider are given in Tables A.12 and A.13.

TABLE A.12 Key portions of code for service implementation of LMS PoC 5

Service Provider	***Service Provider exposes services that are consumed by the service consumer. Code for service implementation (of Loan Service) is shown below.***
Service Implementation Layer or Services Layer (LoanService.java)	

```
package org.lms.service;

import java.text.MessageFormat;

import javax.ejb.EJB;
import javax.ejb.Local;
import javax.ejb.Stateless;
import javax.jws.WebMethod;
import javax.jws.WebParam;
import javax.jws.WebResult;
import javax.jws.WebService;

import org.lms.ApproveLoanRequest;
import org.lms.ConfirmLoanRequest;
import org.lms.Loan;
```

(continued)

TABLE A.12 (*Continued*)

```
import org.lms.LoanResponse;
import org.lms.LogLoanRequest;
import org.lms.NotifyRequest;
import org.lms.RejectLoanRequest;
import org.lms.dao.LoanDAO;

@Stateless
@Local(LoanServiceIfc.class)
@WebService
public class LoanService implements LoanServiceIfc {

        private static String SUCCESS_MESSAGE = "Request is suc-
cessfully completed";
        private static String ERROR_MESSAGE = "There was problem in
the request execution. ERROR: {0}";

        @EJB
        private LoanDAO loanDAO;

        @WebMethod
        public @WebResult LoanResponse approveLoan(@WebParam Approv-
eLoanRequest request) {
                System.out.println("APPROVE LOAN - Loan No: " +
request.getLoan().getLoanNo());
                LoanResponse response = new LoanResponse();
                try {
                        loanDAO.modifyLoan(copy(request.get-
Loan()));
                        response.setMessage(SUCCESS_MESSAGE);
                } catch (Throwable e) {
                        e.printStackTrace();
                        response.setMessage(MessageFormat.
format(ERROR_MESSAGE, new Object[]{e.getMessage()}));
                }
      return response;
        }

        @WebMethod
        public @WebResult LoanResponse confirmLoan(@WebParam Con-
firmLoanRequest request) {
                System.out.println("CONFIRM LOAN - Loan No: " +
request.getLoan().getLoanNo());
                LoanResponse response = new LoanResponse();
                try {
                        loanDAO.modifyLoan(copy(request.get-
Loan()));
                        response.setMessage(SUCCESS_MESSAGE);
                } catch (Throwable e) {
                        e.printStackTrace();
                        response.setMessage(MessageFormat.
format(ERROR_MESSAGE, new Object[]{e.getMessage()}));
                }
      return response;
        }
```

(continued)

TABLE A.12 *(Continued)*

```
        @WebMethod
        public @WebResult LoanResponse logLoan(@WebParam LogLoanRequest
request) {
                System.out.println("LOG LOAN - Loan No: " +
request.getLoan().getLoanNo());
                LoanResponse response = new LoanResponse();
                try {
                        loanDAO.createLoan(copy(request.get-
Loan()));
                        response.setMessage(SUCCESS_MESSAGE);
                } catch (Throwable e) {
                        e.printStackTrace();
                        response.setMessage(MessageFormat.
format(ERROR_MESSAGE, new Object[]{e.getMessage()}));
                }
    return response;
        }
        @WebMethod
        public @WebResult LoanResponse notify(@WebParam NotifyRequest
request) {
                System.out.println("Notify - Loan No: " + request.
getLoan().getLoanNo());
                LoanResponse response = new LoanResponse();
    return response;
        }
        @WebMethod
        public @WebResult LoanResponse rejectLoan(@WebParam Reject-
LoanRequest request) {
                System.out.println("REJECT LOAN - Loan No: " +
request.getLoan().getLoanNo());
                LoanResponse response = new LoanResponse();
                try {
                        loanDAO.modifyLoan(copy(request.get-
Loan()));
                        response.setMessage(SUCCESS_MESSAGE);
                } catch (Throwable e) {
                        e.printStackTrace();
                        response.setMessage(MessageFormat.
format(ERROR_MESSAGE, new Object[]{e.getMessage()}));
                }
    return response;
        }
        public LoanDAO getLoanDAO() {
                return loanDAO;
        }
        public void setLoanDAO(LoanDAO loanDAO) {
                this.loanDAO = loanDAO;
        }
```

(continued)

TABLE A.12 *(Continued)*

```
        private static org.lms.bo.Loan copy(Loan loan) {
                org.lms.bo.Loan loanBO = new org.lms.bo.Loan();
                loanBO.setLoanNo(loan.getLoanNo());
                loanBO.setCurrency(loan.getCurrency());
                loanBO.setCustomer(loan.getCustomer());
                loanBO.setDuration(loan.getDuration());
                loanBO.setFixedRate(loan.getFixedRate());
                loanBO.setInterestRate(loan.getInterestRate());
                loanBO.setLoanAmount(loan.getLoanAmount());
                loanBO.setStatus(loan.getStatus());
                return loanBO;
        }
}
```

TABLE A.13 Key portions of code for data persistence of LMS PoC 5

Service Provider	***Service Provider exposes services that are consumed by the service consumer. Code for accessing data persistence of service is shown below.***
Data Persistence Layer (LoanDAOImpl.java)	

```
package org.lms.dao;
import java.util.List;
import javax.ejb.Local;
import javax.ejb.Stateless;
import javax.persistence.EntityManager;
import javax.persistence.PersistenceContext;
import org.lms.bo.Loan;
import org.lms.bo.User;
@Stateless
@Local(LoanDAO.class)
public class LoanDAOImpl implements LoanDAO {
        @PersistenceContext
        private EntityManager _entityManager;
        public void createLoan(Loan loan) {
                _entityManager.persist(loan);
        }
        public void modifyLoan(Loan loan) {
                _entityManager.merge(loan);
        }
        @SuppressWarnings("unchecked")
        public List<Loan> fetchLoans() {
                return _entityManager.createNamedQuery("LOAN_
ALL").getResultList();
        }
```

(continued)

TABLE A.13 *(Continued)*

```
        @SuppressWarnings("unchecked")
        public List<Loan> fetchLoans(String loanStatus) {
                    return _entityManager.createNamedQuery("LOAN_
BY_STATUS").setParameter("loanStatus", loanStatus).getResultList();
        }
        public User fetchUser(String username) {
                    return _entityManager.find(User.class,
username);
        }
}
```

A.6 ORGANIZATION OF CD CONTENTS

This book is shipped along with a CD-ROM which includes source code of PoCs which demonstrate the usage of SOA technology elements/products to realize the Loan Management System use cases discussed in Section A.1. These PoCs implement service enablement, service orchestration and service integration using technology options discussed earlier.

Table A.14 lists the LMS PoCs packaged on the CD-ROM and the technologies used for developing the PoCs.

The following section describes the organization of the above-mentioned PoCs code on the CD-ROM.

The CD-ROM consists of three folders corresponding to the PoCs mentioned in Table A.14. Each folder contains code for a PoC. The CD-ROM also consists of readme-first.txt file which explains the organization of code contents. Each PoC folder consists of an instruction document and the PoC code contents. This instruction document contains the instructions to deploy and run the PoCs. For consistency, all PoCs implement the Loan Management system use cases discussed in Section A.1. The PoC folder also contains a source code for reference.

Figure A.30 shows the directory structure for LMS 1 PoC. The directory structure will be similar for other PoCs 2 and 3.

Here the **aqualogic** folder consists of run-time components for deploying proxy service in BEA AquaLogic Service Bus. The **bpel** folder consists of run-time components for deploying business process in ActiveBPEL. The **webapps-runtime** folder consists of run-time components for deploying the UI and web services. The **wsdls** folder consists of various WSDL files used in the PoC.

TABLE A.14 PoCs on CD-ROM (with the book)

Proof-of-Concept	*Technology for Service Enablement*	*Technology for Service Orchestration*	*Technology for Service Integration*	*Technology for Presentation Layer and DB Access*
LMS POC 1	Apache Axis	Active BPEL	BEA AquaLogic Service Bus from BEA.	Struts, Hibernate on Tomcat Server
LMS POC 2	Apache Axis	Active BPEL	WSO2 ESB	Struts, Hibernate on Tomcat Server
LMS POC 3	IBM WebSphere Application Server	Active BPEL	IBM WebSphere ESB	Struts, Hibernate on IBM WebSphere Application Server

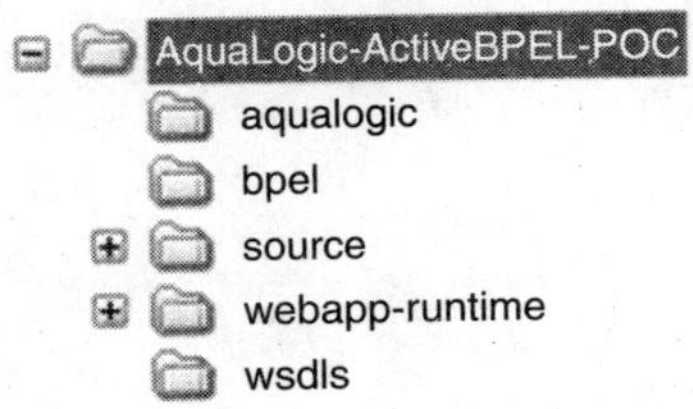

FIGURE A.30 PoC folder structure on CD-ROM.

A.7 ONLINE VALUE

In order to get further and continued insights into SOA and Cloud Computing, a blog has been setup for the book at

http://wileyindiablog.blogspot.com/SOA4EntAndCloud.html

Resources such as implementation details for LMS PoC 4 (Spring Based) and LMS PoC 5 (EJB Based) will be provided at the blog.

Process Orchestration – PoC

B

ANNEXURE

The LMS PoCs presented in Annexure A requires the process service (loan process service) orchestration to be specified. This annexure provides details of the process for visual representation of orchestration and the complete listing of BPEL code.

B.1 VISUAL REPRESENTATION OF ORCHESTRATION

Process orchestration engines usually provide visual tools to specify orchestration.

For example, ActiveBPEL too provides an IDE for this purpose. The loan approval process may be created with an ActiveBPEL IDE as follows:

1. Create a new project in ActiveBPEL.
2. Import required WSDL files into the project. These WSDLs have definition of the services which are referred by business process. Add these WSDLs to web references.
3. Create a new BPEL process.
4. Drag and drop operations from web references to the BPEL editor to create **receive-reply** or **invoke** Tasks.
5. Create **assign** tasks wherever there is need for assigning the data from one message to another.
6. Link these activities in BPEL editor.
7. Create correlation set and assign it to receive activities.
8. Create a deployment descriptor using the wizard available in the IDE and deploy onto the server using Export wizard.

The visual representation of loan approval process encapsulated by *loan process service* is shown in Chapter 8 with detailed description.

B.2 BPEL FOR LOAN PROCESS SERVICE ORCHESTRATION

The complete listing of the BPEL generated for loan process service is as follows.

```
<?xml version="1.0" encoding="UTF-8"?>
<!--
BPEL Process Definition
Edited using ActiveBPEL(tm) Designer Version 3.1.0
(http://www.active-endpoints.com)
-->
<bpel:process xmlns:bpel="http://docs.oasis-open.org/
wsbpel/2.0/process/executable"
xmlns:ns1="http://localhost:8080/axis/services/LoanProcess"
xmlns:ns2="http://localhost:8080/aqualoans/services/
LoanService"
xmlns: xsd="http://www.w3.org/2001/XMLSchema"
name="aqualoanprocess"
suppressJoinFailure="yes"
targetNamespace="http://aqualoanprocess">
    <bpel:import importType="http://schemas.xmlsoap.org/wsdl/"
location="wsdl/LoanProcess.wsdl"
namespace="http://localhost: 8080/axis/services/LoanProcess"/>
    <bpel:import  importType="http://schemas.xmlsoap.org/wsdl/"
location="wsdl/LoanProxy.wsdl" namespace="http://localhost:8080/
aqualoans/services/LoanService"/>
    <bpel:partnerLinks>
    <bpel:partnerLinkmyRole="LoanProcess" name="LoanProcessLPT"
partnerLinkType="ns1:LoanProcessLPT"/>
    <bpel:partnerLink name="LoanServiceLPT"
partnerLinkType="ns2:LoanServiceLPT" partnerRole="LoanService"/>
    </bpel:partnerLinks>
    <bpel:variables>
    <bpel:variable messageType="ns1:logRequest"
name="logRequest"/>
    <bpel:variable messageType="ns1:logResponse"
name="logResponse"/>
    <bpel:variable messageType="ns2:logLoanRequest"
name="logLoanRequest"/>
    <bpel:variable messageType="ns2:logLoanResponse"
name="logLoanResponse"/>
    <bpel:variable messageType="ns2:notifyRequest"
name="notifyRequest"/>
    <bpel:variable messageType="ns2:notifyResponse"
name="notifyResponse"/>
    <bpel:variable messageType="ns1:approveOrRejectRequest"
name="approveOrRejectRequest"/>
```

```
    <bpel:variable messageType="ns1:approveOrRejectResponse"
name="approveOrRejectResponse"/>
    <bpel:variable messageType="ns2:rejectLoanRequest"
name="rejectLoanRequest"/>
    <bpel:variable messageType="ns2:rejectLoanResponse"
name="rejectLoanResponse"/>
    <bpel:variable messageType="ns2:approveLoanRequest"
name="approveLoanRequest"/>
    <bpel:variable messageType="ns2:approveLoanResponse"
name="approveLoanResponse"/>
    <bpel:variable messageType="ns1:confirmOrRejectRequest"
name="confirmOrRejectRequest"/>
    <bpel:variable messageType="ns1:confirmOrRejectResponse"
name="confirmOrRejectResponse"/>
    <bpel:variable messageType="ns2:confirmLoanRequest"
name="confirmLoanRequest"/>
    <bpel:variable messageType="ns2:confirmLoanResponse"
name="confirmLoanResponse"/>
    </bpel:variables>
    <bpel:correlationSets>
      <bpel:correlationSet name="CS1" properties="ns1:loanNo"/>
    </bpel:correlationSets>
    <bpel:flow>
      <bpel:links>
         <bpel:link name="L1"/>
         <bpel:link name="L6"/>
         <bpel:link name="L3"/>
         <bpel:link name="L2"/>
         <bpel:link name="L5"/>
         <bpel:link name="L4"/>
         <bpel:link name="L7"/>
         <bpel:link name="L26"/>
         <bpel:link name="L27"/>
         <bpel:link name="L9"/>
         <bpel:link name="L8"/>
         <bpel:link name="L11"/>
         <bpel:link name="L10"/>
         <bpel:link name="L15"/>
         <bpel:link name="L14"/>
         <bpel:link name="L10_1"/>
         <bpel:link name="L11_1"/>
         <bpel:link name="L10_1_1"/>
         <bpel:link name="L16"/>
         <bpel:link name="L17"/>
         <bpel:link name="L18"/>
         <bpel:link name="L23"/>
         <bpel:link name="L20"/>
         <bpel:link name="L19"/>
         <bpel:link name="L22"/>
```

```
        <bpel:link name="L21"/>
        <bpel:link name="L25"/>
        <bpel:link name="L24"/>
        <bpel:link name="L12"/>
        <bpel:link name="L13"/>
    </bpel:links>
    <bpel:receive createInstance="yes"
    name="ReceiveLoanRequest" operation="log"
partnerLink="LoanProcessLPT"
portType="ns1:LoanProcess" variable="logRequest">
        <bpel:sources>
           <bpel:source linkName="L1"/>
        </bpel:sources>
        <bpel:correlations>
           <bpel:correlation initiate="yes" set="CS1"/>
        </bpel:correlations>
     </bpel:receive>
     <bpel:reply name="ReplyLoanRequest" operation="log"
partnerLink="LoanProcessLPT" portType="ns1:LoanProcess"
variable= "logResponse">
        <bpel:targets>
           <bpel:target linkName="L5"/>
        </bpel:targets>
        <bpel:sources>
           <bpel:source linkName="L6"/>
        </bpel:sources>
     </bpel:reply>
     <bpel:invoke inputVariable="logLoanRequest"
name="InvokeLogLoan" operation="logLoan"
outputVariable="logLoanResponse"
partnerLink="LoanServiceLPT" portType="ns2:LoansService">
        <bpel:targets>
           <bpel:target linkName="L2"/>
        </bpel:targets>
        <bpel:sources>
           <bpel:source linkName="L3"/>
        </bpel:sources>
     </bpel:invoke>
     <bpel:assign name="AssignForLogLoan">
        <bpel:targets>
           <bpel:target linkName="L1"/>
        </bpel:targets>
        <bpel:sources>
           <bpel:source linkName="L2"/>
        </bpel:sources>
        <bpel:copy>
           <bpel:from part="loanNo" variable="logRequest"/>
           <bpel:to part="loanNo" variable="logLoanRequest"/>
        </bpel:copy>
```

```
        <bpel:copy>
           <bpel:from part="fixedRate" variable="logRequest"/>
      <bpel:to part="fixedRate" variable="logLoanRequest"/>
   </bpel:copy>
   <bpel:copy>
      <bpel:from part="startDate" variable="logRequest"/>
      <bpel:to part="startDate" variable="logLoanRequest"/>
   </bpel:copy>
   <bpel:copy>
      <bpel:from part="maturityDate" variable="logRequest"/>
      <bpel:to part="maturityDate" variable="logLoanRequest"/>
   </bpel:copy>
   <bpel:copy>
      <bpel:from part="interestRate" variable="logRequest"/>
      <bpel:to part="interestRate" variable="logLoanRequest"/>
   </bpel:copy>
   <bpel:copy>
      <bpel:from part="customer" variable="logRequest"/>
      <bpel:to part="customer" variable="logLoanRequest"/>
   </bpel:copy>
   <bpel:copy>
      <bpel:from part="currency" variable="logRequest"/>
      <bpel:to part="currency" variable="logLoanRequest"/>
   </bpel:copy>
   <bpel:copy>
      <bpel:from part="loanAmount" variable="logRequest"/>
      <bpel:to part="loanAmount" variable="logLoanRequest"/>
   </bpel:copy>
   <bpel:copy>
   <bpel:from>
       <bpel:literal>NEW</bpel:literal>
     </bpel:from>
     <bpel:to part="status" variable="logLoanRequest"/>
   </bpel:copy>
     </bpel:assign>
     <bpel:invoke inputVariable="notifyRequest"
     name="InvokeNotifyLoanOfficer"
     operation="notify" outputVariable="notifyResponse"
     partnerLink="LoanServiceLPT"
     portType="ns2:LoansService">
         <bpel:targets>
            <bpel:target linkName="L4"/>
         </bpel:targets>
         <bpel:sources>
            <bpel:source linkName="L5"/>
         </bpel:sources>
      </bpel:invoke>
      <bpel:assign name="AssignForNotifyLoanOfficer">
         <bpel:targets>
```

```
      <bpel:target linkName="L3"/>
   </bpel:targets>
   <bpel:sources>
      <bpel:source linkName="L4"/>
   </bpel:sources>
   <bpel:copy>
      <bpel:from part="loanNo" variable="logRequest"/>
      <bpel:to part="loanNo" variable="notifyRequest"/>
   </bpel:copy>
   <bpel:copy>
  <bpel:from part="fixedRate" variable="logRequest"/>
   <bpel:to part="fixedRate" variable="notifyRequest"/>
   </bpel:copy>
   <bpel:copy>
   <bpel:from part="startDate" variable="logRequest"/>
   <bpel:to part="startDate" variable="notifyRequest"/>
   </bpel:copy>
   <bpel:copy>
 <bpel:from part="maturityDate" variable="logRequest"/>
<bpel:to part="maturityDate" variable="notifyRequest"/>
   </bpel:copy>
   <bpel:copy>
 <bpel:from part="interestRate" variable="logRequest"/>
<bpel:to part="interestRate" variable="notifyRequest"/>
   </bpel:copy>
   <bpel:copy>
     <bpel:from part="customer" variable="logRequest"/>
    <bpel:to part="customer" variable="notifyRequest"/>
   </bpel:copy>
   <bpel:copy>
    <bpel:from part="currency" variable="logRequest"/>
    <bpel:to part="currency" variable="notifyRequest"/>
   </bpel:copy>
   <bpel:copy>
   <bpel:from part="loanAmount" variable="logRequest"/>
  <bpel:to part="loanAmount" variable="notifyRequest"/>
   </bpel:copy>
   <bpel:copy>
      <bpel:from part="status" variable="logRequest"/>
      <bpel:to part="status" variable="notifyRequest"/>
   </bpel:copy>
   <bpel:copy>
      <bpel:from>
         <bpel:literal>NEW_DEAL</bpel:literal>
      </bpel:from>
     <bpel:to part="message" variable="notifyRequest"/>
   </bpel:copy>
</bpel:assign>
<bpel:receive name="ReceiveLoanApproval"
```

```
operation="approveOrReject"
partnerLink="LoanProcessLPT" portType="ns1:LoanProcess"
variable="approveOrRejectRequest">
         <bpel:targets>
            <bpel:target linkName="L6"/>
         </bpel:targets>
         <bpel:sources>
            <bpel:source linkName="L7">
               <bpel:transitionCondition>$approveOrReject
Request.status = "reject"</bpel:transitionCondition>
            </bpel:source>
            <bpel:source linkName="L26">
               <bpel:transitionCondition>$approveOrReject
Request.status = "approve" and $approveOrRejectRequest.
loanAmount &lt; 10000</bpel:transitionCondition>
            </bpel:source>
            <bpel:source linkName="L27">
               <bpel:transitionCondition>$approveOrReject
Request.status = "approve" and $approveOrRejectRequest.
loanAmount &gt;= 10000</bpel:transitionCondition>
            </bpel:source>
         </bpel:sources>
         <bpel:correlations>
            <bpel:correlation initiate="join" set="CS1"/>
         </bpel:correlations>
      </bpel:receive>
      <bpel:reply name="ReplyLoanApproval"
operation="approveOrReject"
partnerLink="LoanProcessLPT" portType="ns1:LoanProcess"
variable="approveOrRejectResponse">
         <bpel:targets>
            <bpel:target linkName="L11"/>
         </bpel:targets>
      </bpel:reply>
      <bpel:invoke inputVariable="rejectLoanRequest"
name="InvokeLoanRejection" operation="rejectLoan"
outputVariable="rejectLoanResponse"
partnerLink="LoanServiceLPT" portType="ns2:LoansService">
         <bpel:targets>
            <bpel:target linkName="L8"/>
         </bpel:targets>
         <bpel:sources>
            <bpel:source linkName="L9"/>
         </bpel:sources>
      </bpel:invoke>
      <bpel:assign name="AssignForLoanRejection">
         <bpel:targets>
            <bpel:target linkName="L7"/>
         </bpel:targets>
```

```
          <bpel:sources>
             <bpel:source linkName="L8"/>
          </bpel:sources>
          <bpel:copy>
       <bpel:from part="loanNo"
variable="approveOrRejectRequest"/>
         <bpel:to part="loanNo" variable="rejectLoanRequest"/>
          </bpel:copy>
          <bpel:copy>
             <bpel:from part="fixedRate"
variable="approveOrRejectRequest"/>
             <bpel:to part="fixedRate"
variable="rejectLoanRequest"/>
          </bpel:copy>
          <bpel:copy>
             <bpel:from part="startDate"
variable="approveOrRejectRequest"/>
             <bpel:to part="startDate"
variable="rejectLoanRequest"/>
          </bpel:copy>
          <bpel:copy>
             <bpel:from part="maturityDate"
variable="approveOrRejectRequest"/>
             <bpel:to part="maturityDate"
variable="rejectLoanRequest"/>
          </bpel:copy>
          <bpel:copy>
             <bpel:from part="interestRate"
variable="approveOrRejectRequest"/>
             <bpel:to part="interestRate"
variable="rejectLoanRequest"/>
          </bpel:copy>
          <bpel:copy>
             <bpel:from part="customer"
variable="approveOrRejectRequest"/>
             <bpel:to part="customer"
variable="rejectLoanRequest"/>
          </bpel:copy>
          <bpel:copy>
             <bpel:from part="currency"
variable="approveOrRejectRequest"/>
             <bpel:to part="currency"
variable="rejectLoanRequest"/>
          </bpel:copy>
          <bpel:copy>
             <bpel:from part="loanAmount"
variable="approveOrRejectRequest"/>
             <bpel:to part="loanAmount"
variable="rejectLoanRequest"/>
```

```
         </bpel:copy>
         <bpel:copy>
         <bpel:from>
               <bpel:literal>REJECTED</bpel:literal>
            </bpel:from>
            <bpel:to part="status"
variable="rejectLoanRequest"/>
         </bpel:copy>
      </bpel:assign>
      <bpel:invoke inputVariable="notifyRequest"
name="InvokeNotifyCustomer" operation="notify"
outputVariable="notifyResponse"
partnerLink="LoanServiceLPT" portType="ns2:LoansService">
         <bpel:targets>
            <bpel:target linkName="L10"/>
         </bpel:targets>
         <bpel:sources>
            <bpel:source linkName="L11"/>
         </bpel:sources>
      </bpel:invoke>
      <bpel:assign name="AssignForNotifyCustomer">
         <bpel:targets>
            <bpel:target linkName="L9"/>
         </bpel:targets>
         <bpel:sources>
            <bpel:source linkName="L10"/>
         </bpel:sources>
         <bpel:copy>
            <bpel:from part="loanNo"
variable="approveOrRejectRequest"/>
            <bpel:to part="loanNo" variable="notifyRequest"/>
         </bpel:copy>
         <bpel:copy>
            <bpel:from part="fixedRate"
variable="approveOrRejectRequest"/>
         <bpel:to part="fixedRate" variable="notifyRequest"/>
         </bpel:copy>
         <bpel:copy>
            <bpel:from part="startDate"
variable="approveOrRejectRequest"/>
         <bpel:to part="startDate" variable="notifyRequest"/>
         </bpel:copy>
         <bpel:copy>
            <bpel:from part="maturityDate"
variable="approveOrRejectRequest"/>
      <bpel:to part="maturityDate" variable="notifyRequest"/>
         </bpel:copy>
         <bpel:copy>
            <bpel:from part="interestRate"
```

```
variable="approveOrRejectRequest"/>
      <bpel:to part="interestRate" variable="notifyRequest"/>
         </bpel:copy>
         <bpel:copy>
            <bpel:from part="customer"
variable="approveOrRejectRequest"/>
         <bpel:to part="customer" variable="notifyRequest"/>
         </bpel:copy>
         <bpel:copy>
            <bpel:from part="currency"
variable="approveOrRejectRequest"/>
          <bpel:to part="currency" variable="notifyRequest"/>
         </bpel:copy>
         <bpel:copy>
            <bpel:from part="loanAmount"
variable="approveOrRejectRequest"/>
        <bpel:to part="loanAmount" variable="notifyRequest"/>
         </bpel:copy>
         <bpel:copy>
            <bpel:from part="status"
variable="approveOrRejectRequest"/>
            <bpel:to part="status" variable="notifyRequest"/>
         </bpel:copy>
         <bpel:copy>
            <bpel:from>
               <bpel:literal>REEJCTED</bpel:literal>
            </bpel:from>
           <bpel:to part="message" variable="notifyRequest"/>
         </bpel:copy>
      </bpel:assign>
      <bpel:invoke inputVariable="approveLoanRequest"
name="InvokeLoanApproval" operation="approveLoan"
outputVariable="approveLoanResponse"
partnerLink="LoanServiceLPT" portType="ns2:LoansService">
         <bpel:targets>
            <bpel:target linkName="L14"/>
         </bpel:targets>
         <bpel:sources>
            <bpel:source linkName="L15"/>
         </bpel:sources>
      </bpel:invoke>
      <bpel:assign name="AssignForLoanApproval">
         <bpel:targets>
            <bpel:target linkName="L27"/>
         </bpel:targets>
         <bpel:sources>
            <bpel:source linkName="L14"/>
         </bpel:sources>
         <bpel:copy>
```

```
            <bpel:from part="loanNo"
variable="approveOrRejectRequest"/>
        <bpel:to part="loanNo"
variable="approveLoanRequest"/>
         </bpel:copy>
         <bpel:copy>
            <bpel:from part="fixedRate"
variable="approveOrRejectRequest"/>
            <bpel:to part="fixedRate"
variable="approveLoanRequest"/>
         </bpel:copy>
         <bpel:copy>
            <bpel:from part="startDate"
variable="approveOrRejectRequest"/>
            <bpel:to part="startDate"
variable="approveLoanRequest"/>
         </bpel:copy>
         <bpel:copy>
            <bpel:from part="maturityDate"
variable="approveOrRejectRequest"/>
            <bpel:to part="maturityDate"
variable="approveLoanRequest"/>
         </bpel:copy>
         <bpel:copy>
            <bpel:from part="interestRate"
variable="approveOrRejectRequest"/>
            <bpel:to part="interestRate"
variable="approveLoanRequest"/>
         </bpel:copy>
         <bpel:copy>
            <bpel:from part="customer"
variable="approveOrRejectRequest"/>
            <bpel:to part="customer"
variable="approveLoanRequest"/>
         </bpel:copy>
         <bpel:copy>
            <bpel:from part="currency"
variable="approveOrRejectRequest"/>
            <bpel:to part="currency"
variable="approveLoanRequest"/>
         </bpel:copy>
         <bpel:copy>
            <bpel:from part="loanAmount"
variable="approveOrRejectRequest"/>
            <bpel:to part="loanAmount"
variable="approveLoanRequest"/>
         </bpel:copy>
         <bpel:copy>
            <bpel:from>
```

```
                <bpel:literal>PRE_APPROVED</bpel:literal>
            </bpel:from>
        <bpel:to part="status" variable="approveLoanRequest"/>
          </bpel:copy>
       </bpel:assign>
       <bpel:assign name="AssignForNotifyCustomer">
          <bpel:targets>
             <bpel:target linkName="L13"/>
          </bpel:targets>
          <bpel:sources>
             <bpel:source linkName="L10_1"/>
          </bpel:sources>
          <bpel:copy>
          <bpel:from part="loanNo"
variable="approveOrRejectRequest"/>
             <bpel:to part="loanNo" variable="notifyRequest"/>
          </bpel:copy>
          <bpel:copy>
             <bpel:from part="fixedRate"
variable="approveOrRejectRequest"/>
          <bpel:to part="fixedRate" variable="notifyRequest"/>
          </bpel:copy>
          <bpel:copy>
             <bpel:from part="startDate"
variable="approveOrRejectRequest"/>
          <bpel:to part="startDate" variable="notifyRequest"/>
          </bpel:copy>
          <bpel:copy>
             <bpel:from part="maturityDate"
variable="approveOrRejectRequest"/>
       <bpel:to part="maturityDate" variable="notifyRequest"/>
          </bpel:copy>
          <bpel:copy>
             <bpel:from part="interestRate"
variable="approveOrRejectRequest"/>
       <bpel:to part="interestRate" variable="notifyRequest"/>
          </bpel:copy>
          <bpel:copy>
             <bpel:from part="customer"
variable="approveOrRejectRequest"/>
          <bpel:to part="customer" variable="notifyRequest"/>
          </bpel:copy>
          <bpel:copy>
             <bpel:from part="currency"
variable="approveOrRejectRequest"/>
          <bpel:to part="currency" variable="notifyRequest"/>
          </bpel:copy>
          <bpel:copy>
             <bpel:from part="loanAmount"
```

```
variable="approveOrRejectRequest"/>
       <bpel:to part="loanAmount" variable="notifyRequest"/>
         </bpel:copy>
         <bpel:copy>
            <bpel:from>
               <bpel:literal>APPROVED</bpel:literal>
            </bpel:from>
           <bpel:to part="status" variable="notifyRequest"/>
         </bpel:copy>
      </bpel:assign>
      <bpel:invoke inputVariable="notifyRequest"
name="InvokeNotifyCustomer" operation="notify"
outputVariable="notifyResponse"
partnerLink="LoanServiceLPT" portType="ns2:LoansService">
         <bpel:targets>
            <bpel:target linkName="L10_1"/>
         </bpel:targets>
         <bpel:sources>
            <bpel:source linkName="L11_1"/>
         </bpel:sources>
      </bpel:invoke>
      <bpel:reply name="ReplyLoanApproval"
operation="approveOrReject"
partnerLink="LoanProcessLPT" portType="ns1:LoanProcess"
variable="approveOrRejectResponse">
         <bpel:targets>
            <bpel:target linkName="L11_1"/>
         </bpel:targets>
      </bpel:reply>
      <bpel:assign name="AssignForNotifyManager">
         <bpel:targets>
            <bpel:target linkName="L15"/>
         </bpel:targets>
         <bpel:sources>
            <bpel:source linkName="L10_1_1"/>
         </bpel:sources>
         <bpel:copy>
           <bpel:from part="loanNo"
variable="approveOrRejectRequest"/>
           <bpel:to part="loanNo" variable="notifyRequest"/>
         </bpel:copy>
         <bpel:copy>
            <bpel:from part="fixedRate"
variable="approveOrRejectRequest"/>
         <bpel:to part="fixedRate"
variable="notifyRequest"/>
         </bpel:copy>
         <bpel:copy>
            <bpel:from part="startDate"
```

```
variable="approveOrRejectRequest"/>
         <bpel:to part="startDate"
variable="notifyRequest"/>
         </bpel:copy>
         <bpel:copy>
            <bpel:from part="maturityDate"
variable="approveOrRejectRequest"/>
      <bpel:to part="maturityDate" variable="notifyRequest"/>
         </bpel:copy>
         <bpel:copy>
            <bpel:from part="interestRate"
variable="approveOrRejectRequest"/>
      <bpel:to part="interestRate" variable="notifyRequest"/>
         </bpel:copy>
         <bpel:copy>
            <bpel:from part="customer"
variable="approveOrRejectRequest"/>
          <bpel:to part="customer" variable="notifyRequest"/>
         </bpel:copy>
         <bpel:copy>
            <bpel:from part="currency"
variable="approveOrRejectRequest"/>
          <bpel:to part="currency" variable="notifyRequest"/>
         </bpel:copy>
         <bpel:copy>
            <bpel:from part="loanAmount"
variable="approveOrRejectRequest"/>
        <bpel:to part="loanAmount" variable="notifyRequest"/>
         </bpel:copy>
         <bpel:copy>
            <bpel:from>
               <bpel:literal>PRE_APPROVED</bpel:literal>
            </bpel:from>
            <bpel:to part="status" variable="notifyRequest"/>
         </bpel:copy>
      </bpel:assign>
      <bpel:invoke inputVariable="notifyRequest"
name="InvokeNotifyManager" operation="notify"
outputVariable="notifyResponse"
partnerLink="LoanServiceLPT" portType="ns2:LoansService">
         <bpel:targets>
            <bpel:target linkName="L10_1_1"/>
         </bpel:targets>
         <bpel:sources>
            <bpel:source linkName="L16"/>
         </bpel:sources>
      </bpel:invoke>
      <bpel:reply name="ReplyLoanApproval"
operation="approveOrReject" partnerLink="LoanProcessLPT"
```

```
portType="ns1:LoanProcess"
variable="approveOrRejectResponse">
         <bpel:targets>
            <bpel:target linkName="L16"/>
         </bpel:targets>
         <bpel:sources>
            <bpel:source linkName="L17"/>
         </bpel:sources>
      </bpel:reply>
      <bpel:receive name="ReceiveLoanConfirmation"
operation="confirmOrReject" partnerLink="LoanProcessLPT"
portType="ns1:LoanProcess" variable="confirmOrRejectRequest">
         <bpel:targets>
            <bpel:target linkName="L17"/>
         </bpel:targets>
         <bpel:sources>
            <bpel:source linkName="L18">
               <bpel:transitionCondition>$confirmOrReject
Request.status = "reject"</bpel:transitionCondition>
            </bpel:source>
            <bpel :source linkName="L23">
               <bpel:transitionCondition>$confirmOrReject
Request.status = "confirm"</bpel:transitionCondition>
            </bpel:source>
         </bpel:sources>
         <bpel:correlations>
            <bpel:correlation initiate="join" set="CS1"/>
         </bpel:correlations>
      </bpel:receive>
      <bpel:reply name="ReplyLoanConfirmation"
operation="confirmOrReject" partnerLink="LoanProcessLPT"
portType="ns1:LoanProcess" variable="confirmOrRejectResponse">
         <bpel:targets>
            <bpel:target linkName="L22"/>
         </bpel:targets>
      </bpel:reply>
      <bpel:invoke inputVariable="rejectLoanRequest"
name="InvokeLoanRejection" operation="rejectLoan"
outputVariable="rejectLoanResponse"
partnerLink="LoanServiceLPT" portType="ns2:LoansService">
         <bpel:targets>
            <bpel:target linkName="L19"/>
         </bpel:targets>
         <bpel:sources>
            <bpel:source linkName="L20"/>
         </bpel:sources>
      </bpel:invoke>
      <bpel:assign name="AssignLoanRejection">
         <bpel:targets>
```

```
            <bpel:target linkName="L18"/>
         </bpel:targets>
         <bpel:sources>
            <bpel:source linkName="L19"/>
         </bpel:sources>
         <bpel:copy>
            <bpel:from part="loanNo"
variable="confirmOrRejectRequest"/>
        <bpel:to part="loanNo" variable="rejectLoanRequest"/>
         </bpel:copy>
         <bpel:copy>
            <bpel:from part="fixedRate"
variable="confirmOrRejectRequest"/>
      <bpel:to part="fixedRate" variable="rejectLoanRequest"/>
         </bpel:copy>
         <bpel:copy>
            <bpel:from part="startDate"
variable="confirmOrRejectRequest"/>
     <bpel:to part="startDate" variable="rejectLoanRequest"/>
         </bpel:copy>
         <bpel:copy>
            <bpel:from part="maturityDate"
variable="confirmOrRejectRequest"/>
            <bpel:to part="maturityDate"
variable="rejectLoanRequest"/>
         </bpel:copy>
         <bpel:copy>
            <bpel:from part="interestRate"
variable="confirmOrRejectRequest"/>
            <bpel:to part="interestRate"
variable="rejectLoanRequest"/>
         </bpel:copy>
         <bpel:copy>
            <bpel:from part="customer"
variable="confirmOrRejectRequest"/>
      <bpel:to part="customer" variable="rejectLoanRequest"/>
         </bpel:copy>
         <bpel:copy>
            <bpel:from part="currency"
variable="confirmOrRejectRequest"/>
      <bpel:to part="currency" variable="rejectLoanRequest"/>
         </bpel:copy>
         <bpel:copy>
            <bpel:from part="loanAmount"
variable="confirmOrRejectRequest"/>
            <bpel:to part="loanAmount"
variable="rejectLoanRequest"/>
         </bpel:copy>
         <bpel:copy>
```

```
            <bpel:from>
               <bpel:literal>REJETED</bpel:literal>
            </bpel:from>
        <bpel:to part="status" variable="rejectLoanRequest"/>
          </bpel:copy>
      </bpel:assign>
      <bpel:invoke inputVariable="notifyRequest"
name="InvokeNotifyCustomer" operation="notify"
outputVariable="notifyResponse"
partnerLink="LoanServiceLPT" portType="ns2:LoansService">
         <bpel:targets>
            <bpel:target linkName="L21"/>
         </bpel:targets>
         <bpel:sources>
            <bpel:source linkName="L22"/>
         </bpel:sources>
      </bpel:invoke>
      <bpel:assign name="AssignForNotifyCustomer">
         <bpel:targets>
            <bpel:target linkName="L20"/>
            <bpel:target linkName="L25"/>
         </bpel:targets>
         <bpel:sources>
            <bpel:source linkName="L21"/>
         </bpel:sources>
         <bpel:copy>
            <bpel:from part="loanNo"
variable="confirmOrRejectRequest"/>
            <bpel:to part="loanNo" variable="notifyRequest"/>
         </bpel:copy>
         <bpel:copy>
            <bpel:from part="fixedRate"
variable="confirmOrRejectRequest"/>
         <bpel:to part="fixedRate" variable="notifyRequest"/>
         </bpel:copy>
         <bpel:copy>
            <bpel:from part="startDate"
variable="confirmOrRejectRequest"/>
         <bpel:to part="startDate" variable="notifyRequest"/>
         </bpel:copy>
         <bpel:copy>
            <bpel:from part="maturityDate"
variable="confirmOrRejectRequest"/>
      <bpel:to part="maturityDate" variable="notifyRequest"/>
         </bpel:copy>
         <bpel:copy>
            <bpel:from part="interestRate"
variable="confirmOrRejectRequest"/>
      <bpel:to part="interestRate" variable="notifyRequest"/>
```

```
          </bpel:copy>
          <bpel:copy>
             <bpel:from part="customer"
variable="confirmOrRejectRequest"/>
          <bpel:to part="customer" variable="notifyRequest"/>
          </bpel:copy>
          <bpel:copy>
             <bpel:from part="currency"
variable="confirmOrRejectRequest"/>
           <bpel:to part="currency" variable="notifyRequest"/>
          </bpel:copy>
          <bpel:copy>
             <bpel:from part="loanAmount"
variable="confirmOrRejectRequest"/>
        <bpel:to part="loanAmount" variable="notifyRequest"/>
          </bpel:copy>
          <bpel:copy>
             <bpel:from part="status"
variable="confirmOrRejectRequest"/>
             <bpel:to part="status" variable="notifyRequest"/>
          </bpel:copy>
       </bpel:assign>
       <bpel:invoke inputVariable="confirmLoanRequest"
name="InvokeLoanConfirmation" operation="confirmLoan"
outputVariable="confirmLoanResponse"
partnerLink="LoanServiceLPT" portType="ns2:LoansService">
          <bpel:targets>
             <bpel:target linkName="L24"/>
          </bpel:targets>
          <bpel:sources>
             <bpel:source linkName="L25"/>
          </bpel:sources>
       </bpel:invoke>
       <bpel:assign name="AssignForLoanConfirmation">
          <bpel:targets>
             <bpel:target linkName="L23"/>
          </bpel:targets>
          <bpel:sources>
             <bpel:source linkName="L24"/>
          </bpel:sources>
          <bpel:copy>
             <bpel:from part="loanNo"
variable="confirmOrRejectRequest"/>
       <bpel:to part="loanNo" variable="confirmLoanRequest"/>
          </bpel:copy>
          <bpel:copy>
             <bpel:from part="fixedRate"
variable="confirmOrRejectRequest"/>
             <bpel:to part="fixedRate"
```

```
variable="confirmLoanRequest"/>
         </bpel:copy>
         <bpel:copy>
            <bpel:from part="startDate"
variable="confirmOrRejectRequest"/>
            <bpel:to part="startDate"
variable="confirmLoanRequest"/>
         </bpel:copy>
         <bpel:copy>
            <bpel:from part="maturityDate"
variable="confirmOrRejectRequest"/>
            <bpel:to part="maturityDate"
variable="confirmLoanRequest"/>
         </bpel:copy>
         <bpel:copy>
            <bpel:from part="interestRate"
variable="confirmOrRejectRequest"/>
            <bpel:to part="interestRate"
variable="confirmLoanRequest"/>
         </bpel:copy>
         <bpel:copy>
            <bpel:from part="customer"
variable="confirmOrRejectRequest"/>
            <bpel:to part="customer"
variable="confirmLoanRequest"/>
         </bpel:copy>
         <bpel:copy>
            <bpel:from part="currency"
variable="confirmOrRejectRequest"/>
            <bpel:to part="currency"
variable="confirmLoanRequest"/>
         </bpel:copy>
         <bpel:copy>
            <bpel:from part="loanAmount"
variable="confirmOrRejectRequest"/>
            <bpel:to part="loanAmount"
variable="confirmLoanRequest"/>
         </bpel:copy>
         <bpel:copy>
            <bpel:from>
               <bpel:literal>APPROVED</bpel:literal>
            </bpel:from>
        <bpel:to part="status" variable="confirmLoanRequest"/>
         </bpel:copy>
       </bpel:assign>
       <bpel:assign name="AssignForLoanApproval">
          <bpel:targets>
             <bpel:target linkName="L26"/>
          </bpel:targets>
```

```
          <bpel:sources>
             <bpel:source linkName="L12"/>
          </bpel:sources>
          <bpel:copy>
             <bpel:from part="loanNo"
variable="approveOrRejectRequest"/>
        <bpel:to part="loanNo" variable="approveLoanRequest"/>
          </bpel:copy>
          <bpel:copy>
             <bpel:from part="fixedRate"
variable="approveOrRejectRequest"/>
             <bpel:to part="fixedRate"
variable="approveLoanRequest"/>
          </bpel:copy>
          <bpel:copy>
             <bpel:from part="startDate"
variable="approveOrRejectRequest"/>
             <bpel:to part="startDate"
variable="approveLoanRequest"/>
          </bpel:copy>
          <bpel:copy>
             <bpel:from part="maturityDate"
variable="approveOrRejectRequest"/>
             <bpel:to part="maturityDate"
variable="approveLoanRequest"/>
          </bpel:copy>
          <bpel:copy>
             <bpel:from part="interestRate"
variable="approveOrRejectRequest"/>
             <bpel:to part="interestRate"
variable="approveLoanRequest"/>
          </bpel:copy>
          <bpel:copy>
             <bpel:from part="customer"
variable="approveOrRejectRequest"/>
             <bpel:to part="customer"
variable="approveLoanRequest"/>
          </bpel:copy>
          <bpel:copy>
             <bpel:from part="currency"
variable="approveOrRejectRequest"/>
             <bpel:to part="currency"
variable="approveLoanRequest"/>
          </bpel:copy>
          <bpel:copy>
             <bpel:from part="loanAmount"
variable="approveOrRejectRequest"/>
             <bpel:to part="loanAmount"
variable="approveLoanRequest"/>
```

```
          </bpel:copy>
          <bpel:copy>
             <bpel:from>
                <bpel:literal>APPROVED</bpel:literal>
             </bpel:from>
             <bpel:to part="status"
variable="approveLoanRequest"/>
          </bpel:copy>
       </bpel:assign>
       <bpel:invoke inputVariable="approveLoanRequest"
name="InvokeLoanApproval" operation="approveLoan"
outputVariable="approveLoanResponse" partnerLink="LoanService
LPT" portType="ns2:LoansService">
          <bpel:targets>
             <bpel:target linkName="L12"/>
          </bpel:targets>
          <bpel:sources>
             <bpel:source linkName="L13"/>
          </bpel:sources>
       </bpel:invoke>
    </bpel:flow>
</bpel:process
```

SOA Best Practices

ANNEXURE C

Several best practices have been identified in analyzing SOA implementations. This annexure summarizes the key best practices that enable successful adoption of SOA.

The best practices are classified under three categories:

1. SOA Strategy;
2. SOA Development;
3. SOA Governance.

C.1 SOA STRATEGY – BEST PRACTICES

An appropriate SOA strategy plays an important role in successful implementation of SOA in an enterprise. The following best practices ensure that the SOA strategy envisioned provides the required focus on critical aspects related to strategy.

1. ***"Don't do SOA for SOA's sake" – Establish a business case:*** SOA is meant to provide value to business through reuse, agility and integration. It is important to establish that reuse, agility and integration are indeed key concerns of an enterprise and that SOA adoption will deliver the estimated cost savings and ROI to an enterprise. SOA requires investments in service enabling existing applications, developing new service-oriented applications and in implementing ESB and process orchestration infrastructure. Approval at enterprise level for such investments is only possible when the ROI is justified.
2. ***Adopt an enterprise-wide view:*** While the principles of SOA can provide benefits to individual applications, substantial benefits related to business agility and reuse can only occur when business processes are externalized and orchestrated beyond the scope of individual applications on the basis of the enterprise-wide view. Hence, SOA-strategy

definition for an enterprise can benefit from techniques and best practices for enterprise architecture definition such as enterprise modeling and governance.

3. *"Start small, grow big":* Enterprise-level initiatives require significant effort in implementation. To ensure that the choices and decisions made in implementing business processes and technology selection are appropriate and that the SOA strategy, in fact, provides the projected benefits, validation is needed through pilots conducted at unit or departmental level before rolling it across the enterprise in a phased manner.
4. *Senior management commitment:* The alignment of business and IT (or lack of it) can cause several challenges in implementation of SOA. In order that the immediate needs of the business do not impact strategic SOA initiatives, buy-in of senior management on the value of SOA is necessary as well as a strong will of senior management to implement it to derive long-term benefits is essential.
5. *Establish SOA guidelines:* SOA can mean "different things to different stakeholders" in an enterprise. In order that there is buy-in of a shared vision, it is advisable that a set of guidelines on SOA implementation and governance with common terminology is prepared and communicated to all stakeholders of the enterprise. This could involve preparation of architecture "Blue Book" that provides the architecture principles and reference architecture for the enterprise.
6. *Educate key stakeholders on paradigm shift with services model:* The services model represents a paradigm shift from the traditional IT applications. The concept of services and need for their reuse needs to be fully understood and operationalized. This requires new policies to be defined in organizations and associated training to fully leverage SOA.
7. *Ensure cloud is part of the architecture vision of enterprise:* Analysts predict that cloud will see increasing support from service providers and a number of cloud services will be available for enterprises to leverage. Therefore, the considerations for enterprise-wide SOA architecture should include potential availability of extensive range of cloud services in future.
8. *Define a roadmap for implementation:* There is a need for clarity on how SOA will be implemented in an enterprise. A roadmap for SOA provides such an approach and hence it is important for well-thought out roadmap to be defined with inputs from all the key stakeholders.
9. *"Buy what you can, Build what you must and Outsource the rest":* At the core of SOA are enterprise-wide architecture, business process alignment with IT, technology decisions, governance and security. In order to implement a roadmap for SOA, it is best for an enterprise to buy solutions and products that are best suited, build only what it must and outsource the rest of development to specialist organizations in the interest of competitive advantage, lesser time to market and lower cost.

10. ***Consider cloud based strategies to improve synergies in global organizations:*** Cloud presents an opportunity to improve synergies in IT capabilities across different business units of global enterprises. Service-oriented applications developed by one unit of an enterprise may be deployed in a private cloud for other units to reuse. In some cases a public cloud (with security concerns suitably addressed) is also an option.

C.2 SOA DEVELOPMENT – BEST PRACTICES

Adoption of the following best practices in SOA development enables standardization, improved productivity and quality along with reduced rework.

1. ***Externalize business processes:*** Business agility in an enterprise is enabled by process orchestration. "Hardwiring" of business processes in IT applications makes it difficult to effect changes to them based on changes to business. Externalizing of business processes through orchestration of workflows specified outside the context of business applications can address this issue and make business processes configurable.
2. ***Create a business process model:*** A comprehensive business process model that correctly captures the business processes of an enterprise is critical to the identification of different types of services and hence is critical to the success of SOA implementation.
3. ***Develop a PoC to validate technology stack:*** While SOA solutions can be built with products from several vendors, the amount of effort required to address requirements of an enterprise can vary on the basis of the choice of products. With vendors continuously enhancing their product suites for competitiveness, it is necessary to build a PoC to determine suitability of products and technologies used in SOA solutions.
4. ***Leverage Open Source to keep the cost down:*** Open Source tools for service enablement (e.g., Axis 2), integration (e.g., WSO2 ESB) and orchestration (e.g., jBPM) have matured significantly over the past couple of years. Many vendors also provide community and commercial editions. Solutions may be developed with open source editions to the extent they deliver value with the option of paid commercial support where necessary.
5. ***Define a reference model and reference implementation:*** Reference models and reference implementations enable standardization by encouraging project teams to adopt a consistent approach for addressing specific type of problem (e.g., service enabling web applications). Project teams get to not only know of *what* needs to be done to address a specific problem but also *how* the solution needs to be implemented.
6. ***Architect and develop services that provide and manage master data:*** A single view of customer is concern of IT applications in many enterprises. Master data management techniques based on services model

can address this concern through implementation of services that may be consumed by all IT applications in the enterprise (such as customer).

7. ***Ensure team members in different roles (architecture, service modeling, service development, integration and orchestration) are adequately trained:*** On account of the paradigm shift caused by services model, it is necessary for development teams to be trained adequately on the following two aspects of SOA development:
   - training on technology-agnostic SOAD process;
   - training on technologies (product suites) identified for development of SOA solutions.
8. ***Take advantage of services model to parallelize development:*** The loosely coupled nature of services involves clear definition of service and data contracts that can serve as an advantage in planning project activities. On completion of business process modelling and service modelling activities of a project, the service definitions become available. Since services are self-contained autonomous components with no (or very few) external dependencies, parallelization of development of services is a clear possibility that can be considered while planning project activities.
9. ***Establish mechanisms to publish and reuse services:*** In order to avoid duplication of effort and institutionalization of reuse, mechanisms for publishing details of services developed (or planned to be developed) are implemented and project teams incentivized to leverage the services infrastructure.
10. ***Consider cloud infrastructure to improve scalability of development environment:*** Several cloud providers (such as Microsoft) offer an option to use development tools (such as Microsoft SQL Services and Visual Studio) on the cloud based on a "pay as you go" business model. Organizations may use this option to scale the development environment when needed to meet the demands of projects while keeping the costs to a minimum.

C.3 SOA GOVERNANCE – BEST PRACTICES

Operational efficiencies of enterprises are dependant on policies and procedures required to meet business objectives and their enforcement to ensure that the objectives are met. The following are some of the key best practices in SOA governance related to process, technology and people.

1. ***Establish a governance team:*** When implementation of enterprise-wide SOA is planned, a governance team is formed with participation of key stakeholders of the enterprise. This team defines policies and

procedures, ensures that SOA guidelines are defined and the policies and procedures are complied with.

2. ***Identify a "Champion" to lead the governance team:*** A non-controversial member of the senior management team is identified as a "Champion" in the organization to channel energies of the governance team to the different units of the enterprise and get the buy-in of key stakeholders.
3. ***Constitute an architecture group:*** Implementing enterprise-wide SOA requires significant experience and expertise in architectural practices. An architecture team with a suitable mix of enterprise, solution and infrastructure architects is essential. The architecture team with the responsibility of establishing guidelines and standards and approving deviations/changes that may needed from time to time is critical to success of enterprise-wide SOA implementation.
4. ***Ensure that the policies for security and change management are defined and operationalized:*** Policies for security and change management are critical in an enterprise context. These policies are defined for SOA initiatives. Further, it must be ensured that these policies are centralized and dove-tail into organizational policies.
5. ***Monitor and measure SOA results against projected benefits – Course correct, if necessary:*** Technologies and tools for SOA governance (e.g., Service Registry/Repository) are implemented and the progress/results of SOA implementation are regularly monitored and measured to confirm that the objectives are being met. Changes to plans and strategy, where necessary, are made to ensure that SOA implementation results in the required value to business.
6. ***Ensure SOA governance takes into account cloud services:*** Run-time governance of services should be implemented and extended to cover cloud services before use of cloud services is permitted. Likewise, security related considerations for cloud services should also be suitably addressed before their use by enterprise IT.
7. ***Conduct service delivery benchmarking to understand health of SOA implementation:*** In order to gain insights into the effectiveness of SOA implementation, it is worthwhile to conduct a service delivery benchmarking exercise, preferably by a specialist group from outside the organization context, to make an assessment on the effectiveness of the SOA implementation and suggest changes based on industry best practices in order to maximize return on investment for SOA.
8. ***Build skills in SOA Governance tools and technologies:*** SOA governance tools and technologies are fairly specialized that require a deeper understanding of IT governance issues to meet organization needs than what is seen in developers involved in traditional development of applications. It is, therefore, necessary for organizations to build skills in effective use of SOA governance tools and technologies.

EA and SOA for Business and IT Alignment

D

ANNEXURE

In the present day context, a significant percentage of an enterprise's budget is allocated to its Information Technology (IT) support systems. Hence, it becomes imperative that the IT support is aligned to the enterprise's business. A well thought out business and IT alignment would not only improve the efficiency of the underlying business processes but also lead to substantial savings in its IT spend.

Alignment programs involve the ability to understand business, make quick changes based on market forces and the ability to support changes to business and environment. An iterative and incremental approach is normally followed in implementing such programs. Tools like Enterprise Architecture (EA) and SOA could be deployed in the alignment process. EA involves modeling the AS-IS and TO-BE states from various perspectives like business, applications, information and infrastructure. A roadmap is defined for transition from AS-IS to TO-BE state. It is mapped to a program that consists of prioritized projects, taking into account the needs of various stakeholders. Governance structures, like *enterprise architecture board* and *program management office,* are defined for the implementation of the program.

The annexure discusses the need for business and IT alignment and highlights the role that EA and SOA can play in business and IT alignment.

D.1 ENTERPRISE ARCHITECTURE

As discussed in Chapter 2, Enterprise architecture is a collection of models that define the structure required for an organization to achieve its objectives. The models that represent EA may be classified under *business, application, information* and *infrastructure.*

EA deals with drawing up a vision for the business, assessing its current strengths and weaknesses, identifying and closing the gaps between the current state and the desired state in a planned manner.

Though EA addresses various aspects of business and IT, the key theme is that the business architecture drives the other architectural models. Several EA frameworks are in practice, the *Zachman* framework and The Open Group Architecture Framework (*TOGAF*) are among the most popular EA frameworks.

The TOGAF describes a method for EA development. The *Architecture Development Method* (ADM) of TOGAF provides an iterative development method for building AS-IS and TO-BE architectures pertaining to business, data, application and technology, considering the architecture requirements. The method ensures traceability of the architectures right from the business vision to the implementation (automated or otherwise). The gaps between the AS-IS and TO-BE architecture are analyzed and an implementation plan is developed; implementation governance provides the mechanism for smooth implementation and change management contains procedures to manage change to architecture.

The *Zachman Framework* describes the models/artifacts that are required to represent EA. It does not recommend any method but is a schema that constitutes an intersection between two classifications that have been in use. The first is answers to fundamentals of communication found for *what, how, when, who, where,* and *why* that enables the comprehensive, composite description of complex ideas. The second is *reification,* the transformation of an abstract idea into a model (Zachman, 2010).

D.2 NEED FOR BUSINESS AND IT ALIGNMENT

A business entity realizes its business vision through the implementation of business processes that are supported by IT. In the current day context, it is quite evident that business and IT alignment is necessary for growth. The businesses where IT and business objectives are aligned do not just grow but are efficient and responsive to market conditions. Though efforts to align IT with business have been taken up by a large number of business entities, in terms of percentage of the entire business population there is a wide gap.

The State of the CIO 2007 survey conducted by the CIO magazine reports that "Only one out of five CIOs said he's aligned with his business's strategic goals". Further, it states "CIOs who said they were aligned with the business reported that IT had enabled a new revenue stream more than twice as often as those CIOs who said they were not aligned (24 percent versus 11 percent). More important, more aligned CIOs said they had used IT to create a competitive advantage for the company than unaligned CIOs (38 percent versus 23 percent)" (Holmes, 2007).

D.3 EA AND SOA FOR BUSINESS AND IT ALIGNMENT

Business and IT in organizations will be aligned when:

1. Business processes are designed to meet the business goals and drivers.
2. Business processes are externalized and configurable to meet the changing needs of business.
3. Single view of business critical data (such as Customer) is maintained across the enterprise.
4. IT applications are flexible enough to accommodate new business models as and when they emerge.
5. IT applications that implement the business processes are strategic in not only being able to address the current business needs but also needs anticipated over a 3–5 year time horizon.
6. Technology platforms that host the IT applications bring economies of scale while bringing competitive edge to business.
7. Business processes implemented in IT applications can be orchestrated based on the configured business processes.
8. Efficiencies in IT applications are brought through "build once and use many times" approach. For this to happen, it should be possible to expose functionality in an IT application by other applications.
9. IT applications integrate and interoperate based on the needs of the business processes.
10. Enterprise level view of the performance of business and IT is tool-driven

While the above list of factors is only meant to be indicative but not exhaustive, it does show that some factors (e.g., 1 to 6) can be effectively addressed by the principles and techniques of enterprise architecture and few others (e.g., 7 to 10) by the principles and practices of SOA.

Enterprise architecture principles help optimize the fragmented legacy processes (both manual and automated) into an integrated environment that is responsive to change and supportive of the delivery of the business strategy. The business architecture view of enterprise architecture contains details of business processes, functions and organization structure. The other perspectives of the enterprise architecture capture the IT related aspects and ensure traceability with the business perspective.

SOA too plays an important part in aligning business and IT. Focus in SOA is on business processes and addressing the three dimensions, *reuse, agility* and *integration,* all key to aligning Business with IT.

Thus, EA and SOA are effective tools that aid business and IT alignment. In order to ensure that these tools are effectively leveraged, a holistic approach is required that combines the principles of business and IT alignment provided by EA and SOA. Chapter 11 discusses such an approach in detail.

REFERENCES

Holmes (2007) *The ROI of Computing,* http://www.bita-center.com/node/310

Zachman (2010) *The Zachman Framework™: The Official Concise Definition,* http://www.zachmaninternational.com

Index

A

B

C

D

E

F

G

H

I

J

L

O

P

Q

R

S

T

X

Z